THE NATURE OF RELIGIOUS MAN:

Tradition and Experience

THE NATURE OF RELIGIOUS MAN:

Tradition and Experience

A Symposium organized by the
Institute for Cultural Research

Edited by D. B. FRY

THE OCTAGON PRESS
LONDON

ISBN: 90086067 7

Photoset, printed and bound in Great Britain by
Redwood Burn Limited
Trowbridge, Wiltshire

The Trustees of the Institute for Cultural Research gratefully acknowledge the co-sponsorship and collaboration of the Institute for the Study of Human Knowledge, U.S.A., with respect to this Symposium.

CONTENTS

CONTRIBUTORS

Part I: The Realm of Tradition

Anthony Dyson, B.D., M.A., D. Phil.   *Protestant Christianity*
Dr Dyson was Principal of Ripon Hall, Oxford, from 1968 until 1974,
and a Canon of St George's Chapel, Windsor Castle, from 1974 to
1977. He is now Samuel Ferguson Professor of Social and Pastoral
Theology in the University of Manchester. His publications include
Who is Jesus Christ?, *The Immortality of the Past* and *We Believe*.
He is a specialist in European thought of the 19th and 20th centuries.

Riadh El-Droubie   *Islam*
Mr El-Droubie is an author and journalist who was born in
Baghdad. He is Director of Minaret House, a voluntary and independent
educational organization producing a considerable range of
teaching materials. He has worked for many years in the field of
world religions and as publication manager to the New London
Central Mosque and the Islamic Cultural Centre.

John Harriott, M.A., S.T.L.   *Roman Catholicism*
Mr John Harriott was previously a Jesuit priest. He is a writer,
broadcaster and commentator on religious and international affairs
and a member of numerous committees concerned with problems of
social morality. He is author of *Fields of Praise* and *A Pride of Periscopes*.
He read English language and literature at Oxford and
philosophy and theology at Heythrop College. He is currently an executive
member of the Catholic Institute for International Relations
and on the staff of the Independent Broadcasting Authority.

Dow Marmur   *Judaism*
Rabbi Dow Marmur was born in Poland and spent the war years in
the U.S.S.R. He studied in London for the rabbinate and is currently
serving the congregation of the North Western Reform Synagogue,
London. A frequent lecturer in Jewish and non-Jewish circles,
Rabbi Marmur has edited two collections of essays, *Reform Judaism*
and *A Genuine Search*.

Shivesh C. Thakur, Ph.D   *Hinduism*
Professor Thakur was born in India, studied at the universities of
Patna, Durham and Oxford and taught philosophy at various uni-

versities in India, Britain, New Zealand and the U.S.A. He is now Professor and Head of the Department of Philosophy at the University of Surrey. He is author of *Christian and Hindu Ethics,* and editor of *Philosophy and Psychical Research.*

Chairman: Professor D.B. Fry, Ph.D.

Professor D.B. Fry is Professor Emeritus of Experimental Phonetics at the University of London. He is a Trustee and a member of the Council of the Institute for Cultural Research.

Part II: The Realm of Experience

Carmen Blacker, M.A., Ph.D.   *Zen*

Dr Blacker became interested in Japan while still a child and began to study the language and culture at an early age. After taking a degree at the School of Oriental and African Studies in London, she studied in Japan at Keio University and has lectured in Japanese at the University of Cambridge since 1955. She is the author of *The Catalpa Bow* and *A Study of Shamanistic Practices in Japan*. At present she is engaged in a study of the phenomenon of pilgrimage to holy places.

dom Silvester Houédard   *Christian Mysticism*

dom Silvester, who is himself a poet, introduced the concept of 'concrete poetry' into England. He is Vice-President of the National Poetry Society, has contributed to most of the international poetry reviews and has held exhibitions of his work in Edinburgh and Newcastle as well as in the Victoria and Albert Museum in London. He has been a Benedictine of Prinknash Abbey since 1949. His publications include a number of articles on the wider ecumenism, especially on harmonies between Western and Eastern traditions of contemplation.

Vamberto L. Morais, B.M., B.A.   *Yoga*

Dr Morais studied in Brazil and came to London in 1946 as a British Council Scholar to study psychiatry. He holds a degree in ancient history from the University of London and is a writer and broadcaster. He is the author of *The Emancipation of Women* and *A Short History of Anti-Semitism*. He is a Committee Member of and lecturer for the Albion Yoga Movement.

Angela Tilby, B.D.   *Personal Christianity*

Miss Tilby has worked for the BBC religious Department since 1973. In 1977 she produced and presented the Radio Three series *The Long Search Continues*. She was born in Nigeria, educated in England and read theology at Cambridge. She is at present writing a book on religious education.

Chairman: Colin Wilson

Mr Colin Wilson's reputation as a writer has grown steadily since the appearance of his first book, *The Outsider*, in 1956. His long list of publications includes books on literature, on psychology and on mysticism, which is his major interest.

FOREWORD

Throughout the thousands of years of recorded history there
is ample evidence of man's continual recourse to ritual behaviour. The context of this behaviour has naturally varied
a great deal and in the early stages ritual was inevitably
linked with the struggle for survival and subsistence which
was the lot of the hunter-gatherers. The cave paintings of
southern Europe, those at Lascaux, Marsoulas and Niaux,
and those at Les Eyzies mentioned by John Harriott in his
contribution to this volume, show that early man evolved
rituals connected with hunting, for it is clear that the paintings are no mere representation of life as it is; they express
an awareness of the existence of some form of reality beyond
the scenes and events of every day, the recognition of supra-
normal and supernatural forces which influence the life of
man and his community and the belief that these forces may
in turn be influenced by ritual behaviour. In a word, they
testify to the religious nature of man. The pattern is continued in the fertility rites, the celebration of the seasons, the
worship of the Great Mother and all the other observances
that characterize the stage of animism. To early man it was
self-evident that success and safety in the hunt, the harvest-
ing of crops and the raising of the family, dependent though
they might be on his own efforts, involved a vast area of
unpredictability governed by unseen powers whose might
infinitely surpassed his own meagre capacity to control the
march of events. The response to this situation was not
simply a natural fear and a desire to placate the powers that
be, but also a feeling of wonder and awe in the face of the
unknown and the unseen. In the course of time this led to the
evolution of a whole pantheon of gods and goddesses who, in
their earlier guises, were the direct representatives of
natural forces – Earth, Sky, Rain, Fertility. With the
growth in the size of human communities and the development of a more complex social life, they became more diverse

in their functions and more strongly characterized, as was the case in the Greek pantheon, where Zeus ruled as the supreme power but was surrounded by such figures as Poseidon – who ruled the ocean; Apollo – the Sun God; Aphrodite – Goddess of Love; Athene – Goddess of Wisdom; Demeter – who ruled the harvest; Ares – who ruled over battles; Hera – marriage and the home; Artemis – nature and the hunt; and many more. Many of these had their counterparts in the Roman pantheon and it is interesting that a similar basic pattern can indeed be seen in such widely diverse frameworks as those of the Norsemen in Europe and of the Hindus in Asia.

An important factor in the early evolution of religion, as indeed throughout its history, is man's attitude to the death of the individual and the question of belief in life after death. Among the traces of almost every civilization are to be found evidences of funerary rites, from the well-known contents of ancient Egyptian tombs to the Stone Age grave goods found at Chapelle-aux-Saintes and Le Moustier, in the Viking ships of the dead and in the long barrows of England. These artefacts and the rituals that they imply show how long standing is the belief in survival after death and the conviction that death may be not an ending, but the prelude to a different kind of existence. These two strands, which are very much intertwined – a strong awareness of the existence of some reality beyond the confines of ordinary earthly life and a belief in at least the possibility of life after death – run continuously through the history of religion: from the primitive rites of early man and their surviving forms in present-day Africa, Australia and the Pacific, down to the complex rituals and practices of the great world religions. By following these threads man advanced from animism by way of polytheism and pantheism to the prevailing monotheistic religions. Such continuity bears undeniable witness to the essentially religious nature of man.

From its very beginnings religion has evinced a double aspect, the one social and the other individual; and the weight given to the one or the other has varied with the period and with the particular religion. Ritual behaviour presupposes a human group. In every culture and every community the tradition and the ritual which formulate relations with the supernatural serve to bind together the members of the community and to shape many aspects of social behaviour. In a primitive community the bonds are especially strong because forms of ancestor worship link the living with the dead in a very specific way and give rise to strict taboos, often reinforced by *rites de passage* of one kind or another. In more developed cultures, commonality of worship and religious practice remains a major factor in social cohesion: the moral constraints which religion imposes may be less absolute; they are nonetheless very powerful. While it is of the essence of religion to be concerned with the 'otherworldly', it has always had the important function of enabling men to live together in relative peace, of maintaining society and of allowing the continuance of the natural order of things as they exist. History shows indeed that a major change in the religious sphere brings in its train a change in the whole character of a society, such as took place with the coming of Christianity to the Ancient World and in Arabia with the coming of Islam.

The religions of today perforce fulfil this social role, though they may differ in the degree of overt emphasis that is placed upon it. Even the religions of India, which stress the illusory nature of life on earth, recognize, through the doctrine of *karma*, its importance as the only medium through which change for the individual can be brought about. In some religions, however, the actual coming together of people for worship, the corporate nature of the 'church', plays a much more significant role than in others. At one end of this scale stands the Roman Catholic Church, not only constituting an entity of immense social and even political importance, but also assuming great weight in the life and worship of individual members. In contrast one can cite the case of Islam, which has no priesthood and is entirely concerned with the direct relationship between the individual Moslem and God, as is clearly brought out by the contribution of Riadh El-Droubie. All religion is based ultimately on the convictions and practices of individuals; the distinction here is between those religions which focus attention on this aspect and those which show a great concern for and with the community formed by the individual adherents. One might expect to find a correlation between this feature and the complexity of the rituals involved in worship, but the matter is clearly not so simple. While it is true that worship in the Roman Catholic Church entails elaborate rituals, the rituals of Moslem prayer and other ceremonies in Islam are also quite complex. On the other hand, the Quakers, who eschew ritual altogether, even on such an occasion as a marriage, regard the corporate nature of the Society of Friends as fulfilling a most important function in their religious practice.

The influence of the individual is in evidence not only in those religions which owe their origin to a single outstanding figure but in the long lists of names that appear in the history of every religious movement: Jesus Christ, the Buddha, Mohammed, the great figures of the Old Testament, the Christian saints, Martin Luther, Samuel Wesley and George Fox, who founded the Society of Friends. Again and again great changes, both in religious belief and practice and in social conditions, have arisen out of the personal experience of a single being. Such transformations would not be possible were it not for the nature of the material on which such people were able to work, that is to say were it not for the religious nature of man. It takes both the leaven and the dough to make the finished loaf. Religion itself can exist only because of certain potentialities which are present in every man and woman: the ability to entertain the idea that the reality represented by everyday life and the perceptible world may not be the only reality, that beyond this may lie a greater reality, that life on earth may not be the sum total of existence for man, that life after death and, as many believe, life before birth are part of this greater reality; a capacity for assimilating experiences which bring both knowledge and a perception of other dimensions of existence; the potentiality for the permanent transformation of the nature of the individual man or woman. In many a religious person such formulations might find little echo, but nevertheless these are the potentialities that spring from the religious impulse and from which that impulse itself arises. The appeal of the great traditional religions, at least for those to whom their practice is something more than a mere social activity, is twofold; it lies in the possibility that right action by the individual may bring real benefit to his fellows and the community, and that single-minded devotion to his faith, and all that that implies, may bring about change for the better in the man himself. It is in the nature of things that this second objective is not that of the majority, but all the religions afford the means by which the task may be carried out; the tradition of monasticism and the life of contemplation, Christian, Moslem, Buddhist, is largely directed to this end, to achieve the 'mind-turning' referred to by dom Silvester Houédard; in India, among both Hindus and Buddhists, it is traditionally common for men at a certain stage of life to divest themselves of all worldly possessions, to renounce family ties and to wander alone in order to try to reach the state of emancipation.

There have long existed independently of the established religions, or rather independently of communal worship and ritual, religious practices and techniques of which the sole objective is the transformation or 'development' of the individual, that is to say the full realization of some of the potentialities mentioned above. Such are the various forms of yoga, the practices of Zen Buddhism, the diverse techniques of meditation, the psychological methods employed by different 'schools' for personal development. A prominent feature of life in the past decades has been a very widespread realization of the existence of such objectives and such methods and a corresponding upsurge of interest in every technique available, including the use of hallucinogenic drugs and the application of 'biofeedback' – the method of acquiring control of certain physiological processes by relaying to the brain information about them which the subject is normally quite unaware of. To some degree the kinds of experience which in former times were called 'mystical' and were judged to be the prerogative of the religious man and the fruit of religious exercise have come to be regarded in a way more in keeping with the formulation of William James when he wrote: 'Our normal waking consciousness, rational consciousness as we call it, is but one special type of consciousness, whilst all about it, parted from it by the filmiest of screens, there lie potential forms of consciousness entirely different'; one can now find quite frequent references in the psychological literature to what are termed 'altered states of consciousness.'

The history of all religions is replete with accounts given by individuals who have undergone out-of-the-ordinary experiences. Such accounts are naturally written in the language of the particular traditional religion practised by the person concerned. This fact makes it all the more striking that common features in these accounts should so constantly recur, indicating that there is indeed some underlying experience possible for man which transcends the confines of our ordinary senses. That this experience varies in its intensity is quite clear; what is less certain is whether, with different people and on different occasions, it differs in its essence. In the case of the long line of great saints and mystics of the past, of whatever creed, one would not hesitate to regard the capacity for such experiences as part of the nature of religious man. Yet for every saint there are millions of other worshippers, who devote themselves to the practice of their faith and who may have religious experiences of a different and a lesser kind, but who must surely be looked upon as religious men and as sharing the same nature. There are yet others again who belong to no church or community but who take what is now termed the experiential approach to religion.

The contributions to this volume are the record of a seminar designed to examine these various aspects of the nature of religious man. They endeavour accordingly to throw light on a series of questions: Are there distinguishing features that mark the major traditional religions? What makes men and women follow a particular creed? What is it that religion offers and how far does this differ between creeds? What characterizes men and women who pursue the inner goal, outside rather than within the traditions, and do they differ essentially from those who remain within? The contributors are men and women who have a knowledge of and an involvement with religion and who are able to speak out of first-hand experience either about the established world religions or about one of the experiential methods which are current today. The first part of the book deals with Protestant and Roman Catholic Christianity, Hinduism, Judaism and Islam; in the second part there are chapters on Zen training, Yoga, the classical Roman Catholic tradition of contemplation and on the relations between the religious traditions and personal religious experience, together with a commentary from Colin Wilson, who has made a lifelong study of the relationship between psychology and mysticism. Both parts contain a report of some of the questions asked by those present at the seminar and the answers and comments of the speakers, in the separate sessions and in the course of panel discussions.

Dr Anthony Dyson, having warned against any facile assumption of homogeneity in the body of Protestantism, points out the rapid and significant developments which took place after the Reformation. He sees in the Protestant Church and among Protestants a number of tendencies which, though they are not peculiar to adherents of this religion, when taken together characterize the Protestant outlook. These include a preoccupation with individual salvation as depending on personal encounter with God, coupled with a basically pessimistic view of man's position with respect to God and to the external world; a degree of moral rigorism; a reliance upon the Bible as the only channel of direct divine authority and a corresponding suspicion of historical institutions and of traditions which seem to claim this authority.

Mr John Harriott places Roman Catholicism in its historical context, not only that of the Christian era but of the thousands of years that preceded the life of Christ. The Roman Catholic Church itself is the most highly institutionalised in the world; for this reason the social and political role of the Church inevitably looms very large for non-Catholics and even for some Catholics. The relation between the Roman Catholic Church and contemporary society is the basis of a number of the debates in recent years which have become a matter of deep concern to Roman Catholics and have occupied the attention of the world at large. John Harriott discusses the relevance of these issues to the essential nature of the Catholic faith, which is most often of the intellectual kind and stresses conviction, somewhat in contrast to the Protestant faith, which stresses trust.

Professor Shivesh Thakur graphically contrasts the nature of Western religion, including Islam, and that of Hinduism, with its inherent pantheism and its freedom to embrace every kind of personal response, from mysticism to atheism. Having outlined the doctrine of Hinduism, insofar as it may be said to involve doctrine, and the notions of *karma, dharma* and the possibility of liberation from the cycle of re-births, Professor Thakur goes on to discuss the probable character of the future post-industrial society and the way in which Hinduism might interact with it. In such a society, with the emphasis that it is likely to give to individual freedom, tastes and inclinations, other traditional religions which place reliance upon institutions, dogma and doctrine, are not going to have much appeal. Hinduism, if so modified by the march of events as to get rid of its caste

xix

system, might well have a distinctive contribution to make to the world of the future.

The account of Judaism is given by Rabbi Dow Marmur, of the Reform Synagogue, who shows how modern Judaism represents the reconciliation of what might at first sight appear to be conflicting factors: the age-long monotheism of the Jews recognizes that each individual must find God for himself and hence perceptions of God are necessarily different, personal and limited; the veneration for tradition and history, which is the hall-mark of the Jew, is nevertheless combined with a willingness to face the present and the future; respect for the past acts as a guide but not as a strait-jacket. The Jew of today relies upon the accumulated wisdom and tradition of the Jewish past; his recognition of the Jewish capacity for and perhaps liability to suffering makes him more sensitive to the pain of others; in his quest for God and for spiritual integration he identifies himself with the congregation and the community, but he views membership of the chosen people as involving an obligation rather than conferring a privilege.

The meaning of Islam is submission and hence surrender to God is the theme of Mr Riadh El-Droubie's contribution. Evidence of this surrender comes through a man's actions and his conduct and, despite their differences of doctrine and belief, the various religions can work together to raise moral standards in the world today. Man has free choice in his actions and they must be regulated by three relationships: that between man and God, between man and man, and between man and himself. In addition to surrender to God, Islam stands for love between man and man and for peace within the inner man.

The second part of the book, dealing with experiential religion, begins with Dr Carmen Blacker's account of Zen training in Japan. She discusses the nature of the genuine religious experience as that of 'an all-embracing reality which pervades and transcends the world of phenomena in which we live our ordinary lives' and distinguishes it from other unusual states of consciousness which may be psychological in origin. The religious experience is incommunicable in words; to some individuals it is granted, as it were, as a gift, but for others it is necessary to seek the kind of bridge to it which is afforded by the different religions, among them Zen Buddhism. Basing herself on her own experiences during Zen training in a Japanese monastery and under Japanese masters, Dr Blacker describes the main features of this training. The motive for wishing to embark on the training is very important and among the Japanese is likely to be found in some overwhelming, perhaps tragic, experience in life. The method is based on the *koan*, a verbal statement which cannot be understood by the reasoning mind and on which the aspirant has to dwell for long periods in an attempt to make the leap to another kind of mentation. Several times a day the student has a confrontation with the Zen master, who is an indispensable element in Zen training. He is one who has himself made the journey to the state of enlightenment and is able to check at every stage the genuineness and effectiveness of what the pupil is experiencing.

The current popularity of some forms of yoga has given rise in many minds to a distorted impression of the nature and purpose of yoga. Dr Vamberto Morais reminds us that yoga is essentially the union of man with the divine, the return of the human being to his source. Although yoga is a system of mental and physical control, its objective is a spiritual one, the emphasis is on devotion and the state at which it aims is that of 'the mind in the heart', also spoken of at length in the contribution by dom Silvester Houédard as part of the classical Christian tradition. An important feature of yoga is the wide variety of approaches it affords to this single goal. The fact that some of these approaches have been taken up in contemporary society for the purpose simply of relieving tension does not alter their function as a means of deepening spiritual life. Meditation is one such method, with its intimate connection with consciousness and with breathing; for the true yogi there is no discontinuity between meditation and life, and here again there is a parallel to be seen with the literature of Christian devotion.

dom Silvester Houédard traces much of the history of Christian monastic devotion in the early centuries AD as a means of illuminating the character of the classical tradition of Christian mysticism particularly as it was formulated by S. Benedict. Union with God is seen as requiring withdrawal to the centre of the self in order to perfect the human image of God within. But since man is part of creation, the mind is turned not away from creation but towards it, the flight is not from the world, but through the world. The path which leads to union with God, to the Kingdom Within, is our life, and on this path contemplation and prayer are all important in 'turning the mind to the presence of God'. dom Silvester quotes extensively from the early Christain fathers on the various stages of the path and adds many examples of the mantras which they recommended for use in contemplation.

Angela Tilby examines in some detail the relations between experiential religion and institutional religion and asks what are the means, if there be any, of testing for oneself the genuineness of a religious experience. The trend of the present day is to accept as genuine any kind of experience and to regard its relation to established or traditional religion as irrelevant. But people brought up in different religions live in different worlds, and do have different experiences. Miss Tilby argues that often theology precedes and colours experience, yet in the Western tradition, particularly of Christianity, the theologian has become detached from religious experience and is seen simply as the rationalist. In Eastern religion, on the other hand, the theologian is first and foremost a man of prayer, who prays 'with the mind in the heart' and the integration of theology with experience is acknowledged. The real danger of the current preoccupation with experience and the view that it is the antithesis of creed and doctrine is that it tends to do away with the ability to be self-critical.

These diverse and yet curiously consonant views of religion, both institutional and experiential, will inevitably raise many questions in the minds of readers. A proportion of these at least will be found to be dealt with in the reports of discussion sessions. One of the traits of religious man which is self-evident is that he is a man of conviction. All too often, especially in the West, this means that he is also intent on convincing others. The contributors to this volume have rendered invaluable service by their willingness to present their views without any desire to convince or to proselytise in any way. This not only adds immeasurably to the value of what they have to say, but is itself the most telling proof that these are true exemplars of the religious man and woman.

D. B. FRY

THE REALM OF TRADITION

Protestantism

Anthony Dyson

The suffix '–ism' warns of all manner of problems for the
student of religion and religions, and in this respect Protestant*ism* is no exception. Many of the words with the
suffix '–ism', where used of particular religious traditions,
are inventions of the modern Western academic community.
Increasing knowledge of these traditions suggests that
'–ism' words, however convenient, are at best imprecise and
at worst flagrantly misleading. It is agreed, for example,
that 'Hindu*ism*' is a misnomer if it refers to *a* religion as this
is conceived of in the West: it is a highly unsatisfactory
abstract term for the long and infinitely heterogeneous
Indian religious tradition. Now I am of the opinion that
many of the cautions which Wilfred Cantwell Smith has
advised about the uses of '–ism' words with regard to *Eastern*
religious traditions can profitably be borne in mind in
thinking about Christian religious traditions in the *West*.
Bearing this in mind, it is tempting to insist that many important preliminary issues must first be clarified in detail
before direct discussion of Protestantism can begin. But
such preliminaries could with ease absorb a whole lecture,
not least because they concern matters where scholarly consensus is hard to find. However, avoiding this temptation, I
shall confine myself to indicating two areas of procedural
difficulty – one more general and one more particular.

First: the term 'Protestantism' embraces a volume and a
variety of phenomena which defy definition and categoriza-
tion in any simple way. One writer has asserted that Protestantism has always shown 'great variety and rapid
change', and this is no exaggeration. Another writer, at
greater length, has remarked as follows: '... Protestantism
is not "there", it is all over the place. It does not have recognizable boundaries; it is extremely difficult to know when an
individual or a church has ceased to be Protestant... Protestantism does not have discernible practices; at least the
ones that can be discerned are so inconsistent that it is diffi-

cult if not impossible to find a unifying principle of interpretation. Nor does Protestantism have infallible dogmas; at most it has a body of shared convictions, but it also has sharp differences about convictions that are not shared.' There seems little doubt that ecclesiastical polemic on the one hand and, in a paradoxical way, the ecumenical movement on the other hand, have helped to create an allegedly homogeneous entity called 'Protestantism' which can hardly be said to exist in reality. For, if we use the label 'Protestantism' for those churches or religious groups which, since the 16th century, have not been part of Orthodoxy nor in communion with the See of Rome, we must at the same time acknowledge that such a labelling has to include bodies as different as 16th century Calvinism and 20th century Quakerism, 19th century Liberal Protestantism and 20th century American fundamentalist sects. Further, if we leave on one side sociological or institutional definitions of Protestantism and explore such notions as Protestant *theology*, Protestant *spirituality*, Protestant *worship* or Protestant *monasticism*, the picture becomes even more complicated. For using *these* criteria we can identify similarities and differences which cut right across organisational and sociological definitions of denominations. On these other criteria we can see all sorts of Catholic elements in Protestantism and vice versa. In the light of this, I suggest that the most helpful procedure may be to reserve the adjective 'Protestant' first and foremost for certain tendencies of Christian thought and outlook which are found and sometimes not found in the Protestant religious bodies, and are present or absent in other religious traditions too. Thus I am arguing that what we call 'Protestantism' refers to certain movements and attitudes which are found in all religious traditions, and that only by historical circumstances and even historical accident have these movements and attitudes come to be mainly identified with certain churches and denominations in a rather exclusive way. If the approach which I am here suggesting tends to untidiness and complexity, I can only plead that it is more respectful of the evidence before us.

Second: if we are to come to terms with Protestantism as a contemporary religious phenomenon, it is important to be aware of the relative irrelevance of the mainstream 16th century Reformation. Though the character of the Refor-

4

mation is still much in debate, I must risk a few judgments as these bear closely on my later remarks. The Lutheran and Calvinist reformations were essentially of a pre-modern character in as much as, in respect of belief and polity, they were debates conducted within the late medieval framework. Both Lutheranism and Calvinism offered a vision of Christianity and a picture of the Christian society which were a variant of, not an alternative to, prevailing medieval notions of *Christendom*. The radical and innovatory movements are rather to be found in the sects of the 16th and 17th centuries. So the developments which we call Protestantism cannot be adequately grasped unless we recognize that the classical Lutheran and Calvinist ideals soon faded in many important respects, and that those classical traditions later accommodated themselves to the left-wing groups which were undergoing their own developments under internal and external pressures. In all this process we have to allow that political, social and economic factors were at least as important as religious impulses. For, from their beginnings, the new movements were caught up in the destinies of nascent sovereign states and so were intimately involved, for better or for worse, in the breakdown of medieval Europe, in the period of the Enlightenment, and in the advent of popular revolution and democracy. For reasons which I shall examine later, the so-called Protestant churches were much more exposed to such developments than was Catholicism – hence the variety and rapid change in Protestantism referred to above. All in all, therefore, so profound have been the changes in Protestantism over four centuries that the 16th century mainstream Reformation can no longer serve as the principal basis for discussion. Against this background I want now briefly to indicate nine tendencies of Christian thought and outlook which may deserve the label 'Protestant'.

(1) There is a tendency to adopt a strongly pessimistic view of the predicament of man vis-à-vis himself, the world and God. Along with this goes a tendency to emphasize the majesty, justice and radical otherness of God. Within the framework of institutional Protestantism, however, we also find examples of vastly more optimistic estimates of man.

(2) There is a tendency to focus the event of salvation upon the individual, interior encounter with God – an encounter in which the emotive, non-cognitive element is

dominant. This tendency leads to suspicion of a sacramental system or a church hierarchy which might claim to control or pre-determine this personal encounter with God. In much actual Protestantism this encounter is often subtly routinised and becomes itself a kind of system.

(3) There is a tendency to view the Church as a spiritual holy community set apart from, and gathered out of, the world – a community into which man is rescued from his predicament. This holy community is not coterminous with an historical institution: there is always a mismatch between the visible and the invisible church. In practice the Protestant churches have for the most part become settled historical institutions.

(4) There is a tendency to react adversely to the claim of *tradition* to serve as a major criterion for Christian authenticity. Theoretically the sole formal criterion is the Bible which judges traditions and whose meaning is self-evident. But there is also a tendency to appeal to more spontaneous, charismatic grounds of authenticity which are held to derive directly from the work of the Spirit. This hesitancy about tradition is matched in principle by a belief that the Church must be subject to continuous reform – *ecclesia semper reformanda*. In practice Protestant groups tend to canonise their own tradition.

(5) Given the primacy of faith and of the existential character of the encounter with God, there is a tendency to regard with disfavour metaphysical speculation in the religious sphere. For speculative confidence stands in opposition to the view of man's rational incapacity as one of the products of sin. But precisely because Protestant thought has lacked a firm metaphysical framework, it has sometimes entered into liaison with alien systems which have embodied quite alien values.

(6) There is a tendency sharply to challenge all ideas and practices which might seem to promote the possibility of *idolatry*, i.e., the worship as God of entities less than and other than God. The natural and material order is thus accorded a low status (with a dependence on verbal rather than on tactile or visual symbols), and a certain asceticism in manners and piety is cultivated.

(7) Given the awesome reality of divine judgment and the sense of the Church as a less than stable historical institution, there is a tendency for eschatological and apocalyptic

elements to arise from time to time, offering important challenges to the *status quo* in the Church and in society.

(8) There is a tendency towards moral rigorism, a suspicion of complex systems of moral casuistry, and a deep moral conscientiousness about the fulfilment of one's secular calling.

(9) Running through all these tendencies is often a sense of man's radical inability to deal with his own guilt, a sense of the sheer gratuitousness *and* severity of dvine action towards humanity, and thus a sense not so much of divine-human cooperation as of radical human dependence upon God. The world is not so much to be transformed as to be replaced by a superior reality. (For these reasons, Protestantism exhibits in theory a deep suspicion of *religion*, tending to regard it as a man-made device, as an expression of *hubris*. In practice, of course, Protestantism is as involved in religion as any other religious group.) This sense of man before God provokes the problem of *authority* which has always been acute for Protestantism. It will be clear, from what I have said so far, that the Protestant outlook depends upon the availability of direct, divine authority, unmediated by historical institutions. For historical institutions, always damaged by sin, are unreliable mediators of divine revelation. Thus the Bible alone as the revealed Word of God or the internal testimony of the Holy Spirit provides access to this direct and available divine authority. As I shall observe later, this question of authority has reached a state of crisis in Protestantism, as, in different ways, in other religious traditions.

Now the nine tendencies which I have briefly mentioned are not of course unique to what is popularly called Protestantism. They reflect emphases and possibilities which are open to Christian existence at any time. Examples of those tendencies can be found in the Biblical writings and in the subsequent history of the Church. In themselves (I would argue) those tendencies are neither true nor false; they only make sense when they stand in active dialectical relationship with their opposing tendencies. But when these Protestant tendencies are taken as the sole bases of Christian existence, the danger of profound distortion and extreme ossification can hardly be avoided. I should judge that precisely this has happened at various critical stages in Protestant history. For a complex variety of political, social, economic and ecclesiastical reasons, the Protestant tendencies to which I have referred have often ceased to be features of a dialectical process, but have instead become fixed in historically distinct institutions and there defended as definite characteristics of the true church, with the result of an alarming loss of proportion and inner dynamics in belief and practice. I want now to look briefly at some of the consequences for Protestantism, as it sought to subsist on these tendencies alone, and when it encountered major challenges in the modern world. I will mention four such topics – the rise of nationalism; the rise of secularism; the rise of the natural sciences; and the rise of historical-critical Biblical science.

(1) The breakdown of the medieval *Corpus Christianum* and the emergence of the nation-state came to pose profound problems for Protestantism. In theory modern Protestantism sees the Church as very distinct from culture. But having taken root in different countries by various kinds of settlement with the state, and lacking a visibly universal character, Protestant churches have been closely identified with nationalist sentiments and national ways of life, often leading to social and political conservatism. This tendency has adversely affected the prophetic calling of Protestantism and has brought about a rigidity strangely at odds with the conception of *ecclesia semper reformanda*.

(2) I have already noted the sharp distinction in post-medieval Protestantism between the world and the gathered community, reason and faith, nature and grace, man and God. This outlook treats the world as a profane secular reality. Sacrality belongs only to the holy community and to the Bible. The rise of a secular point of view in European society, by which I mean the tendency to explain phenomena in this-worldly terms, is therefore in a sense affirmed by Protestantism. At the same time this has had the effect of marginalizing the Protestant churches in society and of reducing the explanatory and prophetic power of the Church's gospel both in intensity and scope. Thus we have witnessed a progressive Christian withdrawal into the gathered Church community as the sole sphere of authentic Christian existence, with the accompanying loss of a spirituality which deals with human life in the day-to-day world. It is not surprising, therefore, that, postulating a non-sacral, worldly reality and postulating a radically transcendent

8

and unmediated God, the tenuous bond between the world and God can easily snap. leading to Protestant affirmations both of the death of God and by way of substitute, of the religious character of secular society as such.

(3) Protestantism's relative independence of tradition and its non-sacral view of the world has made it, in principle, not unsympathetic to the rise of the sciences. I say 'in principle' because Protestantism's dependence upon the Bible has of course in some circles meant a collision with the world of the sciences and a flight towards irrational fundamentalism. Where Protestantism has come to terms with science, it has in fact often conceded (even welcomed) a thoroughgoing naturalistic interpretation of all phenomena except those of faith. In so doing it has left itself little room for doctrinal reconstruction and has found itself unable to offer a comprehensive *religious* account of the world. (Not surprisingly, this has provoked, within Protestantism, countering theologies of radical divine immanence and religious experience.) All in all the Protestant search for human meaning has, perhaps predictably, moved little beyond the experience of individual faith, typified recently by Protestantism's relationship, in some circles, with existentialism – a philosophy which does not deal with man's place in nature nor with the meaning of human community.

(4) I have already drawn attention to the centrality of Biblical authority for much of Protestantism. Thus the development of Biblical criticism in the 19th century (mainly in Protestant circles) has produced a major crisis of conscience. For the picture disclosed by Biblical science is quite incompatible with earlier theories of the whole Bible as the divinely revealed, directly inspired, and self-interpreting Word of God. Three options have presented themselves: (a) the way of fundamentalism, in a strong or weak form, with a rejection of all or some of the presuppositions, methods and results of Biblical science; (b) the search for an alternative central authority consistent with the Protestant outlook; (c) along with a commitment to Biblical science, a re-evaluation of the role of reason and tradition in Christian faith and life. It is likely that a large proportion of Protestantism will continue to take the fundamentalist option. The third option is less clear-cut and, to the extent to which it is pursued, must inevitably lead to a loss of Protestantism's principal historical characteristic.

I have been asked to include in my lecture some remarks of a more personal nature. Perhaps I can pose to myself the question 'What implications has the foregoing account of Protestantism for personal faith and life and what are its future prospects as a religious tradition?' I do not (readily) call myself a Protestant or a Catholic. I believe that the reality of Christianity and its future is too important a matter to be reduced to a choice between these two religious traditions *in the form in which we inherit them today*. I am of the opinion that neither the characteristic tendencies of Protestantism nor those of Catholicism can stand in isolation. *If* there was a historical context where that was possible and necessary, it has been totally overtaken by the course of events. Maybe there are some signs of an interpenetration of Protestant and Catholic tendencies in contemporary Christianity, though much of it appears to be in the form of replies to out-dated questions, and such interpenetration will certainly lead to a hardening of position on both extremes. Though I can foresee the continuing strength of certain forms of fundamentalism, providing personal reassurance in a technologically dominated culture fraught with psychological and economic uncertainty, I find it difficult to imagine that Protestantism on a wider front will be a cohesive force at the end of the century. This leaves the urgent and vital question as to whether and how the Protestant tendencies, which are crucial to the health of any theistic religion, can become part and parcel of a Christianity renewed amid a world of many faiths. I doubt whether many of us can understand the degree of Christian transformation such a renewal would involve. The potential tragedy is that Protestantism and Catholicism will remain slaves to the forms and loyalties in which they came to birth as medieval and post-medieval realities out of particular circumstances, questioning and accident which have now been comprehensively overtaken by other needs and issues. Such idolatry towards the past is a recipe for the death of a religion, and there is plenty of historical precedent for the death of religions.

Discussion

Q: You have stated that you believe the nine tendencies

you have mentioned to be crucial to any religion. Why?

A: I see these tendencies as being on one side, at one pole of a relationship, so that if you have a religion with a tendency to emphasize a very spiritual, holy community idea of the church, it is important that that should be in tension with a view of the church as a visible, concrete, historical, worldly institution. When these two tendencies are in tension with each other, people are never allowed to fall completely into one or the other and I believe that is a recipe for a living religion. One could show in the case of all the nine categories or tendencies that I mentioned, that they represent one side of an important dialectical relationship. Similarly, it seems to me that if you have only one principal organ of authority within a religious tradition, this will lead almost inevitably to one form or another of religious totalitarianism within that tradition. Therefore I think it is important to see that there are different organs and principles of authority within a religious tradition which have to live in a relationship of tension and hopefully of creativity with each other. That is the way I would state the crucial nature of these Protestant tendencies within a wider framework.

Q: If interpenetration takes place between the two faiths, Protestanism and Catholicism, why will this lead to a hardening of attitudes as opposed to greater conciliation between the two faiths?

A: I said that it would lead to a hardening of attitudes at both extremes. It seems to be in the nature of religious developments that where there is an increasing accommodation between two groups in the middle ground, there is further splintering on each wing of both bodies. This has happened in the past in the history of religious bodies and in traditions other than the Christian one, and there is sufficient evidence to suggest that it will happen again. We already see signs today that various forms of *rapprochement* between middle of the ground Catholicism and middle of the ground Protestantism are in fact leading to an increase of what I would call fundamentalism both of a Protestant and a Catholic kind on the wings. This just seems to be one of the patterns of religious development.

Q: Do you see a time approaching when the orthodox Church will move away from the literal interpretation of the Bible to a much greater extent that is now the case? Do you yourself see this as necessary for an authentic renewal of

Christianity?

A. This is a very searching and difficult question because it seems to me that the rise of Biblical science and its treatment of the Bible, although in some respects an intellectual necessity, has led in other respects to different kinds of scepticism and rationalism which are not particularly fertile seed-beds for belief. A considerable move away from the literal interpretation of the Bible has already taken place, except in some sections of the Christian churches, as I mentioned. I do see a coming to grips with this question of the nature of our relationship with Biblical writing as a very urgent question, just as I think it is an urgent question for Judaism and an urgent question for Islam. Religious renewal always comes about at the end of the day through an encounter in the present with what is held to be the living God; any kind of commitment or loyalty which in a sense inhibits that encounter in the present with the living God is bound to militate against renewal. There is a curious sense in which commitment to the Bible, or to certain kinds of institution, can be a form of idolatry and prevent this encounter. I think therefore that we have to work out very clearly in what way our responsibility to holy traditions, holy books and holy institutions can be given only a certain relative status and not an absolute one and may consequently not inhibit our response to the challenge which comes to us in the present. This is the kind of area which it seems to me has to be tackled.

Q. In what form would you see a revival of true religion taking place?

A. This is obviously a monumental question and I suppose my short answer is that I do not see a revival of true religion taking place solely in what we call the religious sphere. What we call revival takes place, I believe, out of a human encounter with God in the actualities of our life in the world; this then expresses itself in religious forms and in religious institutions. I am very suspicious of leaning upon and pressing religious traditions as such very hard, in the hope that we can somehow squeeze revival out of them like juice out of a lemon. Revival is something which happens to man rather than something which he creates; I believe it happens as he seeks to respond to what is happening in the world around him in all sorts of contexts and in that he finds an encounter with the living God.

Q. Is there much value in concentrating so much on man's inherent guilt, rather than looking to man's moral improvement?

A. From the way in which I have approached this theme in my lecture you will perhaps perceive that I would not be happy about such an either-or question. Christianity and indeed Western thought is littered with all kinds of dubious doctrines of progress and optimism and of human perfectibility which we do not now regard as very credible; equally the Western tradition is the graveyard of extreme pessimistic views of man. In the Christian tradition we are dealing with a paradoxical state of affairs in which at one and the same time man is recognized as being in a state of extreme but free defection from God, from the source of his being, and yet at the same time is affirmed by God, and is regarded as having within himself the possibility, with divine assistance, of growth and transformation. If you separate those two things and give exclusive attention to one or the other, all sorts of distortions are going to arise, not simply at the level of belief, but at the level of practice, of self-understanding, social policy and political thought.

Q. Should not all available compatible authority be considered along with the Bible, as judged by effective results in life?

A. The question of authority is a very complex one and is exercising, I suspect, nearly all the major religious traditions today. Some of the major religions have a very firmly defined understanding of authority as related to particular organs of authority. Once these are challenged in one way or another, this obviously leads to great uncertainty. Religious traditions in the past and in the present have spent a lot of time seeking a single, unambiguous authority; we have to realize that no such thing is available to man. We have to think rather, at least in Christian terms, of God making his own authority available to man in a whole range of secondary mediated authorities, and it is to these that we have to relate ourselves. I agree therefore that it is not a question of a single authority but of a variety of authorities. But we have to be a bit cautious of a purely utilitarian approach to authority, asking whether it leads to effective results. This begs the question 'What is effective?' and also it is the case that bad causes can sometimes produce good results. I think there are certain truth questions about authority that have

13

to be tackled quite regardless of their particular consequences.

Q. Do you consider an inherent tendency to pessimism as
peculiar to Protestantism or as inherent in the physical environment of Western Europe?

A. I do not think that it is simply confined to the physical
environment of Western Europe. In fact some of the great
origins of Western Christian pessimism are found in North
Africa, in Augustine and of course in Egypt from the beginnings of monasticism, so I do not think that the climatic and
geographical argument holds, nor do I think pessimism is
peculiar to Protestantism. There is no doubt that in the
Middle Ages there were some very profound strands of
cultural, philosophical and social pessimism. This is hardly
surprising when one considers what was happening in the
Middle Ages, economically and in other respects, and in
view of events such as the Great Plague. I think some of that
cultural pessimism came through and expressed itself in the
origins of Protestantism; but similar things happened in the
4th century so I do not think it is peculiar to Protestantism.
As so often happens, certain social and cultural tendencies
allied themselves with certain religious tendencies. What
strikes me very forcibly about Luther is that he was concerned to look quite fundamentally at man's position before
God, challenging a whole framework of cultural, social and
religious ideas and asking absolutely fundamental
questions. This involves putting man totally in question
before God and in a sense that is what that kind of pessimism is all about. Pessimism in religion is a very complex
thing and is found in all religious traditions and in all sorts
of physical environment. As I said earlier, there is a kind of
polarization towards optimistic or pessimistic tendencies; it
is when oscillation between the two becomes extreme in particular circumstances that obsession with pessimism and
guilt sets in and becomes as dangerous to the religious temperament and to religious possibilities as are obsessive per-
fectionism and obsessive concern with human progress.

Catholicism at the Crossroads

John Harriott

Two weeks ago, on Holy Saturday, I went to a concert of sacred music in a small twelfth century church in a tiny hamlet in the Dordogne. The musicians, it must be regretfully admitted, were not very good, but the music was ambitious and ranged from Monteverdi's setting of the Good Friday Lamentations through seasonal pieces by Couperin, Bach, Vivaldi and Handel. It ended with a spirited rendering by a local Perigordian choir of César Franck's *Dextera Domini resuscitavit me*. In wave after jubilant wave the various sections of the choir repeated the mighty statements that 'The right hand of the Lord has raised me up'. In the gentle light within those ancient walls that robust, joyful proclamation of faith made a powerful emotional impact.

For me the impact was heightened because less than a dozen miles away lay Les Eyzies, the womb of pre-history. And I had just spent several days visiting the caves and tunnels which honeycomb the surrounding cliffs, looking with wonder at the mortal remains, the tools and weapons, and above all the paintings and engravings traced on cave walls, left behind by men and women who lived fifteen, thirty, or even more, thousands of years ago. The previous day, on Good Friday, I had in my fashion descended among the dead at Rouffignac where a tiny rickety railway carries visitors along two of its ten kilometres of tunnels, once gouged out of the hill by rushing waters, down to a round, flat-roofed cavern, a 'temple' where primitive men once gathered for some, now unknown, form of worship. Its roof is patterned with paintings and drawings of mammoths, reindeer and horses, the animals which played some part in those ancient rites. One's skin prickled at the thought of the men and women who had once picked their way by torchlight down those damp Stygian tunnels to express some sense that their struggle for survival in a comfortless world, racked by climatic convulsions and roamed by strange, enormous creatures now extinct, yet had some meaning.

15

Nothing can or could convey the moving quality of those messages, with their confident, singing lines, their sense of colour and volume comparable with any of the world's great art, transmitted from man to man across those unimaginable years.

For those few days the services of Holy Week – recalling and re-living the life, death, descent among the dead, resurrection and ascension of Jesus Christ – were interwoven with reflections on the dizzying stages of the earth's own birth in time, and man's own equally dizzying evolution: on the contrast between the hundreds of thousands of years during which man made no discernible technological advance on the most rudimentary stone tools, followed by a quickening which has led to inventions like the aeroplane, jet engine, television, nuclear weapons and the computer, all within less than a human lifetime; the contrast between those far-off days when nature threatened man with extinction, and our own day when man's activity threatens nature; on the curious gifts of language, invention and art which set man apart from the rest of creation and enable him – even when engulfed by barbarism and savagery – to create music, painting, sculpture and architecture of breathtaking beauty, charged with faith and hope, in defiance of time and time's destruction. On the fact that the same questions about life and death, human purpose and human worth, which drew prehistoric man into that underground temple at Rouffignac are those which still today put us on our knees, draw us into places of worship, and are the essential concerns of all the great world religions.

Yet another change of perspective during that affecting week was to see once again, and far more vividly, the youth of Christianity when contrasted with the long history of man and the longer history of the planet. Against that enormous cadence of the years the Christian era is only the blink of an eye. We think of the passion, death and resurrection of Jesus Christ (in themselves beyond the wildest dreams of men who lived aeons before) across the crowded events that have stemmed from them, as ancient and remote. But Christianity is in truth a puking infant of a religion, and if mankind does not kill itself by its own hand, which it now has the means to do, human history may yet stretch tens of thousands of years into the future and the Christian religion evolve and mature in ways as undreamable to us, as Christ himself was to early man. That at least is my own belief, even if a touch on the nuclear button could tomorrow leave such confident speculations in tatters.

If, then, I speak today of Roman Catholicism, it is as a Roman Catholic well aware that the Christian religion found room for itself in an already crowded field and subsists alongside far more ancient beliefs and ways to God which cannot be simply shouldered aside as obsolete, like old-age pensioners by a pushy youngster. I speak too as a Roman Catholic who most genuinely believes in the three primary Christian statements that Christ has died, Christ is risen, and Christ will come again, and that the first two of these are historical events which have already incomparably affected human hopes and self-understanding; but that no man can prophesy when the third will befall, and that in the intervening time the understanding of Catholic belief and the institutional expression of the Catholic Church will evolve and change as much as and more than they have done in the brief two thousand years that lie behind us. If it were not so, we would be speaking not of a living organism but a religious fossil, a curio fit only for some grand museum of mankind. But above all I believe that Catholicism will thrive or decay in the degree that it sheds light on the basic human concerns which modern technological man shares with Stone Age man: life and death, human achievement, human suffering, the workings of the human psyche, the building of the human community, and – central to them all – the existence, presence and power of God.

Perhaps of all the great world religions, Catholicism is for the outsider the hardest to see as primarily concerned with God. It has frequently been said, and it would be hard to deny, that it is the most institutionalized of all religions. And the sheer size and scale of its institutionalism can provoke presumptions and expectations which to the insider seem marginal and accidental. It can and does scandalize as the world's most overblown bureaucracy; a sympathetic judgment may see it as an alternative International Red Cross Society under religious auspices, a less sympathetic judgment as a – usually sinister – political power; and many see it as a closed ideology, an authoritarian system which shackles the human spirit, an obstacle to human curiosity, inventiveness and achievement. Others again see it in a kindlier light as a supreme generator of artistic achievement and the chief guardian of mankind's heritage of art and learning. There are many facets to the Catholic faith and the Catholic Church and it is easy to see one only to the exclusion of the rest. Even Catholics themselves can demand of the Church the exercise of the one function dearest to their hearts and dismiss the remainder as of little or no account, or as impediments to the single function they recognise as valid. I mention a broad cross-section not to refute or brush them aside, even the most critical, for each, even the harshest view, has some substance in fact, but to turn the picture inside out and suggest that such a variety of concerns, occupations and enterprises – and, yes, even such colossal mistakes and corruptions – are evidence of a mysterious vitality and an equally mysterious capacity to engage men's hearts and minds. And perhaps as a gentle warning against supposing that one can judge the inner working of the ship from a casual inspection of the super-structure or some part of it.

What then are the engines, the driving-forces, of Catholicism? First the belief that God revealed himself in a particular man, in a particular place, at a particular moment in time, and revealed himself in a way more complete and intelligible than any other. 'He who has seen me has seen the Father' is the utterance which gives such weight to everything Christ said and did, and such urgency to our attempts to understand every nuance of those words and deeds. The baldest summary of the mystery of Christ and its meaning is, of course, the Creed, but Catholics believe that the implications of its propositions can be endlessly unravelled. To help them understand and live out their response to this divine revelation Catholics also believe that Christ founded a distinct, visible community to preserve that revelation intact, meditate on it, and tease out its inexhaustible meaning. Further they believe that Christ is not a dead historical personage but a living, contactable presence whose spirit operates continuously in human society and every area of human activity; a presence which is also the promise of a further stage of existence.

Here and now I have no intention of tracing all the ramifications of Catholic doctrine or its historical development; nor of offering a sociological map of the Catholic community as it at present exists. But perhaps that Minima Theologica may be sufficient background for what I do want to do, that

18

is focus on the issue which it seems to me is the most important in Catholicism today: the nature of faith itself.

Ever since the Second Vatican Council it is no secret that the Catholic Church has been the theatre of tumultuous debate: over the social role of the Church as an institution, over doctrinal issues like infallibility, over its liturgical practice, its administrative system, pastoral techniques, and not least the role of its clergy. Familiar features have disappeared, and new movements, institutions and expressions of faith have come into being. Commentators have often labelled the parties to these debates as 'conservatives' and 'liberals', but it would be somewhat more accurate, I believe, to label them as 'spiritualists' and 'humanists'. And though some of these changes may appear, even to Catholics themselves, as merely a shifting round of the furniture, I also believe that what underlies them all is a changing conception of the nature of religious faith.

I would not, of course, claim that difference, or at least difference of emphasis, is a sudden eruption. The central doctrine of Christianity, that Christ is truly God and truly man, is itself a bit of a tight-rope walk. It is easy to slip from the tight-rope either by emphasizing the divinity to the virtual exclusion of the humanity, or vice versa; and such a slip is the common factor among most of the great heresies. But the same tight-rope walk is required in the Catholic idea of the church, conceived of as both divinely instituted and guided and yet a very human organization; or the idea of man as holding something in common both with the pure spirits called angels and with the brute creation; and in the idea of sacraments, vehicles of God's power and presence instituted by him, yet performed in visible rites that have been culturally conditioned. The Mass itself, in Catholic eyes the profoundest Christian mystery, God's most precious gift, and the point of closest encounter between man and God, centres on simple human materials, bread and wine, and its ritual coat is woven of threads from the ancient synagogue, from the daily life of Rome and the courts of Charlemagne, Byzantium and the High Renaissance.

The Catholic theory has not been that any of these things are either divine or human, but that in each the divine is incarnated, enfleshed, in the human. Nevertheless the instinct has been a strong one to polarize the two, to make them an either/or, and, so some critics would claim, the instinct has been reinforced by the influence of a non-Christian, Hellenistic dualism which early entered the Christian bloodstream. The idea that in Christ, God was only encased in a human envelope, or that the human soul was in Descartes' phrase 'a ghost in a machine' are but two familiar examples. Similarly there has been a tendency to sharpen the division between the society of the Church and human society at large, by concentrating on the divine or mystical character of the Church to the point where it seems neither to touch, nor to be touched by, ordinary human concerns, and to be removed from the scope of ordinary human analysis or criticism. Such an emphasis not surprisingly gives the Church an appearance of self-sufficiency, exclusiveness and arrogance which have often roused strong feelings of antagonism. Worse, the combination of an immense dynamism and vitality, which I think even its critics would admit, with an equally strong sense of a divine mission and divine guidance has often led Catholicism into violent and aggressive ways which I for one would regard as contradicting its essential message – the love and compassion of God for his creatures.

It was growing unease with this dislocation between the Church as an institution and the rest of human society, including its other great religions, which prompted the Second Vatican Council. As the American theologian, William Dych, has remarked, the Council's first concern was the relationship between the Church defined as 'a community of men united in Christ and led by the Holy Spirit on their journey towards the kingdom of their Father' with the world defined as 'the human family with all its energies, tragedies and triumphs' or as 'mankind and its history'. To explain the link between these two histories could not be done by reference to some timeless essence of the Church, or to its history and tradition exclusively, but only by some understanding of the contemporary world.

This internal unease was reflected in two powerful contemporary challenges to religious faith, those of Marx and Freud. They forced contemporary Catholics to ask not only 'Is this faith true?' but also 'Does it work?'. Marx did so by denouncing religion for distracting men from this world's sufferings and its causes, which they could do something about, to pie-in-the-sky promises of a just and satisfying life after death. Freud on the other hand criticized religion for impeding the proper functioning of the human psyche; for him religion was 'illusory'. Neither is actually concerned with the objective truth of religious faith, but only with its effects. In their view it does not work, but is an obstacle on the one hand to the betterment of the social order, on the other to the healthy operation of the human psyche. And whatever the academic theologian's response to such challenges might be, the fact is that many people recognized some truth in them in the light of their own experience. Catholics have often been reluctant to face both the awkward question and the awkward fact, but it is to the credit of the Council that it did face them and attempted some kind of answer. The essence of its answer lay in these lines:

'While we are warned that it profits a man nothing if he gain the whole world and lose himself, the expectation of a new earth must not weaken but rather stimulate our concern for cultivating this one. For here grows the body of a new human family, a body which even now is able to give some kind of foreshadowing of the new age. Earthly progress must be carefully distinguished from the growth of Christ's Kingdom. Nevertheless, to the extent that the former can contribute to the better ordering of human society, it is of vital concern to the Kingdom of God.'

There is, the Council also declared, 'a true and intimate link between the Christian community and secular history' because where improvements and developments in the social order are concerned 'God's Spirit, who with a marvellous providence directs the unfolding of time and renews the face of the earth, is not absent from this development', and because 'Jesus was crucified and rose to break the stranglehold of the Evil One so that this world might be fashioned anew according to God's design and reach its fulfilment'.

This intimate link was even more tersely expressed by the International Synod of Bishops in 1971 which declared that 'action on behalf of justice is a constitutive element in the Church's mission.' It must, however, be admitted that other statements in conciliar documents seem either to contradict this intimate link between the Church's mission and secular activity, and even in the wording I have quoted the ghost of

21

the old isolationism peeps through. It is really only since the Council that the nature of the intimate link has been systematically explored, often in response to such questions as 'What has the Church to do with the Third World?' or to justify heavy Church involvement in such issues as human rights, racism, or the condition of labour.

But why is the difficulty there in the first place? Is the pursuit of holiness a parallel activity to human wholeness which itself requires decent conditions of life? And why did the Council make such heavy weather of it? Primarily, I suggest, because its members had only traditional but in some respects inadequate definitions of religious faith to draw on, and because the kind of definition they needed had only just begun to surface, partly because of the stimulus they provided. To illustrate the difficulty I would like to draw freely on the work of Fr. Avery Dulles, another American theologian, whose name alone should guarantee that he is free of any Marxist bias.

Dulles distinguishes between two traditional theories of faith: those of an intellectualist kind which stress conviction, and those of the fiducial kind which stress trust. Catholics, on the whole, lean towards the former. Protestants, on the whole, to the latter. The intellectualist tradition stems from Augustine's famous dictum 'I do not seek to understand that I may believe but I believe in order to understand. For this I also believe – that unless I believed I should not understand.' A modern version is Bernard Lonergan's definition that 'faith is the knowledge born of religious love'. The ultimate goal of those who hold this theory is contemplative union of the soul with God, a complete knowledge which fully satisfies the mind. And the business of the Christian is to create conditions in which he can achieve this contemplative union. It has been the mainspring of the eremetical and monastic traditions, and indeed one criticism of it is that it seems to make the monk's life normative for all Christians, clerical or lay. A second major criticism is that it establishes the contemplative life as intrinsically superior to the active, and man, with some smack of the Hellenistic dualism aforementioned, as first and foremost an intellectual being.

Another variant on the intellectualist theme is summarised in the first Vatican Council's famous definition: 'We believe the things that God has revealed to be true not

22

because of their intrinsic truth perceived by the natural light of reason, but because of the authority of the revealing God himself, who can neither deceive nor be deceived.' Here it is not hunger for union with God but respect for divine authority which is the essence of the matter. Not 'I want to know' but 'I believe what you tell me' and what you tell me, one must add, beamed through the earthly teaching authority of the Church. This theory is the one most commonly associated with Catholics, and it has certainly encouraged the kind of Catholic rationalist who has no natural taste for religion but nonetheless believes.

Neither of these theories, for all their strength, suggests any strong motive for playing a vigorous part in secular affairs. The first encourages retirement from the noise of the world in order to hear the still, small voice of God speaking to the soul. The second makes faith a matter of obedience to authority – another kind of passive role. Though in the first instance knowledge gained may prompt social action, and in the second thoroughgoing obedience involves doing what authority asserts to be just, in both cases secular life is marginalized, and there seems no compelling reason why faith should not be practised in isolation from human society as a whole.

Certainly as a matter of observation, those deeply influenced by popular versions of these theories often see faith simply as a quest for orthodoxy, and salvation exclusively in the area of sacred doctrine and worship. Sometimes they shy away from any kind of social or political action as contaminating, or because they do not see it as any part of their religion. Others defend such action mainly on the ground that if they are not seen to do good, no one will find them credible. Such results seem inevitable when the spiritual and the secular are seen as separate realms.

But have the fiducial theories done better? It would appear not. Neither Luther's definition of faith as 'an absolute reliance on the saving merits of Christ who freely bestows the gifts of salvation on those who trust in his grace' nor Calvin's that 'faith is a firm and certain knowledge of God's beneficence towards us, founded upon the truth of the freely given promise in Christ, both revealed to our minds and sealed upon our hearts through the Holy Spirit' provide such guidance in themselves on how that faith should influence our dealings with the visible world. This absolute trust in God is very attractive, and can lead to a deep devotional life, but it does not seem to impose any duty of bettering human society. On the contrary modern theologians have been uneasy with it for this very reason, Bonhoeffer and Barth among them, and Ernst Troeltsch is very sharply critical:

> 'Lutheran Christian individualism has retired behind the line of battle of all external events and outward activity, into a purely personal spirituality.... As soon as the Christian believer turns from this spirituality to take part in real life, he can only express his inner liberty through submission to the existing order, as a method of manifesting Christian love to the brethren, and to society as a whole, or as something evil to be passively endured and accepted.'

It was this kind of reading which underlies the judgment of Niebuhr that the Lutheran divorce of heaven and earth, and its stress on passive righteousness, had paved the way for Nazism. In passing it is worth perhaps remarking that just as the Church's complacency in face of Nazism prompted a new breed of theologians like Bonhoeffer, so it is the Church's apparent complacency in face of the poverty and dependence of the world's poor that has triggered off new thinking on the Catholic side.

It is to this we must next turn, especially the Liberation theologians of Latin America, such as Hugo Assman, Segundo Galilea, Gustavo Gutierrez and Luis Segundo – though perhaps to lump them together is itself an act of injustice. It is among them that the divorce of faith from secular life, the effects of an exclusively interior and individualistic faith, have been most keenly felt and severely condemned.

Their view is that faith must involve commitment, that any given act of faith must correspond to the actual historical situation in which it is made. Or to put it more dramatically and perhaps less precisely that faith cannot operate in a social void. Their characteristic, and it is one which has deafened many ears to their message, is to couch their theology in terms borrowed from Marxism. Thus they say that the word of God comes to us through the historical situation which mediates it to the believer; in Latin America that means it is the cry of the poor and oppressed which mediates the word of God, and only by coming close to these afflicted ones can we hear what God is saying to us and demanding of us. Next, faith requires commitment to *praxis*, that is the sum of those human activities capable of transforming human society. When this is not done the word becomes distorted and alienating. It is only through this commitment that we can recognize what needs to be done here and now for the bettering of society, and the possibilities for shaping the future, even though we shall never know the full truth until God's kingdom is finally consummated. As for the goal, it is liberation (a biblical usage based on that for the manumission of slaves) – liberation of oppressed nations and social classes, liberation of mankind in the course of human history, and liberation from sin and total reconciliation with God through Jesus Christ. Commitment to this liberation constitutes the warm welcome to God's word required by faith.

In its present rough-hewn form, liberation theology has been the target of many critical arrows, not only on account of its Marxist vesture. Dulles himself, by no means unsympathetic, lists a number of objections. That it seems to leave out any question of God making himself known directly to the human spirit, despite the long tradition of Christian mysticism; that here faith seems like a response to the historical situation rather than the call of God; that it does not take account of the psychological complexity of the human mind, though in fact people can believe one thing and yet do another; and that poverty, degradation and dependency can take many forms, not just those which so rightly anguish the theologians of Latin America.

This said, the theory also has many strengths. It has a decent Biblical foundation exemplified in John's 'Whoever does what is true comes to the light' or Paul's 'faith working through love' which suggests the transforming effect that faith can have on the world. Most notably, instead of being bemused by the continuous fluctuations of ideas and activity that occur from one generation to another, or dismissing them as irrelevant (as more static and passive theories of faith are inclined to do), the liberation theory makes actual experience of the contemporary human struggles a primary text along with scripture and tradition. Again it chimes in with our contemporary sense of the power of human initia-

tive to shape the course of our lives, and with the related
sense that God wishes man to take the responsibility for his
future into his own hands. In this it is true to the nature of
Christianity which is a non-fatalistic religion in the sense
that it believes man to be responsible for his acts, and does
not regard him simply as a puppet in the hands of God or
Fate. In short it is a theory which matches some of the
deepest feelings of contemporary man, and allows us to live
at ease with the main thrusts of this modern age without the
constant temptation to think that nothing matters, human
activity is pointless, human achievements unserious, and
human insights only of curiosity value, because the
interior, spiritual, life is all that matters.

Even more positively it insists that meeting the great
challenges of our own day, challenges to mankind's very
survival, is not an optional extra for Christians with a taste
for that kind of thing, nor social concern an auxiliary dimension of the true inner life which really counts, but that the
quest for justice is indeed a constituent element of the
Church's and the individual Christian's mission. Christians, in short, are not asked to lead a double life or to suffer
divided loyalties.

This view is reinforced by another modern theological
insight. It is the thesis, germinal in Protestant theologians
like Bonhoeffer but worked out in recent years by theologians like Karl Rahner, that God is not known as another
object, an extension of creation, but by co-naturality, that is
by engaging in God-like activity. Wherever there is genuine
love and compassion for the neighbour, God is being loved in
the quality of the relationship. Godlike being and doing is
the way in which God becomes known as through a glass
darkly. The same is true of our knowledge of Christ. The
surest way of knowing Christ is in the experience of an existence spent in selfless service of others. Through such experience, a participation in God's life, grace and truth are known
as one, and so too knowledge and love. It is important to
notice that this is not the same thing as saying that we serve
others because we see Christ in them, or for his sake, both of
which motives have often been invoked to encourage Christian charity but both of which suggest that the neighbour is
only loved because of his perceived relationship to Christ.
But, as Dych shrewdly observes, those who are saved in the
Gospel because they have cared for their neighbour are sur-

prised since they were not aware that they were serving Christ in so doing. Here again is more than a hint that human activity, especially loving activity, is good in itself. It does not need a sprinkling of holy water to make it so.

I would claim then, that liberation theology, though embryonic, represents a genuine advance in our understanding of the relation between the spiritual and the secular. It breaks out of the dualism which creates so many tensions in Christian life, and out of the 'garden of the soul' type of spirituality which makes religion an essentially private, individual activity. I believe too that even if the liberation theologians have applied their own insights too narrowly, because of the appalling social situation in which they find themselves, the insights themselves will gradually be recognized to have a wider validity. Most especially their recognition that the liberation which Christ brings is meant to cover every aspect of human existence and not just the internal taboos, guilts, fears and limitations we suffer, is of permanent importance. So too the allied notion, also biblically soundly based, that the kingdom of heaven is already here among us and not simply a Heavenly Utopia which we can reach only after death and to which secular activity is entirely irrelevant. They bring forward the day when we recognize that the quest for holiness and for human wholeness are not two separate quests but one.

The implications of this not only for Catholicism but perhaps also for other world religions are considerable. Certainly the various theories of faith are likely to co-exist for a long time to come. The more traditional theories have a strong grip, and I for one believe they still contribute something vital to a total concept of faith. But it may be that Christians have taken an exceptional experience as the standard, and so created unreal ideals and expectations sufficiently far removed from actual human experience as to undermine the credibility of Christianity itself. Sharp divisions between the spiritual and the material, holiness and humanity, the Church and the human society, have all encouraged the idea that the Christian must lead a double-life and struggle with conflicting loyalties. The essential unity of the human person, human experience and human destiny have been lost sight of. Yet for the time being tensions will remain between those who see religion as a separate compartment of life, and those who see the whole range of human interest and occupation as essentially spiritual and God-filled. And the tension between the two will lead, as it is doing at present in the Third World, to clashes over the Church's ecclesiastical policy, church organisation, liturgy, and above all the social dimension of its mission. But I do believe that even if it is time for slow digestion, the present time is also a watershed in Christian history and mankind's religious understanding. Within the Catholic Church itself this re-definition will I think lead to greater flexibility in its relations with other Christian bodies and the other great world religions, as well as those engaged in both old and new sciences.

What is more, many of the insights of these Latin American theologians seem to me to be a natural growth from certain traditional Catholic characteristics. The very word 'Catholic' suggests something all-embracing, a faith that can penetrate and illuminate every aspect of human existence and be at home with every human culture and enterprise. Again the Catholic characteristic is, as I have already suggested, to render the spiritual in material terms, the invisible in visible terms. In my view that instinct is now pushing Catholics towards a clearer recognition that God's taking of human flesh and sharing in human experience have graced the whole visible creation, revealed the intrinsic goodness of human activity, and provided a solid ground for our convictions about the dignity of the human person, as well as offering a sure promise that we and the whole of creation will ultimately reach that state of completion of which our deepest dreams and desires speak to us.

I spoke at the beginning of Rouffignac man and of how little he could have foreseen of the things that were to come, least of all the coming of Christ. Christ was born into the world after an almost interminable period of human gestation. Before he comes again perhaps there must be a period of human maturation almost as long. That cave is also a striking testimony to the antiquity of man and his slow evolution; to the antiquity also of the religious instinct. There can never be a point when we say that all truth is grasped and that we can rest on our journey. I believe we ourselves are living through one of the most important stages on that journey and that Catholicism, for all its failures, weaknesses and mistakes, is revealing yet again its immense stores of vitality, and in so doing, helping humanity as a whole to chart the next stage of its long and mysterious course.

Discussion

Q. If something is true, why should it require faith in order to believe it? Does not faith imply belief based on insufficient information, like that of the savage who believes in a 'cargo cult'?

A. I will not go into a disquisition on 'cargo cults' and how they arose. The real point is that the act of faith is a very complex one, and this is partly the difficulty of trying to define it. It does have some intellectual content because it is an act. We have many parallels in human experience and in our human relationships. If you go along to the doctor, you may know that he is qualified, you may know that he has a good history of curing his patients, you may like the look of him, you may like his approach, but there has to come a point where you say to yourself 'I believe this man can cure me'; there is an element of trust when you say 'Doctor, my life is in your hands'. It is not simply a detached intellectual judgment, as it might be, for example, if you said, 'I can hear the noise of a railway train; I can see in the timetable that a train is due to arrive at such a time and somebody has already told me that there is a train at this particular moment', and then go on to make the judgment: 'Yes, there is a train coming into the station now'. It is not a purely intellectual judgment; it is in a sense an act of faith if you cannot actually see the train. It is a combination of these things, and I think the problem is that certain vital elements become separated out. What it certainly is not is just a kind of wild 'I will believe this nonsense', or something which on balance seems to be nonsense, simply for the sake of believing. This is why one cannot dispense with the traditional theories entirely and say they have been supplanted by a new one. The important thing about the new kind of definition is its stress on faith as a commitment of the whole person and the fact that it suggests very strongly that we come to know God, not as something in addition to what already exists in creation, in other words as another created object, but that we come to know Him most intimately and deeply in the actual living of our lives and in our ordinary human relationships. If those relationships are of a certain

29

kind, we meet God in them and I think that is a very profound and very necessary perception.

Q. You described the Mass as the point of closest encounter between man and God, yet at another time you described contemplation as the union of the soul with God. Is there here a difference of kind or of degree?

A. It is really a difference of degree. In Catholic belief, God makes himself available to us in countless different ways; that in a sense is the thesis of the whole of my lecture. But in the particular form of the Mass, God does so in a way which man himself could never have invented. God makes himself known in a way which makes it certain that He is here present; here we are in the closest possible contact with Him and through a ritual that makes very plain sense to us. It has so many echoes: bread, the staple of life; the meal, an activity which creates bonds of friendship and trust and a sense of responsibility to those we eat with, and so on. There are all kinds of levels of meaning in eating and in meals which are at the back of our minds when we take part in the Eucharist; in a sense, the fact that that kind of meeting takes place in the Eucharist, throws into a rather different light all those other meetings, from the simple 'Would you like something to eat?' to the family banquet.

Q. You said 'the Kingdom of Heaven is among us'. Is not the Biblical text 'The Kingdom of Heaven is within you'? Do you see these as meaning the same thing?

A. Here we are up against the problem of Biblical translation. In more recent translations it is the habit to say 'The Kingdom of Heaven is among you', not 'within you'. I do not think that these are mutually exclusive, by a long way, but I think the second translation perhaps emphasizes that the Kingdom is something which comes about through social activity and is not simply a seed buried in our own individual hearts. This is something again which is characteristic, not simply of modern Catholicism, but of modern Christianity: to recognize that there is a social dimension to salvation and it is not simply, if you like, fishing individual souls out of time's waters. We stand or fall together as a human race and it is the race which is redeemed and not just the individual human being. That said, of course the building up of a kingdom or a society of love and justice depends also very greatly on the movements within our own hearts and minds.

30

Q. You said or quoted that 'a man could be a believer without having a taste for religion'. Do you agree that one can have a taste for religion without being a believer? How can we reconcile the two things?

A. A very clear example of a self-confessed believer who had no religious instinct was Hilaire Belloc, and perhaps one might say of him that one would not want too many of the same kind, but that was in fact his situation. I have myself met people who claimed to feel no strong sense of God, no great taste for any kind of communication with God, and yet believed that there was a God, believed that Christ was who he claimed to be, believed that the Church was something which he founded, and so on. If one is to take people at their own estimation, one must accept that you can believe without having much taste for religion. On the other side, again, I have certainly met people who had an extremely strong academic interest in religion and kept an open mind as to the possibilities it offered of answering some of the questions that troubled them, without actually believing, in the sense of thinking that this or that of religion's main claims were true or subscribing to any particular religious practice. I am not sure that I have not on occasion met Christian theologians who would fall into that category, who treated theology as another science like geometry, without apparently being profoundly committed to religion or being very markedly affected by it.

Q. 'Rendering spiritual material which is invisible, visible': is this an explanation of the place of ritual within the Catholic Church?

A. My instinctive answer is to say 'Yes' but it is linked too with other kinds of human conduct. The movements of the interior spirit are constantly expressed in visible gestures, posture, facial expressions and activities like handing a gift to someone. In the practice of religion that kind of gesture and action becomes formalized, and so in the main ceremonies of the church there is always an important function for ritual in trying to find the appropriate gesture or sign or movement to express some invisible motion of the mind or the heart. Sometimes those signs can be outgrown, and then they no longer express what they were originally seen as expressing. This brings us to the point which I mentioned briefly in passing of the cultural conditioning of so much religious expression; this is something we are more aware of

31

nowadays than we were, say, fifty years ago. There comes a point where certain kinds of gesture, expression or action, which we perhaps feel fond of simply because they are familiar, have lost the power to communicate what they are meant to communicate. It is the characteristic of Christianity, and of Catholicism most especially, to make the invisible, visible, to put it in a sense within human reach. We should not see the doctrine of the incarnation and the sacraments of the church, the physical organization, as disparate but as all part of a continuous process. This goes back to the Catholic belief, and one by no means exclusively Catholic, that in Jesus Christ, God did in a sense cast off his cloak of invisibility and speak to us through human words, human gestures, a human life, and that as a human being, he shared in the human experience. Thus through the whole of Christian history there has been the tendency to continue the process of making the invisible, visible and expressing the spiritual in material shapes and forms

Q. Do Catholics believe that God did not reveal himself to man in the many thousands of years before Christ?

A. No indeed, quite the reverse. One of the strongest Catholic beliefs is that God has been revealing himself to man for countless ages and in all sorts of ways, most especially of course, though it seems a truism to remark it, in his dealing with the Jewish people. As the scriptures themselves say, 'He spoke to them in signs and in words and through the prophets.' The coming of Christ was in a sense the culmination of a long process of preparation of that people in particular to recognize what was happening to them when Christ came, a process of gradual self-revelation so that enough would be known about God to make Christ recognizable when he came. Modern Catholic theology would say that the coming of Christ had effects on early man and on man in all his stages of development, that certain things happened to man because Christ came eventually into the world, though man himself was unaware of and could not have identified these effects. I do not want to suggest in the slightest way that Christ's coming can be divorced from the whole religious history of mankind, either before or since. Any of you who have travelled in Asia, for example, will have shared the embarrassment which I personally feel over the way that Christians, and especially Christian missionaries, have crashed into worlds which

32

they did not understand and have pushed aside great religions, great ways to God, full of deep understanding and wisdom, in a most arrogant way. Not very long ago I was in Thailand at a dinner attended by a lot of tourists (like all tourists, I did not feel that I was quite a tourist). One of the evening's entertainments was some extraordinarily beautiful dancing by Thai dancers. I would have thought that even Goths and Vandals would have sat there in awe at the beauty of it, but in fact a large number of Americans and Frenchmen – those two nationalities I could identify at the time, but perhaps there were more – leapt around the building, taking photographs, making a noise, laughing and chattering and even getting in the way of the dancers so that they had to stop. That sort of brutish Western behaviour has a religious parallel. Very often we Christians, instead of sitting down quietly and first listening and learning and reaching for areas of agreement, have just crashed in and smashed up what we did not understand or dismissed it as primitive.

Hinduism in a
Post-Industrial Society

Shivesh C. Thakur

In view of the diversity of beliefs and practices found among
even the major religious traditions, one may doubt whether
it is possible to speak of the nature of religious man in any
general and useful way. Even without the inclusion of
Hinduism among the world's religions, the picture may be
confusing enough. Once Hinduism has been added, however,
the situation is nothing short of chaos.

We are told[1] that Al-Biruni, 'the first Muslim to make a
thorough study of the phenomenon of Hinduism at a time
when Islam was making its first sanguinary excursions into
India', in the 11th century AD, was, to say the least, puzzled.
He wrote:

'They [the Hindus] totally differ from us in religion, as we
believe in nothing in which they believe, and vice versa. On
the whole there is very little disputing about theological
topics among themselves; at the utmost, they fight with
words, but they will never stake their soul or body or their
property on religious controversy.'

That Hindus, by and large, fight with words rather than
swords has been amply demonstrated by their history:
almost any race of people prepared to use their swords or
guns could vanquish the Hindus at will. And if the British
had not been so over-sensitive as to be injured by words, one
wonders if they need ever have folded up their empire in
India! At least the persecution and harassment of an individual merely because he holds different religious views has
not been the Hindu's typical temptation. This was, it seems,
true in Al-Biruni's time and, in spite of recent shameful
examples to the contrary, remains by and large true today.
To anyone from a background of faiths of Semitic origin, the
Hindu's lack of dogma, of certainty in the truth of his own
beliefs and his readiness to accommodate obviously inconsistent ideas and practices, must have been baffling. The
fact is that even with the passage of nearly a thousand years
and the many revolutionary advances in the means of com-

munication and transport, Hinduism is still a baffling phenomenon to non-Hindus.

Al-Biruni would have been bewildered to find – as would be a modern visitor to India with rigid concepts of religion – that a follower of Hinduism could be a mystic, a theist, an agnostic or even an atheist. Only Hinduism, I think, would be likely to furnish the example of supreme irony that it was its school dedicated to the preservation of orthodoxy that denied the existence of God.[2] The argument was in essence the application of Occam's razor: that given certain other principles and entities for the explanation of the world and its workings, God was quite simply redundant. One can sympathize with Al-Biruni for failing to appreciate how the Hindu was unlikely to be worked up about questions such as: Is there one God or are there many gods? God, according to him, is not a thing or a finite entity susceptible of exact quantification. Given who you are and where you stand on the scale of understanding, you could say either that there was one God, or that there were two or three, five or fifty, three hundred or three hundred and thirty million or billion. It is like asking how many units of air there are. In a sense there can be as many units of air as you wish to create by raising walls and barriers to separate the air in this room from that of adjoining rooms, of this city from that of other cities, of this country from that of other countries. But the fact remains that air is, in the end, one all-embracing entity. I wonder how many people watching '330 Million Gods', the first episode of *The Long Search*[3], got this message!

Staying with *The Long Search* for another few moments, do you remember the inimitable Mr Sharma taking Ron Eyre on a guided tour of the religious landscape of Benares? Mr Sharma says that in worshipping clay or other images, it is not the clay that the Hindu worships but what it symbolises. The image is a symbol, a pointer, and you only keep your finger pointing, he says, until your companion has seen the object you are trying to draw his attention to. Ron Eyre interjects, 'What if the person does not see the object at all and keeps looking at your finger?' Mr Sharma replies, smiling calmly, 'For him God is in no hurry!' Al-Biruni must have been nonplussed by these 'idolaters' (as he must have called them) who went to no end of trouble installing clay and other images of gods and goddesses for the explicit

purpose of worshipping these; and yet at the end of the appointed few days or hours unceremoniously drowned or
burnt them; and, to crown the sacrilege, did it all so cheer-
fully and in good fun!

I must be forgiven if I have given the impression that
Al-Biruni was in any sense an ignorant man or dim-witted.
On the contrary, he was a profound scholar and narrator
whose understanding of the complexity or subtlety of
Hinduism has not often been paralleled. From now on,
therefore, our guided tour of Hinduism, necessarily a brief
package-tour, had better be conducted for the benefit of a
lesser man, a modern tourist from another culture. What
further paradoxes may Hindu society present to this
tourist's view?

Our tourist may notice that the Hindu believes that not
only humans but all creatures have souls and, more strik-
ingly, that all these souls are eternal and uncreated, though
from one birth to another they may change their material
bodies or forms – a process which may continue almost endlessly, until an individual soul, through a personal awakening or wisdom (*jnāna*), attains liberation and thus steps off
this cycle of births and deaths and suffering. At this point I
cannot resist the temptation to tell the story of a European
scholar of Hinduism who, when asked by the interviewer on
American television, 'How can you maintain that no new
souls are being created when in America alone the human
population is nearly 200 million now as against so much
less, say, a hundred years ago?' Our scholar replied, 'Well,
you must take into account the souls of the innumerable
Indians who were killed by the whites and whose souls are
being reborn.' The interviewer was not satisfied, 'The
number of Indians killed, even on a wild estimate, would not
make up the difference between the population a hundred
years ago and the present two hundred million, surely?'
Replied our intrepid scholar, 'And what happened to all the
buffaloes do you think?'[4] This fascinating account of the
world's population explosion may not appeal to a demogra-
pher but it is bound to warm a Hindu's heart!

But to return to our tourist. He will notice that the Hindu
believes that this cosmic transmigration of souls (*samsāra*)
across all forms of life is governed by inexorable law
(*karma*). One's actions, attitudes and functional position in
the order of things in this life largely determines at least the

outline of the next. But, surprisingly, this law is not so inexorable after all, for otherwise, no one could ever be liberated and thus lift his eternal soul (*ātman*) right out of this mess. The law only operates and has binding power so long as the soul is under the veil of ignorance (*avidyā* or *māyā*). Once it has acquired the redeeming wisdom that it is not separate from the essence that forms the ground of the whole universe (*Brahman*), it enters the realm of freedom and bliss. Space, time, causality and other limiting conditions of this world become impotent, as fried seeds lose their power to germinate.

What is the nature of this liberation (*moksa*) and how may it be attained are questions which, once again in true Hindu style, elicit many different answers. The vast majority of Hindus take this liberated state to be a kind of super-heaven where the redeemed souls live in eternal happiness, and in close proximity to and loving dependence on God. It is believed that this state comes about through the redeeming love and mercy of God which He in His glory bestows on His devotees. The duty of one who aspires to the membership of this 'commune' is to live in utter submission to the will of God and to love, cherish and adore Him and to chant His name ceaselessly. But there is also the belief that even if you do nothing and have in fact been the greatest of rogues, God, if He so chooses, may still redeem you, just as the cat picks up its kitten by the scruff of its neck and the latter does not even have to hold on to the mother. Others believe that the way to this blessed condition is to discharge your duties (*dharma*) ceaselessly and without attachment to the rewards or fear of punishments that the performance of such duties may bring forth. That is the main purport of Krishna's advice to Arjuna in the *Gītā*. Is this state to be attained by renunciation and mortification of the flesh? Yes, as witness the ungainly sights of so-called yogis spending much of their life-time lying on beds of nails. And yet there are Tāntrics who swear that the only way to heaven is through indulgence, to the point of saturation, in the delights of the five *m*'s: *māmsa* (meat), *matsya* (fish), *madirā* (intoxicants), *mudrā* (wealth) and *mithuna* (sex). Not for them the vegetarianism, abstinence and renunciation so typical of the rest of Hinduism! But perhaps the interpretation of liberation and the path appropriate to it that has elicited the assent and loyalty of some of the most admired of

37

Hindus, as well as non-Hindus, is not that of a climb to a heavenly abode of bliss. Indeed, this has been regarded by them as a descent into a state of slumber from which it may be excessively difficult to wake up. Heaven, according to them, is the ultimate ensnarement and clinging to *samsāra*. The soul's full destiny lies in its mystic absorption into the one *Brahman*, through the acquisition of redeeming wisdom, by the study of Vedānta and the practice of yogic meditation. Only thus can one pierce the veil of ignorance.

All this, however, only relates to the 'doctrinal' side of Hinduism, if the phrase is at all appropriate here. If our explorer of Hinduism moves in the direction of noticing the social organization of its followers, what he will see may be truly confounding. These Hindus who vaunt their excessive tolerance in matters of belief are, on the social side, ossified into a rigid class and caste structure. Everyone must be either a Brāhmin (scholar-priest), a Kshatriya (warrior-prince), a Vaishya (farmer-tradesman), or else a Shūdra (the lowly chap who does all the hard dirty work). The Brāhmin who happily preaches the essential oneness of all souls practises a degrading form of discrimination against some of his fellow Shūdras. This is the Hindu system of the four classes (*varnas*), infamous all over the world as the caste system. Along with the four *varnas* has traditionally gone the system of the four stages (*āshramas*) which every individual Hindu (or at least those of the top three classes) must pass through. He must spend the first twenty-five-odd years of his life being a student; the next twenty-five or so being a householder – marrying, procreating, being the guardian of all social and ritual duties befitting his class; then for the next few years gradually withdrawing from the hurly-burly of worldly life while preparing his children to take over the reins; and, finally, renouncing the world of conventional duties and ties altogether in order to devote himself to transcendental concerns. This system of stages, especially the last of these, is rarely followed now and even when it was, exceptions were allowed. Enlightened individuals, like the great Shamkara, were allowed to pass directly from the first to the last stage. Exceptions to the class system, however, only seem to have occurred in myths and fairy tales!

How does one tie up together all these incommensurables, and many more that we have not even mentioned? The Hindu himself has never, or hardly ever, seen this as a problem. But our tourist could be expected, with good reason, to be raving by now. So let us leave him to regain his composure, while we move in another direction.

If this sketch of Hinduism as a religion has strained your credulity, I must warn that there is worse to come as we enter, now, the fantasy world of projections about the post-industrial society. This is the world of the Herman Kahns and the Daniel Bells whose phantasmagoria of futurology is designed to keep our optimistic spirits up in the face of inflation, unemployment, depression (in all senses of the term) and general economic chaos in the so-called developed part of the world – not to mention hunger, malnutrition, inadequate housing and a numbing feeling of general helplessness in many of the developing countries. Thanks to our ingenuity, we are told, we will all have everything we could care to have: it is only a matter of time. Instant information and services at the touch of a button, oceans of leisure we will almost not know what to do with, long – perhaps immortal – lives free from most diseases, interplanetary, even intergalactic travel for fun, all this and much more form part of the picture of the good life that our grandchildren, if not our children, are going to be heirs to. We may be humans ourselves but our progeny are certain to be fairies, flitting about from one colony to another in space (or is it heaven?), in eternal youth and happiness! Now, I am not against science fiction nor am I repelled by the thought of heaven. Quite the contrary, I enjoy *Star Trek* and *Star Wars* and *2001: A Space Odyssey*, not least because of the glorious female androids who seem to combine so miraculously beauty and grace, brains and wit with unquestioning obedience and the desire to please. But as a philosopher, it is, I could say, almost my duty to be a spoil-sport. A free trip to one of these space colonies, as a treat, I would relish immensely. But the prospect of living in this sphere of suspended animation does not fill my heart with delight.

But, more seriously, the trouble with these futuristic projections is that their assumptions are all wrong. The surplus resources required for these collective dreams to come true presuppose a continuous annual overall economic growth rate of at least 4 per cent. This just simply has not been the case. If Japan and, say, Germany are achieving these targets, or doing better, at any given time, they are, and can only be, doing so at the expense of Britain, the United States and France, not to mention poor Italy, Spain and Greece or the rest of the world. You see, there are no longer four 'spare' continents from which to extract the resources for the dream-lives of a fraction of the population of America and Europe. These pictures of the post-industrial society seem to have taken no real notice of the physical limits to growth so ably argued by the Club of Rome.[5] Trends in the world economy have come out unquestionably in favour of the line taken by the Club. Since these over-optimistic forecasts were made in the mid-sixties, not once has the world's overall growth rate, or even of the affluent societies as a whole, approximated those targets.

Even supposing, however, just for the sake of the argument, that they turn out to be true in the near future, even then this post-industrial cornucopia is unlikely to come about for the masses; nor, in the most unlikely event of that happening, is it going to produce the promised state of 'economic satiety', and therefore happiness and content- ment for the masses. This has been most persuasively and forcefully argued by the late Fred Hirsch in his superb book, *Social Limits to Growth*.[6] Let me quote a passage:

'The most evocative rendering of the theme of growth as a dynamic equalizing agent has been offered by two British sociologists, Michael Young and Peter Willmott. Building on the analysis of Daniel Bell, in turn inspired by de Tocqueville, they represented the growth process as a marching column. The ranking of the column reflects the income distribution, which stays more or less unchanged over time, as the column as a whole advances. The people at the head are usually "the first to wheel in a new direction. The last rank keeps its distance from the first, and the distance between them does not lessen. But as the column advances, the last rank does eventually reach and pass the point which the first rank had passed some time before.... The people in the rear cannot, without breaking rank and rushing ahead, reach where the van *is*, but, since the whole column is moving forward, they can hope in due course to reach where the van *was*."'[7]

This quotation ends with the telling comment by Hirsch,

'Evidently, the vanguard is not the place for the proletariat: quite the contrary.' The point of his argument is that this process of the vanguard for ever moving on, with the proletariat for ever trying to catch up and, worse still, finding, when it has at last reached the previous target, that its destination has by then been divested of all its appeal – is frustrating, pointless and self-defeating. The Seychelles may now be a tourist paradise, but, by the time everyone has come to be in a position to have a holiday there, it may not be worth a spit! There is no doubt that in the past increased productivity and, consequently, increased social welfare has been made possible by individual free enterprise in a market economy. But the point has long been passed, he argues, when this could continue to keep happening. One of Hirsch's reasons why this can no longer be taken for granted will be dealt with in a while. But let me conclude this particular argument of his in his own words. 'The crude concept of economic growth', he says, 'neglects such complications and sees national growth as individual economic advance writ large.'[8] The Kahn-Bell variety of futurism, in so far as it is meant to be a picture of the proletariat's eventual paradise, is nothing but a mirage.

My objection to this blue-print of post-industrial society, however, is not simply on account of the falsity of these assumptions. I regard the whole approach itself as misconceived. For it takes no real account of what is basically wrong with the industrial-technological way of life, buttressing and buttressed by capitalist free enterprise. In this approach every task, however subtle or abstract, is seen as a problem of engineering: mostly of physical engineering or technology, but occasionally of economic or social engineering. In the face of any problem, including that of human happiness and fulfilment, the search is invariably for either a gadget or a method of analysis and control. For the accompanying belief is that, given sufficient time, our ingenuity will always come up with some mathematically precise means of solving or dissolving it. There is no doubt that engineering has had immense successes in acquiring certain basic amenities, like food, heating, lighting, housing, transport and communication. But just because of its successes, the problems of an industrial society no longer happen to be of this dimension. The new challenges relate largely to what has come to be known, in popular parlance, as 'quality of

41

life'; and the problems raised here are ecological-environmental, moral, metaphysical, religious and ideological.

Let me go back to Hirsch again for a moment. The reason why in the past individualistic economic advance and collective advance (that is, social welfare) have gone hand in hand (to the extent they have), and the reason why this can no longer be the case, is this. In the words of Adam Smith, '[Men] could safely be trusted to pursue their own self-interest without undue harm to the community not only because of the restrictions imposed by the law, but also because they were subject to built-in restraint derived from morals, religion, custom and education.'[9] Today, however, the only restraining factor is the law, for 'contemporary liberal celebrations of the dominance of self-interest'[10] have divorced economic individualism from its moral-religious base. Milton Friedman is perhaps the best (or worst?) exemplar of this new philosophy of naked self-interest. His attitude as well as Hirsch's pungent comment are summed up in the following extract:

> 'In discussing principles of income distribution, Friedman makes the point that a man who finds a sum of money in the street will not generally be expected to share his windfall with the less fortunate who have made no such find. Two other possible courses of action that an earlier bourgeois virtue would have demanded – that the finder should take the money to the police station or else burn it – receive no mention. The individual, in effect, is invited to choose the morality as well as the God of his choice.'[11]

How can a blue-print of post-industrial society even begin to be worthy of consideration if it fails to eliminate the main evil of an industrial society, namely, its disruption and destruction of the environment, its almost total disregard of ecology and its callous neglect of the symbiosis between man and nature? And the stark fact is that the Kahn-Bell models of post-industrial society are, in principle and practice, quite incapable of assimilating this dimension. For they are based on the arrogant human chauvinism which regards nature as the object of human control, conquest and colonization. Nothing seems to have been learnt about the organic relationship between humans and the rest of the eco-system; and, worse still, the history of imperialism and domination seems to have taught nothing either. Colonisation and exploitation – whether of one country by another, of one planet by another, or of nature by man – always produces short-term benefits for the coloniser; but the long-term price paid in the process requires a very high degree of wisdom for a proper calculation. If you ruin nature, nature will ruin you, if not today, then tomorrow; if not in this generation, then in the next.

But I am far from suggesting that mere considerations of self-interest or prudence will ever enable an adequate transition from the philosophy of control and mastery over nature to that of respect for and co-operation, even partnership, with it. The change required is in moral, and ultimately, metaphysical attitudes. Seen in bland, abstract terms, this may not look self-evident. For one may say 'Yes, I see that we should respect nature, care for her. But what does this have to do with metaphysics?' So let me explain, even at the risk of being tedious. It is easy to give assent to respect for nature, where nature is seen in an abstract, obscure fashion. But when you look around you see that this nature that you are supposed to respect consists of worms and insects, sticks and stones, mountains and rivers. Respect for these, without particular sorts of metaphysical, religious commitments, is not only hard but barely even makes sense. But if you are, let us say, an animist who truly believes that all of these things, imperceptibly but definitely, hide in themselves whatever it is that happens to be your own essence – life, spirit, psyche, or whatever – then wanton tampering with and violence to nature could become out of question for you. For the benefit of those that will not countenance animism – only fit for 'primitives'! – let me put in another picture. If you happen to have the conviction that the same God that resides in your heart also has His abode in the rest of nature, then you may perhaps be in a position fully to appreciate what your commitment to respect for nature really entails. That caring for nature has this metaphysical dimension is not, I understand on good authority, grasped even by editors of journals dedicated to ecology; and it's time it was!

Much more no doubt can be said, but I think I have talked enough about the sort of post-industrial society I do not want, and, by implication, the kind of society that I would like to see. Let me now speak somewhat more directly about the features of my own outline. A post-industrial society must, in some respects, be like a pre-industrial society; only, it will be a genuine synthesis of the best features of both. It will have a firm moral, religious and metaphysical base; not metaphysical in the sense of obscurantist, but in the sense that genuinely alternative articulations of life-styles will be welcome. It will not be against the production of things; but the mere fact that silicon chips can be readily and cheaply made, will not be a sufficient reason for every individual having a computer; or just because Windscale can be financed, and even earn some Japanese yen by reprocessing their nuclear garbage, the incalculable hazards of proliferating nuclear power and its processes will not be countenanced. It will not be against technology, but will only tolerate technology that is 'sensitive' to human needs and aesthetic tastes, to the natural resources of a given region and, above all, to the symbiosis between man and nature; technology will not replace but meaningfully supplement and enhance man; as artistic creation does. Such a society will be socialist, in some important sense of the term, but will not tolerate centralisation and state-control that take away men's basic freedoms. And it certainly will not be a 'monoculture' where people can only understand 'advance' in economic terms, and, therefore, find themselves, perforce, in a rat-race for economic goods for the sole reason that its 'élite', in their self-interest, had decided to 'wheel in a new direction', that is, towards the pursuit of certain new technological goods or gadgets. Hopefully, in this society economic values will not even be dominant, though everyone's basic necessities will be provided for.

Does this sound like another dream, of a different kind, when I have dismissed alternative conceptions partly because they were unlikely of fulfilment? If so, you will appreciate why I cannot see it that way: it is always easier to label someone else's dreams as such. More importantly, however, if it is a dream, I certainly do not entertain any unrealistic expectations that some simple miracle will bring this state of affairs to fruition. A great deal of effort is required in order to orient us in this direction. And unless we wish to find ourselves in the chaos rather romantically portrayed by the TV series, *The Survivors*[12] (with the inevitable collapse of industrial society which is bound to come one day), we had all better start endeavouring – individually and collectively – to prepare for the gradual ushering in of the kind of society I believe we need for the future. The changes required will be in the hearts and minds of people, not in the advent of a revolutionary technology.

Let me, at last, come to the question of how Hinduism might meet the challenges of such a post-industrial society. In a way, the simple answer is: very well, indeed. During the last few hundred years of its long history, Hinduism may never have met any challenges squarely. But it has bumbled along! It has survived, and awkwardly coped with, conquests, natural catastrophes, imperialistic indignities, over-population and even industrialization. Indeed, we are told that India has become the tenth industrial power in the world. The fact that its industrial 'might' has got it nowhere does not here matter: it is just one more example of bumbling along that I mentioned earlier. If I seem to be guilty of equating Hinduism with India, it is not because I am unaware of the vast non-Hindu population in the country nor of its immense contributions. It is just that etymologically, the word 'Hindu' is simply the Persian for 'Indian'. So 'Hinduism' literally means, or meant, the religion or religions of the people of India. Only foreigners called Hinduism by that name: the Hindus themselves called it *sanātan dharma* (eternal religion), another ubiquitous and amorphous term. However, let me return from this digression. If, in asking how Hinduism might meet the challenges of a post-industrial society, all I had in mind was whether it will be able to bumble or bungle its way through, I would not be wasting my time or yours. Of course it will. What I have in mind, however, is whether it will have something distinctive to offer.

I intend to look at only three major aspects in any detail, and I will spell these out shortly. But before I do so, let me point out in passing that, in spite of official India's progress on the industrial front, most of Hindu society is still at the pre-industrial stage. This, while regrettable in some ways, is not altogether an unhappy state of affairs in our present context. In so far as the post-industrial society, as I envisage it, will in important respects have affinities with pre-industrial ones, Hindu society may find the transition to a post-industrial phase rather less painful than its industrially advanced counterparts. At least economic individualism will be, as it is now, less rampant and virulent in the heart of Hindu society, that is, in its villages. Also the traditional moral and religious base of these villages (though not of the bastardized cities, alas!) is still largely intact. Consequently, in these parts, the much needed moral and religious corrective to economic individualism is still readily available, even though (and happily, I think) the long arm of state law is largely ineffective, if not inoperative. Equally, there is still a traditional and instinctive distrust of, even animosity towards, anything too big, or too powerful; and, as a deeply conservative society, as indeed for other good reasons, change or innovation, for its own sake, is unlikely to be seen by Hindus as progress – a symptom so readily observable in contemporary affluent societies. Small-scale industry and 'sensitive technology'[13] – in the sense of tools and equipment that are seen as answering felt needs, and only these – for the use of small, self-sufficient communities, will find themselves on very hospitable soil. Moreover, traditional Hindu society has never been one where economic values have either been dominant or made the yardstick of progress; the pursuit of wealth (*artha*) and pleasure (*kāma*) has always had to take a position inferior to morals (*dharma*) and liberation (*moksa*). Indeed, poverty was the virtue cultivated by Brāhmins; and Kshatriyas earned their respect by their valour in war and their readiness to fight for justice. Hinduism has not been a monoculture in the sense outlined earlier.

I must, however, now return to the three major aspects mentioned above. The first relates to the nature of religious belief in a post-industrial society. I suggested beforehand that I envisage, for good reason, a return to moral and religious commitment. But I, personally, doubt that over-institutionalised, dogmatic or doctrinaire forms of religion could have much appeal to this new society. All the indications already seem to point towards the growth of forms of belief which answer an individual's own taste, temperament and inclination. For religion, as I see it, should be an individual's personal or private response to the reality around him: this cannot, and should not, be dictated by an external agency, even with the best of motives. The freedom of belief and response to the reality, however, must be tempered by utmost restraint when it comes to social behaviour and obligations. For I may be free to believe in whatever religious ideas I like, and to choose my own form of worship and salvation, but, as a social being, I cannot be free to do what I like. My inclinations and my obligations need not match: indeed, mostly they do not. If this is a correct anticipation of a post-industrial society's needs, then I think Hinduism might answer these quite adequately. For, while allowing the greatest possible latitude in respect of forms of belief and worship, it is relatively unyielding in the matter of an individual's moral and social obligations (*dharma*). The variety of metaphysical and epistemological theories, the many interpretations put on personal salvation, and the many 'officially' acknowledged paths to one's religious goal – these could be said to be the most distinctive feature of Hinduism. This non-dogmatism or variety that confounded Al-Biruni or our hypothetical tourist is not just a historical accident. The *Vedas*, the most sacred of Hindu scriptures, themselves declare, 'Truth is one but wise men call it by different names.'[14] The *Gītā*, another revered scripture, has God Himself saying, 'I respond as appropriate to the many ways in which my devotees approach me.'[15] And yet the same *Gītā* has Krishna, the Lord, announcing, 'I incarnate myself from age to age for the re-establishment of *dharma*'.[16] *Dharma*, a truly comprehensive word, means law, morality, justice and the rule of righteousness. It is not Arjuna's inclination to fight his kith and kin, but Krishna's advice, as Lord and counsel, is clear and unambiguous. As a member of the Kshatriya class, whose duty is to protect justice and law, fight he must. It has nothing to do with his inclinations. This is what accounts for the paradoxical nature of Hinduism; that is why it combines the most liberal, non-doctrinaire approach to faith and worship with the most rigid system of classes and stages. It is because the latter is the sphere of *dharma* wherein there is no room, or hardly any, for liberties. I am no apologist for the class or caste system, as the sequel will show. But the principle of complete personal liberty in matters of religious belief, combined with a well-structured and relatively unbending framework of moral and social behaviour, could serve our post-industrial society very well.

I now come to the metaphysical framework for man's proper relationship to nature, i.e., one of partnership and co-

47

operation and the attitude of respect or reverence for nature. It is well-known, I think, that Hinduism, in common with its sister religions, Buddhism and Jainism – though perhaps to a lesser extent – is committed to the principle of *ahimsā* or non-violence, made famous by Gandhi in recent years. While a negative sounding concept, and perhaps practised by Hindu society in a somewhat negative way, i.e., by simply refraining from killing, it is in fact a very positive ideal. According to Patanjali, the term means 'a complete absence of ill will to all sentient creatures irrespective of time or place.'[17] Hindu practice could undoubtedly benefit from a more positive concept of love and caring for creatures, or at least the addition of Buddhist compassion. But the principle of non-violence is not a bad start.

Non-violence itself, however, is in need of justification. Why must we be non-violent towards creatures? Why must we care for them? Because, according to the Hindu, 'all the [world] is enveloped by the One Lord.'[18] Even Manu, the author of one of the most influential Hindu treatises (and no great liberal, by the way), says, 'That knower of the Self who perceives the Self in all sentient beings and all sentient beings as equal to his own self, attains to his sphere [liberation].'[19] So you see the Hindu's traditional vegetarianism does not derive simply from his fear of eating his grandparents, possibly reborn in animal form, though even that should help the right approach to living beings. The *Brahman*, the all-soul, does not, however, just pervade life, he is in, or he literally is, the whole universe. Nature, in any of its forms, and man are not related as prey and hunter but as one organic whole. Let me quote Paul Deussen, one of the greatest scholars and admirers of Hinduism.

> '"Thou shalt love thy neighbour as thyself" is the requirement of the Bible. But on what grounds is this demand to be based, since feeling is in myself alone and not in another? "Because", the Veda here adds in explanation, "thy neighbour is in truth thy very self and what separates you from him is mere illusion. . . ."'[20]

Metaphysical beliefs of the right sort may not by themselves be enough, but they certainly are necessary if we are to establish, nurture and practise the principle of respect for nature; and Hinduism, it would seem, is certainly well equipped on that score.

The third of the features of the new society I consider as fundamental is socialism. It is no longer morally permissible, and it never should have been, that vast sections of the human population should live in hunger and poverty, and devoid of dignity, while constantly working to the benefit, economic betterment and the enhancement in other ways of the powers and privileges of the few. Socialism in this minimal sense and in that of the equality of opportunity and dignity of treatment for all, should, for the post-industrial society, be a datum. As we have seen, even in the capitalist, industrial society, with its overall ethos of individual economic advance, collective advance, at least in the form of social welfare, has had to be incorporated; even if this operates only minimally in parts of the world and even though socialism is hardly synonymous with social welfare. The post-industrial society, therefore, could, in my opinion, be scarcely worth having without this fundamental tenet. This I do not believe requires argument. But, equally, what would seem not to require any explanation is that Hinduism, as it stands in practice now, will fail this test miserably. Hindu society, with its many classes, in the form of castes alone, organised into a rigid hierarchy in which one's human worth seems to derive primarily from one's place therein, and where the Shūdras, at the lowest rungs of the ladder, are hardly treated as humans – either in economic or moral terms – is as far as you can get from the idea of socialism. This hereditary ordering of people and the consequent degradation of some is the most detestable feature of Hinduism, and for which it is justly ridiculed. The caste system, or its precursor, the system of the four *varnas*, has been central to the organisation of Hindu society from the days of the *Rig Veda*, and is not just a later accretion, though untouchability may well be. Its lofty ideal of the oneness of all forms of life has been rendered hollow by its practice of discrimination; and nothing that I say later should in any way be seen as a defence of this calumny. But, let us face it, no religion has, to my knowledge, been socialist in practice. They have all had to learn to live with it, *post facto*, and it is only to be hoped that Hinduism will eventually get rid of its obnoxious practice of the unequal treatment of people on the basis of their caste. But I have a few more things to say on the subject of socialism and its consistency or otherwise with Hinduism.

While talking earlier about the incompatibility between individualistic economic advance and collective social advance, it seemed clear that the former cannot be an instrument of the latter. For the continued well-being of society, the notion of individual pursuit of profit or wealth has either to be abandoned, or, at least, drastically curtailed. This indeed was the original context in which 'socialism' arose. According to G.D.H. Cole, the author of the classic, *A History of Socialist Thought*:

'The "Socialists" were those who, in opposition to the prevailing stress on the claims of the individual, emphasized the social element in human relations and sought to bring the social question to the front in the great debate about the rights of men....'[21]

It has to be said that in this sense of socialism, Hinduism has been nothing but socialist. Individuals have, on the social plane, as indeed have classes and castes, been merely instruments in achieving the stability, functional interdependence and self-sufficiency of society as a whole. When one reads the works of Owen, Fourier and Proudhon, later to be called the 'Utopians', the similarities between their ideas and those forming the social organisation of Hindu society appear quite striking. 'Owen envisaged a society consisting of small, self-governing, co-operating communities....'[22] Hindu villages are nothing if not that. What is missing from Hindu social organization is that it is not 'established by the free and rational consent of all, of whatever class or station'.[23] Quite the contrary. In Hinduism individuals are forced into roles simply by virtue of their birth, often when they have the least aptitude or inclination for it. If somehow Hinduism could move away from its ossified caste structure and move towards the provision of what Fourier called the 'free choice of occupations, within the wide range of alternatives open'[24] to people, then it could approximate socialism, at least in its Utopian form. Fourier, to whose ideas I must confess I am attracted, was, we are told, 'not in the least interested in technology: he disliked large-scale production, mechanization and centralization in all its forms. He believed in small communities as best meeting the real needs of men.'[25] Moreover, 'he held human nature to be essentially unchanging from age to age, and thus denied the doctrine of many of his fellow-Utopians – especially Godwin and Owen – that character could be moulded into almost any shape by environment.'[26] If to these we add that '... Fourier inherited the eighteenth-century proclivity for identifying God and nature, or at any rate for attributing to nature the attribute of being animated and directed by the divine will',[27] it would almost seem that Fourier, this eighteenth-century Utopian and pioneer of socialism, was in spirit amazingly Hindu. So it looks as though Hinduism might, to some extent, approach socialism, even though only its Utopian variety; and that, in view of my image of post-industrial society, might not be such a bad thing, after all.

References and Notes

1. R.C. Zaehner, *Hinduism*, London, 1971, p. 4.
2. The reference here is to the Mīmāmsā, which is commonly regarded as the most orthodox of the 'orthodox' systems of Hindu philosophy.
3. The B.B.C. Television series on world religions broadcast in September, 1977.
4. I owe this story to Ninian Smart.
5. The work for which the Club is most famous is the publication of *The Limits to Growth*, London, 1972.
6. Fred Hirsch, *Social Limits to Growth*, London, 1977.
7. *Ibid.*, p. 167
8. *Ibid.*, p. 169
9. *Ibid.*, p. 137
10. *Ibid.*
11. *Ibid.*, pp. 137–38
12. The B.B.C. Television series broadcast in 1976.
13. For a somewhat fuller account of what I mean by 'sensitive technology', see my article, 'A Touch of Animism', in *Dialectics and Humanism*, No. 3–4/1976, where the term was first introduced.
14. *Rig Veda*, i. 164.46
15. *Gītā*, IV.11.
16. *Ibid.*, IV, 8.
17. S.K. Maitra, *The Ethics of the Hindus*, Calcutta, 1925, p.220.
18. *Ishā Upanishad*, 1.
19. *Manusmriti*, XII.91.
20. Paul Deussen, *The Philosophy of the Upanishads*, authorised English translation by Rev. A.S. Geden, Edinburgh, 1906, p.49.
21. G.D.H. Cole, *A History of Socialist Thought*, Vol.I, London, 1971, p.2.
22. Margaret Cole, 'Socialism', in *The Encyclopedia of Philosophy*, Paul Edwards (ed.), vol.7, London, 1967, p.468.
23. *Ibid.*

24. G.D.H. Cole, *op.cit.*, p.65
25. *Ibid.*, p.62
26. *Ibid.*, p.63
27. *Ibid.*, p.68

The God of my Fathers –
The God of my Children

Dow Marmur

One of the most important prayers in the Jewish liturgy, recited at least three times a day and sometimes more in the traditional scheme of things, includes the words, 'Our God and God of our Fathers, the God of Abraham, the God of Isaac and the God of Jacob.' Does this mean, commentators have asked, that Judaism implies that there is more than one God; that 'our God' is, as it were, not the same as 'the God of our Fathers'? Surely, with the strict monotheism of Judaism that would be an absurd assumption! And yet, whereas the Hebrew language could well tolerate a phrase like, 'the God of Abraham, Isaac and Jacob', our text deliberately repeats the word 'God' before mentioning each of the three Patriarchs. Why? The traditional answer is that although God is the same, each person has to find Him for himself, and, therefore, is bound to perceive Him in a unique and different way. God does not change, but since each man's perception is different, individual, and very limited, he can at best only fathom a facet of the Reality that is God. Thus God – who is always the same – is yet different in the perception of Abraham, and Isaac, and Jacob and all the prophets, sages and scholars, as well as ordinary folk, who came after them. Tradition is the sum total of these experiences, and yet incomplete at the same time: it beckons us to add our own experience to it.

I offer this interpretation of a liturgical text as an introduction to this lecture for several reasons. Firstly, it seems to be an apt comment on an inter-religious seminar in our age of ecumenism. As long as we recognize the One and Indivisible Reality, which the monotheistic religions call God and other traditions know by other names, and at the same time accept the limited perception of each of us and the potential fallibility of our respective religions; as long as we bear in mind both the Divine Reality and the human limitations we can talk to each other and learn from each other.

My second reason for putting before you this interpretation is to make it clear from the very outset that what I may have to say at this conference is not *the* Jewish view – for such a view is not possible – but *a* Jewish view. Other Jews may very well perceive the same tradition and the same facts differently, for Judaism is too rich and too varied to allow an 'authoritative' view only. Whenever such a view is presented, it tends to be nothing more than a legalistic artifact created to serve a particular set of dogmas.

This brings me to my third, and main, reason for starting this lecture in the way that I did. It offers me an early opportunity to illustrate the range of Jewish tradition, which is both 'our God' *and* 'the God of our Fathers'; it is 'the God of Abraham' *and* 'the God of Isaac' *and* 'the God of Jacob'; it is God as perceived by prophets and priests in the Bible, by the rabbis of the Talmud, by philosophers from Philo to Buber, by the codifiers and the preachers through the ages, by mystics and rationalists, by fundamentalists and liberals. Jewish tradition is the sum total of all these in a composite and complex picture that Judaism describes as Torah, instruction. Originally the term Torah was to denote the Pentateuch only, but in time – and here is not the place to describe the development – it came to describe the totality of Jewish tradition. It is as an exponent of that three thousand and more years old tradition that I stand before you today.

Needless to say, I cannot ever do it full justice, let alone in one lecture. I can only look at it from my particular perspective, which is something like this: in certain epochs in Jewish history, e.g., in the Middle Ages, exponents of Judaism have preferred to look back instead of looking forward. For valid historic reasons they sought to chart the past in as great a detail as possible on the assumption that to know what 'the God of our Fathers' wanted of them and who He was for them, would almost automatically tell us who 'our God' is for us and what He wants of us. A popular expression of this kind of religiosity is reflected in the phrase, 'What was good enough for my fathers is good enough for me'. With this follows a deep reverence and piety for the past, which for all its nobility masks a crippling insecurity and leads to a staid, well-ordered and legalistic way of life.

The most effective way for earlier generations to break out from this spiritual strait-jacket was the way of mysticism, which by its very nature – and often despite outward 'respectability' – was daring and experimental. Jewish mysticism almost invariably retained a loyalty to and a reverence for the past, and yet, at the same time, enabled its adherents to find 'our God', not only in terms of 'the God of our Fathers'.

There is much in modernist Judaism which builds on this tradition. However, under the influence of modernity, Jewish movements that emerged after the emancipation of the Jews in the 18th and 19th century were more interested in stressing 'our God' and more prone to criticize, even denounce, the kind of religiosity that hides behind the pietistic phrase, 'the God of our Fathers'. These movements were no longer satisfied with the maxim, 'What was good enough for my fathers is good enough for me'. Instead, their slogan was, 'What is good enough for my children is good enough for me'. In contrast to medieval Judaism, modern Judaism became future oriented. This does not mean that Jewish modernists thought to ignore or minimize the past, but they viewed it differently and refused to be bound by it.

As a Reform rabbi I am speaking to you from this modernist perspective. For me, the past is not, as it is for an Orthodox Jew, the final guide and arbiter but a source of inspiration, the stuff out of which my own religious life can be shaped. The past may be my first Source of religious guidance, but it is not my only one.

Having thus attempted to place my credentials – or their absence – before you, let me now address myself in some detail to the questions posed in the prospectus for this seminar: 'What makes men and women follow these creeds? What appears to be the goal? What, in short, is it that religion offers? And how far does this differ between creeds?' Alluding to the most ancient of Jewish symbols, the seven branched candlestick, let me try to answer these questions by offering seven reasons why Jews adhere to Judaism.

Since Judaism is not a missionary religion, I am not motivated to offer a 'sales talk' on my tradition. My aim is merely to explain Judaism as I know it in an effort to make a contribution to greater tolerance and better understanding. If there is a real thread going through this presentation, it is the question that mystifies non-Jews more than any others: What does it mean to be 'a member of the chosen people'? Hopefully at the end of this lecture the concept of election in Judaism will become clearer, and at least some of the misconceptions – malicious or ignorant – will be removed.

55

(1) A Source of Wisdom

The first reason why Judaism matters to the Jew and fascinates the non-Jew is because it carries a store of wisdom. Of course, other religions too contain wisdom, but the style and content of Jewish teaching is, naturally, different and distinct. It has come to influence the daughter religions Christianity and Islam, and is a strong component in our Western culture. Jewish tradition describes this wisdom as Torah, and I have already referred to it before. Torah manifests itself in two ways: as education – a system of holy study; and as law – a system of codes and practices.

Jewish tradition teaches that Torah is the revealed will of God. Whether you take it literally, which is the Orthodox approach, or metaphorically, which is the modernist way of looking at it, it means that to study the sources of Judaism is to perceive more correctly and more comprehensively what God wants of us. To my fathers this would have meant that every word of Scripture, and of the oral tradition that developed around it (recorded in the Talmud, in the Codes, in Jewish philosophy and literature), had to be taken literally; for my children, and indeed for me, this means that the Torah is a human response to God's call. But for all, the study of Torah is a holy pursuit. It takes precedence over virtually all other religious activities, even prayer, and as such is absolutely central to Jewish religious life. To study you do not even need an *a priori* commitment, just an open mind and a sense of awe and wonder, which is the beginning of faith. Judaism is so convinced about the intrinsic power of the message that it believes that once you study it diligently, you are bound to want to live by its precepts. Conversely, the lack of faith and the lack of piety are often seen as signs of ignorance. A Rabbinic saying has it that 'an ignorant man cannot be pious.'

Moreover, it must be understood at all times that the purpose of study is right action, the carrying out of God's will as revealed in Scripture and commentaries. Therefore, Torah is never just education but always also law, rules and regulations designed to govern every detail of our lives. It is in practice that the commitment is measured, not in dogmatic statements or articles of faith. The principle applies whether you are a fundamentalist or a modernist. The former is bound to try to accept *everything*; he may be weak enough to escape the law but would never try to change it, because to change would imply a challenge to the authenticity of tradition and the veracity of the word of God. If you seek to modify Jewish law, you become almost automatically a modernist.

In this respect, then, I differ from my fathers. On the basis of what I know about Biblical criticism and historic development, I see tradition not as immutable but as a record of the way in which previous generations responded to revelation, to the call of God. Because of what I know, I feel compelled to offer my own response: to learn from them, and to follow them whenever their response is true for me, but modify and change and innovate when that is not the case. It is this that makes me a modernist.

But, whether fundamentalist or modernist, adherence to Torah is basic. The Pentateuch is read in the Synagogue on every Sabbath and Festival, and members of the congregation are called upon to recite a benediction prior to each reading, the central theme of which is praising God for having chosen us from all peoples and given us the Torah. Chosenness, then, is not favouritism, arbitrarily bestowed, but a vocation to study and to practise.

The difference between the fundamentalist, Orthodox, approach and the modernist, Reform, attitude can perhaps be made clear through the following example. I am keen to carry out the religious duty to study Judaism. As a rabbi I am also trained to teach it and dedicated to the task. I am committed to carrying out the precepts of the Torah. One of the most important of these relates to Sabbath observance. For the Orthodox Jew this means a fixed set of rules which have not changed for hundreds of years, which would forbid him to carry a manuscript or to use transport, today. Therefore, he would not be able to come here this afternoon, and perhaps that is why you do not have an Orthodox speaker. By contrast, a Reform interpretation of Sabbath observance does not view it in legalistic terms but regards teaching Judaism as very much in keeping with the spirit of the Sabbath. If that means coming here on a Saturday afternoon by car, it would not be considered, in Reform eyes, a violation of the Sabbath. That is why I am here – not as a renegade Jew but as someone committed both to the spirit of the Torah and the observance of the Sabbath.

(2) A Sense of History

I am able to regard myself in this way because of my understanding of Jewish history. And history is the second of my seven branches of Judaism. To be Jewish means to almost every Jew to see oneself as a link in a long chain. To understand the present and to respond to its challenges means to him to know what has gone before and why. Let me try to explain it in terms of a paradigm.

After many years the Biblical Jacob returns to his home country. On the way he hears that his brother Esau, whom he had left in haste and with much unfinished business, is coming towards him with 400 men. Jacob is confused: Is this to be an encounter between brothers, and the 400 men an impressive guard of honour? Or is this to be a battle, and the 400 men an army to settle an old score? Jacob makes preparations: he sends a delegation to appease Esau with gifts, and he divides his camp into two. The night before the decisive encounter he spends alone. In the course of it a mysterious being wrestles with him, but as dawn is breaking and the attacker cannot prevail, Jacob extracts a blessing from him: he shall no longer be called Jacob but Israel. So Jacob walks away with a dislocated hip from the struggle – but with a blessing.

The Book of Genesis, which tells this story, does not inform us who the mysterious being was. There are many speculations and interpretations. The medieval Jewish commentator, Rashi, summarising Rabbinic tradition identifies him as 'the guardian angel of Esau.' Bearing in mind that in that tradition Jacob represents the Jew and Esau the Gentile, Rashi's interpretation becomes significant: Jacob the Jew, the spirit of Hebraism, wrestles with the spirit of the surrounding Gentile world. By surviving the struggle Jacob becomes Israel. He is maimed but also blessed. Seen in this light the Biblical story in its Rabbinic interpretation becomes a paradigm for Jewish existence: Israel is the result of the struggle between the spirit of Hebraism with the surrounding civilisation. It is both a painful and a beneficial encounter. Only thus can Jacob become Israel.

Jewish history can be viewed as a succession of encounters of this kind. Each one is both a risk and an opportunity. The risk is annihilation; the opportunity is renewal and rebirth. This is not the place to develop the theme in detail. Suffice it to say that we Jews are conscious both of the danger and the opportunity. In our time the former is epitomised by Auschwitz, the latter in the existence of the State of Israel.

To recognize this drama and try to discern its purpose is to perceive something of the essence of Judaism. Again, chosenness not as favouritism but as a peculiar obligation. Part of that obligation expresses itself in the need to honour the memory of the martyrs of our people. To know what happened to us Jews in the Hitler period has become a kind of religious duty. To seek to prevent its recurrence another, and greater, one.

It is in this context, then, that it may be possible to understand the Jewish preoccupation with the Jewish State. I know that it is currently fashionable to accuse Jews of being racist, imperialist, militarist, and to identify us with every possible anti-symbol, but I believe that, sadly, that is the price we must pay for being conscious of history as part of our religious heritage. For us Jews the State of Israel is nothing more than a chance, perhaps the only chance, to remain Jews and to make sure that never again will six million of us be led as lambs to the slaughter. It is possible that in the eyes of our non-Jewish neighbours we may seem somewhat hysterical, but I hope that our friends will understand the reason for it; that they will appreciate the sense of history that evokes this reponse.

In modern Jewish theology survival has become a religious category. In the words of one contemporary teacher, Emil Fackenheim, only by surviving as Jews can we prevent Hitler from having a posthumous victory. The State of Israel is the vehicle of that quest of survival. Only through it can we Jews find purpose despite Auschwitz.

(3)   An Ability to Feel Pain

Reference to martyrdom and suffering brings us to a third characteristic of Judaism, a third line of communication between fathers and sons as reflected in history. Our experience of pain and degradation enables us to feel the pain of others more acutely, and to prompt us to rush to their aid more eagerly. Again and again are we Jews commanded to alleviate the misery of our fellow-men 'because you were strangers in the land of Egypt'. This is yet another way in which election becomes vocation. Precisely because our history has so much to say about how we have been the victims of man's inhumanity to man, we regard it as a sacred

59

duty to remain human, even in the face of provocation, and to seek to alleviate the misery of others. The involvement of Jews, as individuals and as groups, in voluntary work and in the helping professions should be seen as an expression of this tradition. It goes across generations and religious differences.

This talent for remembering our own pain and trying to feel the pain of others is life-affirming, not life-denying. The commitment to seek to alleviate pain helps us not only to find purpose in life but also joy in life. Judaism is a happy religion; its solemnity is never less than joyous. It stands in this respect in sharp contrast to the secularism of our time which, for all its clamour for 'Paradise now', appears gloomy and dull. What is so characteristic of Jewish humour, to be able to laugh with one eye and cry with the other, is a true reflection of the Jewish attitude to life.

(4) Community

Our affirmation of life and our need to care expresses itself in the seemingly ordinary: in the family, the congregation, the community at large. Community, then, becomes the fourth branch of Judaism in this presentation, and as such yet another expression of the link between fathers and sons.

The joy of having survived and being alive prompts all of us to share it with others. We do so by celebrating holy events in the life of individuals and in the history of the people. This helps us to cement relationships and to relive the past. Much of ritual and ceremonial is linked with this sense of community. It offers us a framework of security in the midst of a perplexing and hostile world. For non-Jews it seems at times bizarre and exclusive, and evokes a mixture of envy and hostility on which anti-Semitism thrives. Much of Jewish life, then, takes place in the family and in the extended family we call congregation or community. The rabbi acts here as teacher and catalyst, not as priest. He is also the person who often seeks to find a way of linking 'our God' with 'the God of our Fathers'. The community offers the milieu that makes such a bridge possible.

(5) God

A congregation is called in Hebrew *kehilla kedosha,* a holy congregation. Belonging is not only a matter of survival but also of spiritual integration, of holiness. The Jew who wishes to be a part of the Jewish community identifies with the quest for spiritual integration/holiness. It is the experience of Judaism that God cannot be found on a remote island but reveals Himself in the midst of the people; Scripture insists that the whole Israelite community was present at Sinai. God is not an *a priori* category, a philosophical abstraction with which one has to start one's religious quest. Instead, He is to be sought in the company of like-minded seekers. To belong to a community does not mean, therefore, that you start off with certainties but that you have a desire to look for them – hence the reason why so many seemingly irreligious Jews belong to congregations. Through membership of the community I am exposed to what Peter Berger, the sociologist, calls 'signals of transcendence', intimations of what it means to be with God. Through the community I may be able to experience Him even when I do not understand Him. That is why in this list of the seven branches of Judaism, God is not mentioned first, but only after Torah, history, pain and community.

This does not mean, of course, that belief in God is unimportant in Jewish tradition; the introduction to this presentation should have made that clear. What must be understood, however, is that a philosophical conception of God is not a necessary prerequisite for being a Jew. You start by sharing the wisdom, the history, the pain and the community, and through these you may come to an experience of God. And, as we said at the outset, although God is One and Unique and always the same, we perceive Him differently. That perception, however, becomes pale and at times even misleading if we try to confine it to a definition. God, Jewish philosophers have taught, can only be described in terms of negative attributes: we can say what He is not, but it is impossible to say what He actually is.

Martin Buber reflected much of this in his writings. God can only be *addressed,* he taught; He cannot be *expressed.* We can speak *to* Him but not *about* Him. Buber has shown how we can receive intimations of God – Berger's 'signals of transcendence' – through interpersonal relationships. Via an *I-thou* relationship I can move towards a relationship with the Eternal Thou. By contrast, philosophy and abstract theology can only perceive God as an object, as an *it*, thus becoming a barrier rather than an aid to faith. Jewish tradition bears out Buber's concept of God and, therefore, at no time does it demand a confession of faith, an adherence to dogmas. We are entitled to perceive God differently because we are not expected to define our perception.

We cannot express God, we said, only address Him, and we feel more confident to do so when we are with like-minded people in the midst of a worshipping congregation. That is why the community is there not only to teach the wisdom and the history, and to share the pain, but also to help us to pray together. Prayer reflects tradition and yet stresses immediacy; through it we are able to celebrate our special relationship with God. Chosenness in this context resembles the relationship of lovers. The Biblical Prophets used the image of marital love as a metaphor for the relationship between God and Israel. The Song of Songs was included in the Biblical canon as the perfect allegory of that relationship. The Christian distinction between *eros* and *agape,* human love and divine love is, therefore, unknown in Judaism: the commandment, 'Love the Lord your God' and 'Love your neighbour as yourself' both use the same Hebrew word, *v'ahavta.*

Despite the apparent exclusiveness, everybody can share the relationship epitomised in the dual commandment to love. For God is the God of all mankind. Scripture begins with Adam, the first man, not with Abraham, the first Jew. In this universal scheme of things Israel has a special task: it is to be a kind of catalyst, but its concerns are the concerns of the whole world. Redemption is not reserved for the Jewish people but must come to all humanity. The nations of the world will deserve it by being true to their ancestral faith – in the same way as a Jew has to be true to his religion, Judaism. This fundamentally tolerant outlook has been seen, however, by our enemies as a sign of exclusiveness and a desire to appear superior – which is the very opposite to what we try to be.

(6) Testimony

Our real aim is to testify to the presence of God. This, then, is the sixth branch of our presentation of the seven branches of Judaism. The Jew sees himself as having the duty to testify to the power and the reality of God in the world. Through the study of Scripture, tradition and history I am able to establish a link with the past, a line of communication with the God of my fathers. Through the experience of pain I have to affirm life. One manifestation of this affirmation is the emphasis on human relationships, the family and the community. Such relationships, in turn, point to the source of all love, to God. Through our collective experience of pain we are made to love mankind and to love God. The problem of theodicy is resolved in the determination to alleviate misery. In this way we come to testify to Job's affirmation, 'though He slay me yet will I trust in Him.' This testimony is particularly poignant in our generation when Auschwitz survivors could praise God and speak of His power and His goodness despite all that befell them.

To be a Jew, then, is something of a heroic act. We are not Jews because it is comfortable but, irrespective of whether it is so or not, we discharge our responsibility to God by affirming our Judaism. Being Jewish in the face of persecution and assimilation is in itself a religious act. This in turn brings us beyond the dichotomy of universalism versus particularism. Chosenness is neither self-centred nor smug but a Messianic obligation. Isaiah's suffering servant is the Jewish people itself, a line of exegesis suggests. Israel's history reflects God's plan for the world. Israel seeks to share her insights and experience with others not in order to convert but in order to demonstrate, through autobiography rather than theology, that God is and that He must be adored and obeyed, even when He appears remote and angry.

(7) Hope

All this becomes only possible through the Jewish propensity for hope, the seventh and last in this list of basic Jewish characteristics. It was a Protestant theologian, Jürgen Moltmann, who in his *Theology of Hope* showed that Judaism is founded on the idea of covenant: God says to His people, 'Here are the commandments; if you observe them I will carry out My part of the agreement and take you to the Promised Land.' By accepting my responsibilities and my obligations as a Jew, by living my Judaism, I am stating my conviction that God will keep His part of the 'bargain' and thus bring about a better tomorrow. Hope, then, becomes a function of my religious life. I don't just wait for the Messiah to come but actually walk towards Him.

This message of hope is of particular relevance in our age of gloom, and it is to share this message that I stand before you today. That is the only way in which I can understand Isaiah's injunction to Israel to be 'a light unto the nations', a light in this age of darkness. The sense of personal privilege at having been a Jew is mingled with my universalist sense of obligation to testify to the message of Judaism. My religious commitment enriches my life and encourages me to share the wealth through the act of testimony. Imbued with a measure of Jewish wisdom, Jewish history, Jewish pain, Jewish community, I testify to God and hope in His promise in the conviction that tomorrow need not bring disaster because obedience to God will merit His benevolent intervention. It also, finally, dissolves the apparent dichotomy between the God of my fathers and the God of my children, for the Messianic vision of Malachi has it that on the great day of the Lord, when His intervention will finally become visible to all, 'He shall turn the heart of the fathers to the children, and the heart of the children to their fathers.'

In the meantime the tension between the demands of tradition and the pull of the present has to be retained. I must be able to say 'our God' and 'the God of our Fathers'. But I can only do so if I know that this is an interim solution, a function of my temporal existence, and that beyond there is a reality that transcends the tension and so gives meaning and purpose to my existence.

Discussion

Q. What is the difference between Israel and Jacob?
A. The Bible explains Israel as he who has striven with God and with man. Elie Wiesel, the poet of *The Holocaust* suggests that part of the experience of the Jewish people is to strive with God. You may have watched the *Long Search* programme on Judaism in which he said 'A Jew can be *with* God or against God, but he can never be *without* God.' Israel is part of that dialogue with God which started in the Bible itself when Abraham suggests to God that His proposed treatment of Sodom and Gomorrah is less than justified.
Q. Does the rocking movement at Jew's prayer have any significance?
A. First of all, not all Jews sway at prayer. It is a particular form of expression for which the basis is a verse of the Psalms: 'All my bones shall say....' It is one way of express-

ing prayer physically. It is not my way, personally, and I am in favour of the interpretation that it is not really a Jewish way, because imagine the High Priest entering the Holy of Holies on the Day of Atonement and shaking – he would spill the incense all over the place. It is a particular East European mode of prayer to which no religious significance should be ascribed, but perhaps the psychological observation is worthwhile, in that it helps concentration. One of the problems we have at prayer is how to keep at it, how not to be distracted by the vicar's hairline or whatever; perhaps if one sways methodically, that is one way of doing it.

Q. How do you view the people who follow the essential practices of your religion, including the sharing of experiences with like-minded people, but without formal membership of your religious community?

A. A Jew is a Jew is a Jew, and he does not have to be a card-carrying Jew in order to be a Jew. The definition of a Jew is he who is born to a Jewish mother or converted to Judaism; whether he belongs to a congregation or not in no way validates or invalidates his Judaism. I would suggest to him that he would have better opportunities of expressing his Judaism if he belongs to a community, but it makes no qualitative or quantitative difference whether he does or not. This is one of the things that non-Jews find difficult to understand, that you can, as it were, be a Jew without any formal affiliation, that the synagogue and the community is not a church which is by implication a kind of gateway to salvation. That is not its purpose. It is an institution to provide the facilities and opportunities which may not be available elsewhere.

Q. Why isn't Judaism interested in preaching Judaism to non-Jews? Why do you keep your spiritual gifts to yourselves?

A. I do not consciously keep them to myself, but I believe it would violate my sense of tolerance if I tried in any way to convert or to convince. I work on the assumption that religion is part of one's destiny; one is entitled to change and modify that destiny, but I am not sure that I am entitled in any way to influence *you* in that respect. I am there to present Judaism and to speak of its rich literature; indeed I am here to speak about it and I speak in many other places, but not because I feel that you then have to accept it. My only part is to share with you my own religious path and my

65

own religious feelings, and that in turn has something to do with the Jewish view of redemption – not everybody has to be a Jew for the Messiah to come, as it were. All that we have to try to achieve is to encourage the Christians to be good Christians, the Hindus to be good Hindus, and the Jews to be good Jews, because through their particular Jewish commitment, they can make their contribution towards the fulfilment of that hope I spoke about earlier. This, broadly speaking, is the reason why Judaism will regard missionary activity as intolerant and, in its own salvation-scheme of things, as it were unnecessary; salvation is not to come only to the Jews but to everybody. I know that that is not how the matter has been understood: Jews have been seen as exclusive and secretive, but this is not the true state of affairs, for this would be wholly inconsistent with what Judaism stands for.

Q. How do you interpret the role of Jesus Christ?

A. Judaism can only see the story of Jesus historically and see him in the context of his time as a Jew. Scholars argue as to which party he might have belonged to – the Zealots or the Charismatics or whatever, but in history rather than in metahistory, which is how Christians see him. If I quickly think of an image, it is the way I look at the wife of my best friend: I think she is very nice, but I do not share his love for her.

Q. How will the Jewish Messiah differ from the Christian one?

A. There is a difference in Judaism between hope and calculation: this question implies calculation, for which I have no talent and no resources. Once you speak of hope, you can only have an expression of people's wishes and not of certainties. One of the ideas that runs through all Messianic speculation in Judaism is that when the Messiah comes, all differences will disappear and perhaps that is how we shall know; more than that we cannot know. What Judaism can say is that the Messianic era is not yet; for the evidence we have only to look around us, and therefore to say that the Messiah has come remains for Judaism less than comprehensible.

Q. In what way do you see the surrounding culture as an opportunity?

A. There is no question about it that however critical and despondent we may be about Western civilization, we ought

also to recognize the great opportunities for human betterment and progress that it offers. Anyone who tries to ask the
question about 'the God of my children', and not only about
'the God of my fathers', cannot be locked in nostalgia for the
past but recognizes in the surrounding culture opportunities, as well as dangers, and that is why Judaism and
Jews have been so affirming of surrounding cultures and
have tried to enter and, in some cases, to make contributions
to them.

Q. How does Judaism look at the other great religions of
the world?

A. Judaism never enters into polemics with other religions, except with regard to idolatry, because in any effort to
elevate something human to the level of the divine it sees
moral depravity, whereas any response to God, under
whatever name, which recognizes the metaphysical reality
of that which is beyond, the transcendence of God, is
accepted as a legitimate expression. At the same time we
recognize, and this is what I have tried to talk about here,
that we Jews have a particular task and a particular
destiny. Therefore religions are not interchangeable; they
are just valid as part of people's destiny. I once talked in
some gathering along these lines and someone got up and
said to me: 'Yes, you go ahead and worship God in your way
and I will worship Him in His.'

Q. You spoke of the Messianic hope. How would Judaism
recognize the Messiah?

A. When we talk of the Messianic age we mean something
in which the question whether Judaism recognizes or does
not recognize is no longer valid. If someone says 'How will I
know that I am in love?' it is an interesting question for
those who have not experienced love. For those who have,
they just know. By analogy it is this kind of answer that I
can offer here.

Q. How does the idea of redemption in Judaism differ from
the carrot of 'jam tomorrow'?

A. It is not a calculation, it is not a sort of incentive. I
have tried to say that Judaism, despite all the pain, is life-
affirming. I could also say that it is very much this-worldly;
it never suggests for a moment that we only live for the
beyond. You live on the basis that there is nothing else but
your hope, as if what is here now does not matter and will
not matter; that may sound paradoxical but it is neverthe-

less a true reflection. One of the characteristics of Judaism is precisely this ability to accept the here and now; in fact many critics of Judaism have said that Judaism has no after-life, no beyond at all, there are no carrots, there is no jam tomorrow at all, but only the here and now. That is not true, but what Judaism tries to instil in us is an ability to enjoy the here and now and to affirm it, whether it is sweet or not, and yet at the same time to hope for tomorrow. There is a political expression of this: the leaders of the Jewish community in Palestine, as it then was, fought with the British over the White Paper which restricted immigration into Palestine; then the Second World War broke out and the Jews of course joined forces to fight against Hitler. Ben Gurion once said to the British High Commissioner, 'We will fight the White Paper as if Hitler didn't exist, and we will fight Hitler as if the White Paper didn't exist.' I could paraphrase this and say you live in this world as if the next didn't exist, and you hope for the next as if this one didn't matter.

Q. Will you please tell us about your concept of life after death in modern Judaism?

A. Judaism has a concept of the future which is both collective and individual; in the individual it hopes for an after-life, but refuses to be specific about it on the basis that there is no evidence. Everything I do in this life points to the beyond. There is a hope of eternity, but it can only be a hope; if it were more, we would speak in my terminology of calculation, and Judaism in fact looks askance at those religions that calculate the beyond and chart it in terms of heaven and hell or whatever. But Judaism says there is a pointer in life to the beyond. It would not make sense of what we see happening in this life to assume that the grave is the end, and yet what the beyond is is literally beyond our comprehension and beyond our words.

Q. What convinces a Jew that God is just and caring and loving?

A. I think conviction is a difficulty. You are never convinced; you struggle, you labour, you have your ups and downs. Jewish theologians have often compared what the questioner here calls conviction to love, and have said that you cannot store it up, you cannot keep it and you cannot save it for the future. It is a momentary experience. It is the experience of the here and now, and it is the same with 'religious conviction'. Throughout the Jewish tradition we have the dialogue with God, saying: 'God, how can you do this to me? Are you really good? If you are powerful, why don't you do something?' but saying at the same time 'Glory be to God'. The two things co-exist, and it is accepted that one single individual cannot play over the whole register all the time, that one's existential situation in life places one at different points in the spectrum; so I would not like to speak of conviction. We never in fact speak of Jewish dogmas; there are no articles of faith that the Jew has to accept. He just has to engage in the struggle and in the sharing. Perhaps it is when conviction seems particularly low that I need my fellow men most to help me along, to carry me perhaps over a difficult time, and I know that the time will come when I shall reciprocate.

Q. With its historical sense and its profession of activity, has Judaism specific advice for mankind at this dangerous point in history?

A. It would be presumptuous to speak of advice but I think it would be proper to speak of experience and to say that, whatever the dangers and difficulties may be, if we are able to address God, if we are able to find ourselves in a spiritual community, if we are able to help one another, that is a beginning. And something else, too: Jewish tradition sees in every individual a microcosm; to save one human being, to help one person, to respond to one single situation is, as it were, to save the whole world. The world, says Judaism, is always in the balance, it is always 50/50 whether it is going to be destroyed or is going to prevail. The next action will decide it, yours and mine.

The Islamic Tradition

Riadh El-Droubie

Say ye: 'We believe in God and the revelation given to us, and to Abraham, Ismail, Isaac, Jacob and the Tribes, and that given to Moses and Jesus, and that given to [all] Prophets from their Lord: we make no difference between one and another of them: and we bow [surrender] to God [in Islam].' *Ch.II, v.136.*

The most important aspect of the relation between God and man is the surrender to God. Without any doubt, all religions base this relation on the same principle of surrender. Unfortunately the way of surrender differs from one religion to another. For this reason God the Almighty sent down prophets and a messenger not only to show mankind the way of surrender to Him (God), but also to show how man could be a viceroy on this earth as God wanted him to be.

All revealed religions have the same basis. How can they differ when the source is one and the same? Moslems accept all the prophets mentioned in the above Qur'anic verse and many others mentioned in other chapters of the Qur'an. However, we do believe that the way of surrender to God the Almighty has changed through the ages owing to changes made by man to the original message. That is why God had to send yet another messenger with a renewed message. This acceptance makes no division between them.

The trend of today, for some people, is that all religions are the same and preach the same thing. For me NO, they are different and we must accept this fact; if we first know our differences, then we shall be able to know our common belief. Once we know these two factors, then our understanding of each other will grow deeper and our co-operation will be more mature. I do believe that there are many ways in which learned (religious) people from all religions, in spite of their differences, can come and work together for the betterment of man. This is especially necessary at a time when morals have declined to such a degree that there is nothing to bring man together except personal advantage at the expense of one's partner. The one and only thing which could bring all faiths together is the lifting of the moral standards of man and the addition of spiritual life to materialistic behaviour.

The Qur'an points out this relation very clearly:

'O mankind! We created you from a single [pair] of a male and a female, and made you into nations and tribes, that ye may know each other [not that ye may despise each other]. Verily the most honoured of you in the sight of God is [he who is] the most Righteous of you. And God has full knowledge and is well acquainted [with all things].' *Ch. XLIX, v.13.*

The whole relation of mankind depends on the individual's conduct. Good conduct will be like a shield in life for everyone. The golden rule is 'prevention is better than cure'. The Qur'an refers to this in the following manner:

'We have indeed created man in the best of moulds, then do We abase him [to be] the lowest of the low, except such as believe and do righteous deeds: for they shall have a reward unfailing.' *Ch. XCV, v.4–6.*

This mould in which man was created is the result of two elements – the soul and the body. The first can lift man up to the status of angel; in our everyday life when we see a person truly well behaved, kind, generous etc., we say he/she is an angel because of the high moral standard. The second can bring man down to the lowest of the low, like an animal. Here again, when we see a person behaving very badly we say that he/she is a pig or an ass, in other words an animal.

But God said:

'We have honoured the sons of Adam; provided them with transport on land and sea; given them for sustenance things good and pure; and conferred on them special favours, above a great part of Our Creation.'

This man whom God created and gave the elements necessary to be in the best of moulds, has the capacity for free choice in action – between what he believes is right and what he believes is wrong. God made success possible for man in his choice and not only in his belief, that he might do righteous deeds.

The Qur'an clarifies this:

'By the Soul, and the proportion and order given to it; and its enlightenment as to its wrong and its right; truly he succeeds that purifies it, and he fails that corrupts it!' *Ch.XCI, v.7–10.*

And defines it further:

'That man can have nothing but what he strives for; that [the fruit of] his striving will soon come in sight; then will he be rewarded with a reward complete; that to thy Lord is the final Goal.' *Ch.LIII, v.39–42.*

Nothing more is needed from man but to strive. The result is left to the Almighty. The prophet Muhammad, peace be upon him, said: 'Actions are judged by intention'.

Therefore we could summarize the creation of man and say that God has sent prophets and messengers to regulate the threefold relation:

(1) The relation between man and God;
(2) The relation between man and man;
(3) The relation between man and himself.

(1)   The relation between man and God

We have been told in our childhood the story of a man and his young son, a story which I can still remember vividly.

One day the man asked his son to go with him and help. The task that day was to steal fruit from a neighbour's orchard. The man asked the boy to stand near the gate and to watch out in case someone might be coming that way. The man entered the orchard, walked to a tree, stretched out his arms to pick some fruit. At that moment the son shouted, 'Father, father, someone is watching you!' The man left the orchard in a hurry. By the gate he asked the boy 'Where, where?' The son pointed his finger to heaven and said: 'He is watching you, father'.

This story is related in conjunction with the teaching of one of Prophet Muhammad's (peace be upon him) sayings:

'Worship God as if you see Him. Remember, if you do not see Him, He sees you.'

Moslems feel the presence of God around them all the time, and their behaviour is bound by his presence.

(2)   The relation between man and man

We are like a person in the desert hoping to cross it. During the hard and difficult journey the individual cannot detach himself from the caravan. Moreover, he is part of it (whether he likes it or not). If he stops, the caravan stops; if he moves, the caravan moves.

The Prophet Muhammad said:

'All of you come from Adam and Adam is from dust. There is no difference between an Arab and a non-Arab except in piety.'

Therefore, not place of birth, nationality or lineage, colour of skin or wealth, but piety/righteousness is the root of all relation between man and man. As we said earlier, the best among men in the sight of God is the one best in conduct. Not only that, the Prophet, peace be upon him, said:

'None of you [Moslems] is a believer unless he desires for his brother what he desires for himself.

'None of you is a believer until he loves God more than his father and his sons.'

Islam is the most misunderstood religion in the world today. Many people are under the impression that there is no love in Islam. The love which God has bestowed upon us is far beyond our conception. We have mentioned earlier that He created us in the best mould. He put us on this earth with all that we need and we are free to use it as we please. Moreover, if any of us committed anything displeasing to Him, the only thing we should do is to turn to Him (God) without any intermediary and He will forgive us. The love God has bestowed upon us is so great that we cannot match it.

The only way to please the Beloved is to please Him, and to please Him we have only to obey His prophet, peace be upon him.

'If you love God, follow me, God will love you. . . .'

(3)   The relation between man and himself

Islam has two linguistic meanings which give the essence of its message. We mentioned the word 'surrender' earlier as the first meaning. Now we mention the second one 'peace'. Peace with God, peace with mankind and peace with oneself. Upon this latter peace depend all other relations, because one cannot offer peace if one has not got it within oneself. Our motto for the individual and society is well-being in this world and well-being in the hereafter.

Religion today is in a situation where it is confronted by a great challenge. Can religion face this challenge and if so, how?

For Moslems this challenge, however strong it is, does not matter. The Qu'ran says:

73

'We have revealed the book and We are [its] guardians.'

We consider, in the light of the above Qur'anic verse, this challenge is not to God or His message; the challenge is to us. We should be worthy to carry this message to the coming generation, otherwise we shall perish and there will be others who love God; He will love them and they will carry forward the banner of God.

Discussion

Q. What do you mean by free will and how can a man maintain free will in his actions in society today?

A. Free will means that a man is free in his actions; let me put it in this way: you are set an examination paper and you are given a free hand to answer the questions; if you answer them well, you pass the examination and if you answer badly, you fail. No matter what our actions, we have to remember one thing, that heaven and hell, that is reward and punishment later on, depend on God's mercy. Even the most pious man in Islam will not enter heaven except with God's mercy. We believe that God has bestowed upon us so many things that we can never thank him enough to guarantee our entry into heaven.

Q. How can we know a man's intention?

A. We can see a man's action but we cannot know his intention; that is not for us to judge. We judge a man according to his actions but actually we should not judge him at all; we should leave it to God, since He is the judge. It is better not to judge and to leave it to God who alone knows the intention.

Q. It has been said that Islam is a missionary religion. What is your view of conversion to Islam?

A. The word 'mission' has a special meaning in the minds of Christians. We do not have the same word in Islam; we have what we call *da'hwe*, an Arabic word meaning 'invitation'. This is a very important point: you invite people to Islam; in other words a man has the right to refuse your invitation. We Moslems go and preach but we do not ask for conversion because conversion is in the hands of God alone, guidance is in the hand of God. A man might come to me and say 'I want to be a Moslem'; he is a Moslem even before he comes because his intention is within. That is why we have no priesthood in Islam, because the matter is a direct relation between man and God. Certainly I cannot change you. I cannot do anything to you. The Prophet himself said to his daughter: 'When on the day of judgment every man comes with his own deeds, if you come and say "I am the daughter of the Prophet", this will not help you; only your own goodness will help you.'

Q. How does the Qur'an view family life? Do you feel that the breakdown of family life in the West is one of our biggest problems?

A. Yes, I do. The unfortunate thing is that if we in Islam follow in the footsteps of Western civilization, we shall produce the same result. The breaking up of family life in the West is due to circumstances and not to the wishes of the family itself. This is an unfortunate thing, and I personally would like to see religion having more influence on social life; it might then change the attitude of the industrial mind and make it a more spiritual, an inner mind as well as an outer mind.

Q. Why do you say that Islam is not a mystical religion? Surely all religions have a mystical element?

A. Without doubt all religions have a mystical element. Islam is not a mystical religion, but that does not prevent its having some mystics in it. Nor does it mean that a man should not be with God all the time. There is a balance between what is mystical and what is not, although all our behaviour is for God and to God alone.

Q. Do you think that the Qur'an should be understood literally?

A. The Qur'an was revealed in the language of the Arabs because the Prophet was an Arab. It was a matter of convenience to the Prophet and the people among whom he lived; it was revealed in simple language which the people and the Prophet could understand; had it been revealed in Shakespearian English or in sheikh's Arabic, it might not have been understood very well by the common man. In the beginning of every religion most of the believers are among the poor and the illiterate, and therefore the message has to be as simple and as direct as possible. Without doubt the Qur'an is in the most beautiful Arabic that has ever been written; for the ordinary man it sometimes needs explanation and this is especially true for many Arabs today when people are so neglectful of the literature and the language.

75

Q. Can a woman be a Mulla?

A. Mulla is an Arabic or perhaps Turkish word meaning a religious man. There is no religious man and no priesthood in Islam. A woman can do everything that a man can do, except that she cannot lead men in prayer. In the mosque, the men pray in the front and the women pray at the back, not because they are second-class citizens but because we men are very weak. Our prayers are not like your prayers in church or synagogue; we have to do an exercise, to bow and kneel and stand; imagine doing these movements with an attractive woman in front of me, with a lovely figure: one would not be able to concentrate. It is as a practical measure that we keep the women at the back and do not allow the man to turn his face in prayer; in this way we are safeguarded.

Q. What are the Seven Pillars of Islam?

A. One of the sayings of the Prophet is that Islam was built on 77 pillars. In Arabic the number 77 or 7 simply means a great many or a number. If I say I came to look for you 7 times, it does not mean literally 7, but many times. Thus Islam is built on many pillars. The greatest of them is to believe that there is but one God, and the least of them is to remove from a man's path whatever is harmful; if a man sees a stone in the middle of the road and removes it, this is the smallest pillar of Islam. But the foundation pillars of Islam are only five: To believe that there is but one God and Muhammad is His messenger. This means that the inner part of a man must be free to accept God; a man must not allow himself to be under or to obey any rule which goes against the wishes of God. That is what it means: literally to believe in only one God; not only He begetteth not, nor is begotten, but all life must act in unity with Him.

The second pillar is to pray five times a day. A Moslem has to wash before prayer and then to pray. This indicates three important things: the purification of the body, the purification of the individual – the self, and the purification of the place in which you pray. This is the essence of the second pillar; as I said earlier, God does not need our prayers: it is we who need to pray.

The third pillar is *zakat*, an Arabic word which has no equivalent in English. By prayer you purify the body and soul; *zakat* means the purification of wealth. It is obligatory for every individual who has more than he needs to pay 2½%

to the poor; this applies to any accumulation of wealth – to cash in banks, jewellery a woman owns, land, cattle, farms, everything a man earns in excess of his daily needs. This is of course in addition to any other charities which man is free to make at any time; even if he is poor, this contribution is obligatory on all Moslems.

The fourth pillar is fasting during Ramadan. Once a year Moslems fast for one month, 29 or 30 days according to the lunar year. From dawn to sunset every day a man must fast from everything entering or leaving the mouth, not only from food but from any action which could be a screen between him and God: a man is not even allowed intercourse with his wife during this period. He must fast from everything; not only from food because if he fasts from food alone, he will merely get hungry, whereas if he fasts from everything, he will be purifying his inner self.

The last pillar is the Hajj, the pilgrimage to Mecca. A man or woman must make the pilgrimage once in life if he or she is able. If a person cannot afford it, however, he is not allowed to go; he may not, for instance, buy a ticket on hire purchase in order to go. He must leave behind enough for his family without lowering their standard of living. If you go on the pilgrimage, it must be done to God and to God alone.

Panel Discussion

Dr Dyson *Q*. As few people below the age of fifty find traditional forms of worship and prayer suited to their needs, what alternatives are emerging?

A. I would make three comments on that: first, I think there is emerging a considerable amount of experimentation in small group worship, and here I believe that the Christian tradition has much to learn from the Hindu tradition about the importance of family worship. Second, I think there is an increasing willingness to recognize that more objective and fixed forms of worship must operate in relationship with much freer forms of worship, not as alternatives but the one interpenetrating the other. I think there is a significant development in this direction. Third, I think too that there are many forms of worship belonging to different religious traditions which can with value be taken over and developed by other traditions. In this area I think things are rather in the melting pot at present, and I regard this with optimism rather than pessimism.

Q. The Protestant emphasis is on 'Christ died for me'. This may be individualistic, but does it not also have the power of authenticity?

A. In a way I think the Protestant emphasis on 'Christ died for me' is an over-individualistic reaction and takes a rather atomistic view of the human race. One can say with some truth that Luther distorted St Paul's understanding of salvation by making it a much more individualistic thing than St Paul understood it to be, St Paul seeing it more as the salvation of the new Israel, an organic concept and not an individualistic concept. It is also significant that in Protestantism there has been much more of an emphasis on the death of Christ, whereas in the Catholic and Orthodox traditions this has been strongly balanced by an emphasis upon resurrection and transformation. This emphasis on the death of Christ has indeed the power of authenticity but it presents a danger when it is seen in an isolated way and the whole of one's religious understanding is built upon this single element of belief.

Q. You said that Protestantism is more prone to political and economic pressure than Catholicism. Surely through the ages the latter has been just as prone?

A. I think the Catholic emphasis on tradition has meant that it has had the capacity on many occasions to withstand cultural pressures. There is gain and loss in both directions: the loss on the Catholic side has been that it has sometimes not had sufficient flexibility and creativity in relation to changing structures; the danger on the Protestant side, clearly seen in what we call 19th century liberal Protestantism, is the danger of being swallowed up by the changes and pressures of society. Although Catholicism has sometimes withstood these pressures and appears to have maintained more effectively and more continuously its identity, still it has had its own difficulties. We are left with the very delicate problem of interpreting and understanding the changes in the environment and the culture, with the problem of responding to these changes in a way that is not over-accommodating but which does not ignore the creativity within society and the challenge of God speaking through these movements.

Q. You have not said anything about the death of ideas. Are the ideas originally expressed by Christianity now real?

A. This seems to me a very interesting question. Nietzsche is the outstanding instance of someone who spoke about the death of ideas; what he had to say about the death of God is in fact about the death of the idea of God in human consciousness. The death of ideas has to be taken very seriously. But I am not basically convinced that what is originally expressed by Christianity is in fact ideas. The ideas follow upon certain kinds of much more fundamental experiences. Ideas can indeed die, but those experiences, if they are authentic, can go on living and find expression in different forms. It is a question of the relationship between the fundamental reality and the forms in which it is expressed.

Q. Historically is not the rise of Protestantism connected with the increased emphasis on the individual which is such a characteristic of Western culture?

A. I think that is a true descriptive statement. The rise of individualism in the 11th and 12th centuries in the West had a lot to do with it; this was reinforced later on by the growth of a market economy in Western Europe, a factor which had a very considerable influence on the development of the Protestant religious tradition in contrast with the medieval economy, which was of a very different character.

Q. What do you consider to be radical in Protestantism today?

A. A very difficult question: two things, although I do not think they are confined to Protestantism; the first is a fundamentally new look at the relationship between faith and religious institutions and society. Although some of the outcome of this may be regarded as somewhat unsatisfactory, I think there is a very profound level of searching going on here; I think a lot of what Mr Harriott said in his lecture as to the questions being asked applies also in the Protestant field. Second, within the sphere of theology itself, there is a lot happening that is radical in Protestantism today. I am not referring to what I sometimes call frothy radicalism, which is here today and gone tomorrow, but I do think that in the last hundred years Protestantism has made a very significant contribution theologically.

Q. Can you see the charismatic movement within both the Protestant and the Catholic churches becoming a way of escaping the impasse of dependence upon an infallible Bible or an infallible tradition?

A. My short answer to that question is, with regret, No. The actual form of the development which the charismatic movement has taken so far within Protestantism and Catholicism is something which I have personal reservations about. The charismatic movement has too introverted, too domestic a character; it is something which is happening very much within the internal life of the churches and is characterized by religious phenomena. As the Protestant theologian Pannenburg has said, we have to recognize that the doctrine of the Holy Spirit in Christian theology is not a church doctrine simply; it is what he calls a creation doctrine. Genesis speaks about the Spirit in relation to the whole of creation. To me, the hope for a charismatic movement is concerned with a renewal of the sense of the work of the Holy Spirit within creation, within society and in a sense only secondarily within the church. That is why I find myself somewhat unhappy about it, because I think it runs the risk of creating a third form of infallibility, namely infallible Bible, infallible tradition and a kind of infallible approach to what is technically called pneumatology. I wish this were not the case and it may be that developments are possible and will occur which will indicate a broader outlook and conception.

Q. Why has the personal teaching of Jesus been insufficient to keep the church living and progressing?

A. I do not think it has been insufficient. The personal teaching of Jesus has been one of the factors which has been most influential in keeping the church living and progressing, even though from time to time clearly the church is in the hands of the mortician and is sometimes regressing. We are faced with the legitimate question 'What does the teaching of Jesus mean?' I do think this question needs an answer; it is not self-evident. If the whole of philosophy is a commentary on Plato, it may be that the whole of the church's history is a kind of commentary on the teachings of Jesus. We are faced by very considerable questions of Biblical criticism as we try to assess what is the teaching of Jesus as distinct from the varied theological and other reflections of the early church; we are also faced by considerable problems in assessing the meaning of that teaching even if we could grasp it. That seems to me a very important and worthwhile difficulty for Christianity, that we should be continually exploring that meaning, not simply exploring it in enclosed terms, but out of the changing experience of life, out of our wider knowledge of the world, the world of the sciences, the natural sciences and the human sciences, the world indeed of other faiths, which have shed enormous light and continue to shed enormous light on the original Christian tradition. In all these ways the question of the personal teaching of Jesus is one of the great sources of life and vitality because it is when we think we know, when we think its meaning is self-evident, that the difficulties set in. One of the great features of the present day reconsideration of many of the religious traditions seems to me to be the way in which the original traditions of different faiths are being explored afresh.

Mr Harriott: One of the most interesting things during these two days has been to hear Dr Dyson's exposition, with so much of which I can agree. I think it shows how much traffic there has been between Catholicism and the Protestant tradition which he has been expounding.

Q. Why do Christians regard Christ as a culmination? Does this suggest that in Christian eyes God's revelation has in a way ceased?

A. It is not a question of revelation ceasing but of certain events not being repeated. Christ is regarded as a culmination in the sense that He was not simply a revelation of God such as we might have gained through a sage or a prophet or through some private experience of God, but the most complete self-revelation of God in someone who was at once truly God and truly man. That was a unique event and what we learn through Him is itself unique. That does not mean to say that there is not in a sense a continuous process of revelation going on from one generation to the next, in the unfolding of the meaning of that revelation in the community, inside the Christian community, and of course too in the particular prophetic insights of members of that community, which become part and parcel of the faith. But they are always related to the particular set of events that are Christ's life and the particular mysteries which make it up – those are part of history and they are not repeated. There is a real sense in which Christians believe that Christ was not just a sort of personage who lived for thirty years and then died, and someone we simply look back on over two thousand years; He is a living presence and in that sense continually instructing us and informing our lives.

Q. Church ritual seems designed to stimulate emotion. Cannot this become a substitute for spiritual development and an end in itself?

A. Here one sees something of the curiosity of Catholicism; it is at once a very logically structured religion, with a great emphasis on reason and on logic, and yet it is so commonly identified with intense emotional experience. There is no doubt that in its ceremonies and in its preaching, there has very often been a very strong emotional effect and it is certainly true that there is a real danger of emotions being worked up and clouding our experience. We may go through a period of extreme enthusiasm which can have all kinds of peculiar consequences, and undoubtedly church ritual, music, incense and ceremony of various kinds can have that emotional effect. I think one can accept the dangers latent in that while at the same time saying that emotion does have a part in our lives. We are not simply intellects, and the experience of deep feeling and feeling in community with others is at once an expression of our deepest beliefs and is a form of knowledge. Both kinds of criticism are sometimes levelled at the Catholic: that he is too much of a rationalist who leaves emotion out of account, and on the other hand, that he is too emotional and his judgment is clouded by that emotion.

Q. You say religious ritual is, among other things, to make the invisible, visible. Does this presuppose the need to prepare and invent new rituals appropriate to a new age and the changing nature and conditioning of society?

A. I would say quite certainly, Yes. I think that is one of the most interesting things about Catholicism today. Under the impact of the Protestant Reformation, there was, not just a temptation, but a real failure in that so much Catholic doctrine, both dogmatic and moral, and Catholic ritual was fossilized; the Church went on to the defensive and all kinds of things which are really accidental were elevated to timeless truth and to unchangeable practice. At the present day there is a greater appreciation of the fact that by fossilizing the ritual expression of what you believe, what you want people to understand, what you are trying to express, you render the thing deceptive and open to misinterpretation. Within the church today there are two schools of thought, the one emphasizing the importance of preserving ritual unchanged for the sake of maintaining tradition and continuity, the other saying that if we are going to express what we believe to be the essential truths of Christianity, the essential facts of Christ's life, then we must find a way of expressing it which speaks to people in our contemporary culture. This is very clearly apparent for example in the Philippines, which I visited recently, where there is on the one hand the old institutional hierarchic church, concerned to keep things ticking over much as they have done for many years and seeing liturgy as something formalized, so that people simply go through the motions all the time, and on the other hand the growth of the new popular church which starts with people's own concerns and sufferings, anxieties and problems, and builds the liturgy around that. I think that is in fact the direction in which the church is likely to go; one sees the liturgy as something which is necessarily far more flexible and time-conditioned; we have to be inventive in our liturgy, perhaps even too in the Mass. The essential thing is that, as far as the Catholic is concerned, however improbable it may seem to the outsider, at a certain point bread and wine become the body and blood of Christ. But the actual ritual which surrounds that event can be extremely simple; Mass can be celebrated on a kitchen table, without any particular dressing up, or it may be like Mass in St Peter's on an Easter Sunday – a thing very rich in ritual, music, complicated ceremony, etc. I think it is best to see Catholic ritual less in terms of theatre than in terms of cooking: just as you can have the most simple kind of meal with very little elaboration or a kind of *cordon bleu* meal at the other extreme, so with the Mass itself, it can be done very simply or in a very complicated way.

Q. What do you understand by the concept 'culture'?

A. I would understand by culture a coherent vision of life, of the meaning of human existence, expressed in a coherent pattern of behaviour, of language, of law, custom and ceremonial, a common set of allusions and common terminology. It is something which interprets life to people in a coherent way and I think that at the present day, despite all the divisions and arguments within Catholicism, it has preserved some kind of culture in that sense and in a sense which also makes it easier for Catholicism to carry on a dialogue with other cultures. There is undoubtedly a Catholic culture; we have managed to preserve a language which makes sense to all Catholics and which they all share in; we have managed to preserve an art, a custom, a way of doing things which is universally accepted and which makes some kind of conversation possible between Catholics, no matter which part of the world they come from. At the present time, however, we are all well aware of the breaking down of that sort of coherence, not simply within religious bodies such as the Catholic church, but in society at large, and that does pose new questions.

Rabbi Marmur: The last question on culture has been passed to me and I would subscribe to the answer that was offered, for the same applies to the Jewish culture. But let me also suggest that Jewish culture has continuously encountered the surrounding culture and as a result has developed what in Jewish theology goes under the name of a creative synthesis. This is also an answer to a number of questions as to how Judaism views the community outside and whether Judaism has taken in anything from the outside world. For a long time it has been a fashion with scholars to list pedantically all the borrowings throughout the ages from other cultures into Judaism. It makes one wonder what is left that is typically and significantly Jewish. The answer is that it lies in that wrestling with the guardian angel of Esau that I spoke of yesterday; here what is significantly Jewish, here the true Israel emerges.

A number of questions dealt with the concept of redemption in Judaism, so let me try without citing specific questions to give at least partial answers to some of them. The Jewish theologican, Leon Baeck, has suggested that there are two kinds of Messianism, a twofold thrust towards redemption in Judaism: on the one hand, in the Bible you have something he calls horizontal Messianism – the betterment of man, the fulfilment in time and space, the ideal kingdom which will emerge. But starting with the Book of Daniel, we have another Messianic concept, he suggests – a vertical concept in which redemption will come as it were from outside and from beyond. Writing in the context of his analysis of Christianity, he suggests that in Judaism there is a tension between the two, the emphasis on vertical redemption stemming from the Book of Daniel onwards. The other point that is worth making briefly is that there is a development in Judaism which is concerned with personal salvation, redemption, life after death. It is hard to find clear evidence in the Bible, in what the Christians call the Old Testament, for a personal after-life, but there is no doubt that in the first Biblical period, in the struggle between the Pharisees and the Sadducees, a major issue concerned resurrection and a personal after-life. The emergence of Christianity has to be seen in the context of the Pharisaic victory; the fact that Pharisaic ideas won in the end and the notion of an after-life developed, enabled the Christian frame of reference to emerge in its Jewish historic context. So there are both elements in Judaism, but I think it is fair to say that Judaism has concentrated on the horizontal rather than the vertical concept of redemption. This is not to deny the possibility of knowledge other than intellectual knowledge, but, as it were, having one's reservations about man's ability to integrate and to transmit that knowledge. There have been prophets in the past who have testified to it and have added to it, but there is a tendency in rabbinic Judaism to say that prophecy has ceased – that today anybody who regards himself as having this kind of prophetic knowledge should be viewed with caution; he or she may be over-valuing their own aspirations and ideas and what appears as mystical evidence may in fact belong to the realm of psychology. But what we do know, suggests Judaism, is that this world is a corridor to the world to come and what we ought to do is to try to work towards the conditions which embody the hope in which we trust. The Sabbath is seen as a kind of foretaste of this Messianic future; we are trying to simulate conditions in order to build models for ourselves. The Passover festival is the foretaste of the ultimate redemption; it is the day when we celebrate the beginning of redemption, the exodus from Egypt, and as part of the ritual there is a cup of wine on the table intended for the prophet Elijah, who is tradition-ally the forerunner of the Messiah; at one stage even the door is symbolically opened because one is saying that we expect, we hope for this redemption and try to work towards it without necessarily being able to penetrate the mystery.

'The heavens are the heavens of the Lord but the earth is given to the children of man.' This is one way in which Judaism operates in practice; it tries to concentrate on earthly conditions; this again relates to a number of questions I had, for example: 'How do Jews relate to non-Jews in the world?' The answer to that is that precisely because one hopes for universal peace and a Messianic future, one tries to the best of one's ability to promote it here. It is not possible to achieve it, but Judaism always works in a state of tension, trying to help us to realize our potential and at the same time to recognize our human limitations. To be Jewish means to have a sense of this vocation, but it is not exactly a matter of race. The medieval Jewish philosopher Maimonides, in answer to a direct question on the subject from a convert who asked whether he could recite the prayer with which I began my talk, 'Our God and God of our Fathers', wrote a magnificent philosophical treatise in which he showed him conclusively that this is in fact possible.

Finally, there were several questions on the lines of 'Why are the Jews persecuted?' I do not know the answer to that but I would like to refer you to the answer given by Elie Wiesel in the programme *The Long Search* in which he said 'This is a problem of the non-Jewish world'. Basically, the problem of the Jew in this scheme of things is how to survive, and not to survive just as an individual; on that basis it would be easier to try to cover one's Jewish traces and say that for the sake of survival I will minimize my Judaism or deny it. Though some have done so, by and large this is not the way of the Jewish people; one has only to look at the emergence of Jewish allegiance in the Soviet Union in the face of consistent atheism and anti-Judaism to see that this is not the answer. Survival in the theological sense means to testify to the presence and power of the living God. This is the theological commitment to Judaism, that is what Jews are dedicated to. The fact that, for a variety of reasons on which there is a rich literature, this creates persecution and anti-semitism, suspicion and misunderstanding, is a sad, tragic fact, but it in no way diminishes the quest or the passion on the part of the Jew to work towards being that kind of testimony. We all try to do that in every way that we see as possible and practical, and it is in this context that I see my own goal as teacher and exponent of Judaism.

Professor Thakur Q. Would you agree that Hindu optimism, i.e., ideas of man's perfectibility, is closer to Catholic Christianity than to Protestant pessimism of the Calvinist type? Can you see any way in which these different approaches to the nature of man *vis-à-vis* the world may be reconciled?
A. To speak of reconciling the two presupposes that the two ways are inconsistent: that you can have either one or the other; in itself this reflects a certain kind of thinking. This is one of the things that the Hindu will not do; he does not think that there is just one picture or model of perfectibility. If there are different ones, let them be; time will tell and people will choose for themselves what they like, rather than having one authority, as it were, telling them which might be the better of the two. In that sense, talk of reconciliation does not quite reflect the truth.
Q. How did a rigid caste system arise side by side with the idea of the oneness of all forms of life? What value is placed on wisdom and enlightenment in the face of caste? Is it possible to be of low caste but more enlightened than a member of a higher caste?
A. Some parts of these questions I am unable to answer; a scholar of history might have more clues than I have as to how the caste system arose and what happened. With regard

to the last question, there are any number of stories in the tradition and of course actual incidents in the life of the community which show that, when it comes to enlightenment, inner wisdom knows no caste barriers. Some of the most revered people are of a low caste. There are many versions of the story in which a man decides, rightly or wrongly, that it is time for him to seek salvation; he approaches a guru, whom he has found after wandering for fourteen years in the Himalayas, and the guru as it were turns him round and sends him to X; X sends him to Y and Y sends him to Z. When he reaches Z ultimately, he finds that he is a butcher who presides over a shop. The seeker says: 'Surely I cannot have been meant to come here. What can he tell me?' For the seeker himself is a brahmin, and is much too proud to learn from a butcher. Yet as he sits there he does learn the secret of wisdom, and in the end attains enlightenment simply through having come to the butcher and having talked to him. So the answer to that question is certainly, 'Yes'.

Q. Can you envisage any circumstances that would cause the rejection of the caste system?

A. I hope that in the sort of future that I envisage, when there is more widespread education, particularly in India and in the Third World, and as the result of certain actions being taken, this will happen. In India, since Independence more especially, there is reason to believe that, while there are still strongholds of the caste system among certain classes and types of people, there are other areas where it does not any longer have much of a hold. I hope therefore that this is the direction which developments will take.

Q. Is the Hindu caste system to be understood simply as priest, warrior, merchant and servant, or has it a psychological parallel in terms of the individual's inner development, perhaps during a single lifetime? Would you consider that the Hindu caste system might be an ossification of fundamental differences in human nature?

A. The second question almost gives an answer to the first; it certainly gives an important clue. There is a belief that Brāhmin, Kshatriya, Vaishya and Shūdra reflect, broadly speaking, types of personalities: some are men of the mind or soul, others are men of muscle, and so on. I hold very strongly that there is a mistake in visualizing such a system as applying to individuals; one can easily lose sight of what was important and what the basic insight was. As far as the caste system goes, there is the important element that it is supposed to reflect differences in natural inclination and temperament; clearly Hindu society overdid it. To those who are knowledgeable there is a clear parallel with the system Plato outlines in his *Republic*: some people are better equipped to be philosopher-kings, others to be warriors and fighters and others to be tradesmen; in his case, the Shūdras would presumably be provided by the fourth class of slaves. So there is a similar sort of basis and an assumption that human nature has a part to play.

Q. Even if the Hindu is given more freedom to choose his occupation than is the case within the rigid caste system, can he still avoid economic and moral corruption in the post-industrial society?

A. If the fist part of this hypothetical question is satisfied, that is if the caste system goes, then the answer to the second part will have to be, 'Yes'. I do not see why moral corruption should take place, particularly if it is what I have termed a genuinely post-industrial society.

Q. Experience seems to show that the desirable features of socialism which you mentioned can only be achieved by a strong bureaucratic state machine. Is there any way this can be avoided?

A. That is a very deep and important question, and one which is very difficult to answer. It is true, judging by recent examples of how socialism has developed and proceeded and where it has succeeded, that state bureaucratic control is probably an important if not a necessary means to it. I do not accept it as inevitable. I believe that, given the circumstances of the past – namely the illiteracy of the masses and the tremendous differences between the masses on the one hand and the élite, the privileged people and the power that they wielded in all sorts of terms – it may well have been necessary to impose this kind of socialism. But I see it as being in the future a development that will take place of people's free will. This may be dewy-eyed, but I believe that as education spreads more and more and people are able to think for themselves, socialism of the variety I am interested in will spread and will be established – not with the force of the long arm of the law or the state, but because people have of their own free will chosen this as the better way of doing things. Exceptions will always be there, but if in the main this requirement can be satisfied, I think I shall be more than happy.

Q. The trouble with descriptions of the post-industrial society is that they tend to be static. How would the society you describe accommodate change?

A You will remember that I made the point that one approach sees change as being of value for its own sake: fashions change and there are fashion-designers who make it their professional business to exploit this weakness of human beings and film-makers and text-book writers do the same, as though change itself was something to be considered worthwhile. My assumption is that in the post-industrial society I am dreaming of, that would certainly not be the case. On the other side, given that society is going to be organized on the basis of small, self-governing communities, it should not be impossible to introduce change if change is seen and felt to be necessary. If someone can convince the community concerned that a certain change is good and of the reasons why it is good, then presumably the community being small and once convinced that the change is needful, will act to carry it out. So change would not be ruled out but it would be made much more difficult to introduce change just for its own sake.

Mr El-Droubie: Q. It has been said that Islam is a religion without love. Does this mean without sentiment?

A. What do we really mean by the word 'love'? We very often say that someone is in love and love is a subject we talk about nearly every day of our lives. To me, love means to give up everything for the one I love. Therefore if a man gives up everything to God, he is in love with God. One thing that is important in Islam is that we do not talk about God's love to man, because that is obvious. He gives us so many things, more things than a mother could give her child; the love of God to man is beyond limitation. But we do have to talk sometimes about what we fail in, which is our love to God, and this rests on how much faith we have in Him. This is why the Prophet said 'A man is not a Moslem unless he loves God more than anything in this world'. And to love God means to remember Him. One of the things which is said in Islam is that God has ninety-nine names and we know God through these. No one can really know what God is, in substance, with the human mind, but we know God through his attributes, through what he has bestowed on us.

90

That is why one of the most important names of God is 'The Merciful'. He is merciful, and mercy can only come from love.

Q. Does Islam believe in eternal damnation? Or does it believe that after due punishment, all men will be saved?

A. The fundamental belief here is that everyone will be rewarded according to his life; no one can guarantee to any person any punishment or reward except as God wills. We can put it mathematically: as God has put it to man, if a man does one good deed, God may reward him ten times, or even 700 times – that is manyfold; but if he does one bad deed, he will have one bad mark, and the rule is that good marks always cancel bad ones. Therefore we see God's mercy and love to man, for if a person does only one good deed, he may cancel 700 bad deeds. Further, God is merciful and can forgive anybody. I could not enter Heaven through my own actions and intentions, however good they may be, unless God's mercy enters in. And nobody will remain forever in Hell, except one person who denied the love of God; and we have been told he is the only person who will remain in Hell. But still if God's forgiveness comes to him, he will be saved from it. Therefore punishment and reward all depend on God and on our intentions.

Q. You say men and women are equal in the sight of God, according to Islam. How do you explain the fact that a Moslem man may have up to four wives, while a Moslem woman may have only one husband?

A. Here we are talking of equality before God, and equality before the law, and not equality of ability, which depends on the person. By nature the woman is different from the man; it is important that a child should belong to his father, should know his father and bear his name. If a woman had four husbands, the child will not be able to know who is his father. This is why in Islam adoption in the Western style is not allowed. I am allowed to adopt a child, but I am not allowed to give him my name; he must keep his own name. That is the freedom of the individual; he is not really mine – he has his own identity and he must keep it.

Q. You spoke of the sixth day of creation and of evolution. Will you please describe your view of the evolution of man?

A. Evolution is still a theory and theories have never been proved. Religion is a revelation and revelation for a believer is always right. In Islam, whatever opposes the revelation is not acceptable and whatever agrees with the revelation is acceptable. This is why in the course of history Islam has progressed and developed so many sciences. If we see some theory which contradicts the word of God, we have to develop it until we see if the theory is right. The theory of evolution has not yet been proved but there are certain roots and foundations in the Qur'an which could explain certain aspects of it. God says in the Qur'an, 'We made every living thing from water', and this is a wide foundation. No living thing can exist without water; all the theories say that a part of life is in water; a child is born because of water passed from a man to a woman. Therefore the concept of evolution theory may be derived from the principle of God and of Islam. All science and all the knowledge of man has to evolve in this way, to the honour and benefit and happiness of man and with respect to God and to the law.

Q. What in your view, each of you, makes men and women seek the right way to live?

Professor Thakur: People see around them all these different ways of going about things and in their own personal judgment they believe one to be superior to another. Then of course the question arises of how this way is better than the others, and so the individual becomes reflective; this state of mind pushes and pushes you, and you probably end up being a wise man, a philosopher, a saint or a mystic. I think that is why people seek; it is the urge to justify the answers to certain questions as to why one way of doing things is better than another.

Mr Harriott: I do not think there is a simple answer to the question, but certainly there is a human instinct to distinguish between right and wrong, to feel some kind of general compulsion to behave in a right rather than a wrong way. There is also the feeling that time is at our back and that we want to use the time we have got most productively and richly; that is to some extent a self-interested argument, but the fact remains that it seems to make for a more agreeable life if people treat each other according to some accepted rules and reliable standards of behaviour. In the case of those who believe in God, it is because one sees God as the only absolute and the demands He makes on us as being

92

absolute. I am not suggesting that what God asks of us in the way of a right way of life is something antipathetic to our nature; I think that we have increasingly realized that the demands He makes of us, if we understand them, are those in fact which make for our own fulfilment and enrichment and that of others. The answer is a complex of arguments of that kind rather than any single one.

Dr Dyson: One can accept the two points made by the two speakers, but I think one has to push it all back to a yet deeper level of explanation. As a Christian, I would myself want to say the deeper level of explanation is that in some sense every man possesses within himself an impulse which comes from what we call God. One of the traditional ways of describing this is, of course, the image of God in man, and I want somehow to maintain the extreme paradox of asserting man's radical freedom and at the same time asserting that every man possesses within himself an impulse and a drive which is in its deepest grounds related to or part of the very drive and being which we associate with God Himself.

Q. There is a saying which comes possibly from Islam: 'Do not serve God from desire of Heaven nor from fear of Hell.' Would the panel say how that might apply to their own faith?

Professor Thakur: I do not know that I am particularly anxious to call Hinduism my faith, except that Hinduism is the only faith that will accept me with my views and ideas. The answer of Hinduism to that question would be that one's perfectibility need not be seen in terms of serving God. In Hinduism, God is not central or even necessary. In the context of an atheist or an agnostic, serving God would not be seen as an ideal way of going about things. Hence those who already have this ideal of serving God and finding salvation in this way will presumably differ among themselves.

Mr El-Droubie: The quotation is a saying of a woman Sufi saint, Rabia. It expresses the highest degree of faith that a man could reach in his belief in God and his love and his mercy. As we are human, we are required to act in a normal human manner but we should strive to reach the limit of which Rabia speaks here. It is a mystical saying, not a principle of Islam.

Dr Dyson: It is interesting that this is evidently a common tradition, because St Francis Xavier prays that he will learn to love, not for the sake of gaining Heaven nor of escaping Hell. In the Christian tradition, too, it represents the achievement of the highest pinnacle of selfless love. I think what has been coming out during these two days is the common fact that we all believe that God is the only absolute, that God is the very quintessence of selfless love, of abundant love, and that man's response lies in learning to love selflessly. In our painful efforts to learn what is meant by love and to practise it, we are all too well aware of the degree of self-interest and of selfishness that is in us, but it does establish an ideal towards which we can work, to feel that we might possibly, at least in certain moments, achieve a completely selfless kind of love for others and through others, for God Himself.

Q. Is there a contradiction between the concept of free will and that of reward and punishment?

Mr El-Droubie: I do not think there is a contradiction; rather if there were no free will, there would be no reward or punishment. If it were decided by God that I should do this or that thing, then God could not ask me why I had or had not done it. But He gave me free will and can ask why I have done this or that; for a good answer I am rewarded and for a bad one I am punished. Therefore free will and reward and punishment must go together.

Mr Harriott: In popular Catholic tradition in recent centuries, there has been rather a stress on God as a kind of Judge Jeffries, but I think in modern Catholic theology the older traditions have been re-discovered in which the stress is entirely on the fact that we make our own fate. It is not a case of God sitting there separating us out in a rather cruel judicial way. There are pointers to that, not only in the extravagant lengths that Christians believe He went to to express the degree of His love to human kind, but also in our own judgments of others: very few of us would want to condemn even the worst kind of human being to everlasting suffering. I think the deeper tradition is that it is possible, though one hopes in fact never the case in practice, that someone may become so impenetrable to love that he becomes isolated in himself, and that that is really what is meant by Hell; that it might be possible, by developing a life of total selfishness and disregard for others, to be absolutely incapable of being reached by love or of expressing love, and in that sense perhaps, even God could not break through that kind of shell.

THE REALM OF
EXPERIENCE

Introduction

Colin Wilson

I am going to say a few words of introduction generally about religion and mysticism. All of my work has been concerned in one way or another with the subject of mysticism, and I want to start by trying to give my own definition – particularly because, fairly recently and partly through Idries Shah, I have begun to see some rather new and interesting implications that I still have not had time to write about. In my first book, *The Outsider,* one of the central passages was the one in which I discussed Dostoevsky's Raskolnikov, who said that if he had to stand on a narrow ledge for ever and ever, in eternal darkness and tempest, he would still prefer to do that rather than die at once. It is an absolute certainty that if you were actually faced with immediate death, you would suddenly *know* that life is infinitely valuable, and you would be incapable of boredom. The American gangster and bootlegger, Charlie Berger, who committed a number of murders, said as the trap was about to drop, 'It *is* a beautiful world, isn't it?' If he'd realized this before, he wouldn't have ended up on the gallows – because his life was a catalogue of stupidity and miscalculation, of doing things for the wrong reason, things like killing people. Now, this has always been the central obsession of my work and this seems to me to be what mysticism is. Mysticism is the attempt to get through the fog in our brains to reality. And I don't mean reality with a capital R; I mean to this ordinary reality which surrounds us. We don't see the world as it really exists.

What Shah put me on to about a year ago was an insight about the left and the right sides of the brain. He sent me Robert Ornstein's book, *The Psychology of Consciousness* and I must confess that even then I didn't see the significance of what he told me. I didn't really begin to grasp it until I came across an extraordinary book called *The Origin of Consciousness in the Breakdown of the Bicameral Mind* by

99

Professor Julian Jaynes; a very strange piece of work in which Jaynes argues that our ancestors fairly recently – as recently as, let's say, the Fall of Troy – had nothing that we could call consciousness. What Jaynes says is that they simply responded to events going on around them almost robotically – certainly not by way of asking themselves questions. They had no stream of consciousness, no conscious I, no sense of *being* conscious: this is his theme. Then how did they in fact do all the kinds of things that require a certain degree of self consciousness, of self questioning? Jaynes' answer is that the instructions came through on a telephone line, so to speak, from the right side of the brain – that they heard voices – and that this is the reason why, in the *Odyssey,* the heroes are always talking to the gods or hearing messages from the gods – they do almost everything on instructions from the gods. But the interesting thing I found in Jaynes – that came like a revelation – was the description of some of Sperry's experiments in Los Angeles.

You probably know that Sperry got fascinated by the fact that the right side of the brain appears to be the side of intuition and recognition – you recognize faces and patterns with the right side of the brain. The left side of the brain is the logical, rational side that deals with language, mathematics, that kind of thing. Normally there is a good telephone link between the two sides, a bit in the middle called the *corpus callosum* which is a knot of nerve fibres connecting the two. So there is a constant interchange between the two halves. However, with epileptics they found that it's helpful to sever the *corpus callosum.* It seems to stop a build-up of feedback between the two halves and prevent those curious electrical storms called epilepsy. Now the interesting thing is that when people have the *corpus callosum* severed, the right and the left halves of the brain, the rational side and the instinctive side, now become completely independent. If you showed a person, let's say, an apple with the right side of the brain and an orange with the left side – that is to say you stick a screen in front of the nose so that the one eye can't see what the other is seeing (just to complicate things the left side of the brain governs the right eye and vice versa), and you say to the person 'What have I just shown you?' they will reply, 'An orange'. If you put a pencil in the left hand and say 'Write down what I've just shown you,' they write 'Apple'; you say 'What have you just

100

written?' and they reply 'Orange'. If you show them a dirty picture with the right side of the brain they blush. If you say 'Why are you blushing?' they say 'I'm not blushing' or 'I don't know'. You have two different people sitting in your head in either half of the brain, and the person who is now talking to you is the left side of Colin Wilson and the person who is now listening is the left side of you. There is an amusing story told by Professor Carl Sagan that a man smoking marijuana had the sudden impression that there was a person in the other half of his brain looking at him and he addressed the question to him, 'Who are you?' The answer came back, 'Who wants to know?'

But it is the implications of all this that are fascinating and these haven't been dealt with by Ornstein or Sperry or anyone else. There are some things that we can actually think out and work out – because any intelligent person can instantly begin to *see* what this amounts to. The right side of your brain is the side not only for recognition but for endowing your life with reality. The left side is a scanner. It deals with language, with symbols, with instant emergencies. It is on the alert, looking at the world all the time. It works fast because its business is to be on the look-out. The right side of the brain is much slower. Its pace is easy. It has no sense of time apparently. (My wife is governed entirely by the right side of her brain.) And its chief function – and this is the important thing – the chief function of the right side of the brain is to add a kind of *third dimension* of meaning to the flat photographs taken by the left. Your left side merely scans quickly, glances at things and gives you a series of flat two dimensional grey photographs. When you're in a hurry, when you get over-tense, it's the left side of your brain – which is always in a hurry – that takes over completely, and you now become totally identified with the left side of your brain. When you relax you begin to move over to the right side; and you *can* relax so deeply at times – through certain exercises – that suddenly you see that the left side is not you at all. In other words you can move your centre of gravity from the left to the right. And the purpose of the right is to add meaning.

Now the most fascinating implication of all this is still to come. The right side of the brain appears to have very peculiar powers which are unknown to the left. For example such things as poltergeist effects, which seem fairly well

101

authenticated, certainly do not originate in the left side of the brain. These are powers of the right side which you normally cannot control or summon. Hypnotic phenomena which have never been understood (and hypnotists will still tell you that they don't understand what it is all about), these phenomena are due to the fact that the left side of the brain is put to sleep by the hypnotist, while the right remains wide awake. Your EEG shows you as being still wide awake. The hypnotist can then tell the right side of the brain 'You are now going to lie down between two chairs, three men are going to stand on your stomach and jump up and down, and it won't harm you in the least because you'll become as stiff as board.' And the right side of the brain says 'O.K. fine,' and does it. Because the right *can* do it. Then why can't *you* do it? Why can't the left side of the brain say to the right 'Become as stiff as a board' or 'Produce stigmata on your hands' or 'Produce a phantom pregnancy' or all of these other peculiar phenomena of hysteria? Because the right would not believe the left. And that's because the left does not believe *itself* when it says you can lie across two chairs and become as stiff as a board.

All of these enormous powers appear to be locked up in the right side of your brain with its curious contact with the lower brains – with the limbic region and the cerebellum, and the reptile brain. Down in this area lies the secret, I'm firmly convinced, of mystical and religious experience – which is entirely a right brain phenomenon. The answer somehow lies in achieving such perfect collaboration between the right and the left sides that finally, in a state of total relaxation, the two can build up a peculiar kind of feedback – like two trains on parallel tracks going at exactly the same speed, so that the people can actually lean out of the windows and have conversations. Normally you're in such a hurry identifying with the left side of the brain that you're completely out of contact with the other side, which has the peculiar powers. You can see that, for example, this explains Eugen Herrigel's book *Zen in the Art of Archery*. What Zen is aiming at is to persuade the left half of the brain to go off duty and let the right fire the arrow, because the left side of our brain always screws things up if you let him interfere. What you must do is to slow down the left until he's walking at the same pace as the right – or alternatively, increase the speed of the right by various forms of excitement (like ritual dancing) until it's moving at the same fast pace as the left. Either will do so long as they go at the same pace. I am grateful to Idries Shah for drawing my attention to something absolutely central to religious and mystical experience.

Some Reminiscences of Zen Training in Japan

Carmen Blacker

It is a great responsibility to be the first to speak in this important second seminar on the subject of religious experience, and I feel very honoured that you should have invited me to talk about the attempts I have made in the matter of Zen training in Japan.

I ought to stress the word *attempts*, for you must realize from the outset that I am not someone who has received an *inka*, that is to say a certificate of approval by the Teacher that one is qualified to give instruction in Zen. This is an extremely difficult stage of advancement, especially for any Westerner, for it means that one has been 'passed' in the requisite number of the Zen problems called *kōan*, and that as a result one's insight is so firm that one can pass it on to others. These *kōan*, as I shall later explain, are set as exercises to help the mind make the leap into the other dimension of experience which is the subject of this seminar. I must confess at once that I have not been 'passed' in a single one of these *kōan*.

So all I can tell you is what happened to me in the course of trying to practise this particular discipline, and hope that my remarks may be of interest to you in a comparative way with your own problems of method.

Perhaps I should start by trying to define what I mean by religious experience, because the term is capable of a good many different interpretations. Let us not forget that Sir Alister Hardy when he founded the Religious Experience Research Unit in Oxford was trying not only to discover how frequently this kind of experience occurred to people in this country, but also to try to distinguish a truly religious experience from other types of paranormal or altered states of consciousness.

May I therefore throw out a few suggestions for a definition of what I understand by the term, and which might serve as a preliminary standard by which we can distinguish the real thing from other states of mind deceptively similar?

I suggest that Dr Martin Israel's definition of mysticism may give us a helpful start. 'Mysticism', he says, 'is the experience of an all-embracing Reality which pervades and transcends the world of phenomena in which we live our ordinary lives. The mystic is one who has had this experience and whose life has been transformed by it. The transformation is made manifest by more perfect living and a heightened awareness of relationships.'

Surely this description of mysticism is very much what we mean by religious experience. It is an experience of a different order of reality altogether. We can call this the divine, the transcendent or the ultimately Real according to the tradition in which we live. But what characterises the genuine religious experience, and differentiates it from other states of consciousness which may be merely psychic in origin, seems to be something on the following lines.

First, religious experience is of a reality entirely different from and more real than anything previously experienced. It opens up a different order of existence, a different mode of awareness, by comparison with which everything which has gone before seems unreal, partial, incomplete. Unreal as a magic show is unreal, or as a mirage of water in a desert is found to be not real when one reaches it.

Second, this experience is felt to be taking place on a level of the mind quite beyond that on which our ordinary processes of thought function. All the mental processes which hitherto gave us what we thought to be valid knowledge – perceptions, memory, induction – none of these have any relevance to the new knowledge which has burst upon us.

It thus becomes absurd to imagine that I can use such mental processes to prove or disprove religious experience, or criticise its validity. What I previously thought to be my mind, and by extension *myself*, I now discover to be only a narrow segment of what is really there. I am not at all the entity I believed myself to be.

So, third, it follows that the experience is not communicable in words to someone who has not undergone it for himself. I cannot make you understand what has happened to me by simply describing it in ordinary words. Because there are no words which will do this job. They were all made for something else. They are names or signs for the segments or processes of our ordinary experience. We have no names for what we have not experienced, so that words can only act

105

as hints or pointers in that direction.

It is possible for two people who have undergone the same experience of a reality beyond the ordinary, to use words in a special way – as we shall see later in the context of Zen – but this will make no 'sense' at all to the ordinary person.

These are the characteristics I suggest for genuine religious experience.

Now some people are naturally *given* a glimpse of this other reality. It is as though some marvellous grace reached out towards them and bestowed this priceless gift upon them, and they often have the overwhelming feeling that this is entirely a divine gift, and that nothing that they had done of their own accord, by their own efforts, would have taken them anywhere near this miraculous world. Sometimes it is only a glimpse, and is then withdrawn, leaving these people with the feeling that their lives will never be the same again, and that they must dedicate themselves completely to discovering what this source of help is and how they can reach it once more.

Others, most others, are not so lucky. They can wait and wait and nothing is bestowed on them. So they look for a method, or a bridge, by which they can make the journey into this other world.

All the great religions have provided such bridges, but some are more precise and detailed than others. I think Buddhism stands out among them in so far as the crossing of this divide, the leap in experience over a gap into another world is the central teaching of the Buddha. It is not a peripheral branch, set apart from orthodox doctrine and theology, but the very heart of the Buddha's teaching. The Buddha himself reached this experience, which is given names in English such as release, awakening or enlightment, and for the rest of his life devoted himself to showing how others too could do the same.

So in fact the whole of the Buddha's teaching is in the nature of such a bridge, though the metaphor employed is usually that of a raft to carry you across a river to the Other Side. It is a body of practical instructions as to how one can make the transition to this other realm of experience. Anyone who has looked at the Pali canon will remember how impatient the Buddha was with metaphysical speculation which has no relevance to this practical journey.

Now let us look at Zen, or rather the Zen sect of Buddhism

106

in Japan. It is virtually the only school of Buddhism in Japan which still preserves a valid method. All the others have managed to avoid the real message of the Buddha; they have either erected massive structures of metaphysical speculation round it, or invented various short cuts, like magical formulae, to circumvent it, or they have denied that it is possible for human beings in these degenerate days at the end of the cycle to make any valid effort towards true awakening. Others once had a method, but somehow it had lost its validity; all that is left is the form, without the transmission of the precious substance of the experience.

But in the two schools of Zen in Japan we can still find this 'special transmission outside scripture' which has been the Zen tradition since its beginning. There are still teachers who have received this transmission, and are capable and qualified to pass it on to their pupils by means of the approved method or discipline.

Let me try to pass on to you some of the things I learnt about this method.

I started my Zen practice as long ago as 1952, before anything much was known about it in the West, and certainly before it became the modish and silly form of exhibitionism which we heard so much about in the late 50s and 60s. (Mercifully that era seems to have passed, for we hear less of the rubbish about 'letting go' and 'throwing aside stale old concepts and going straight for enlightenment'. There are now properly qualified teachers with real insight whose instruction can be sought.) Certainly it was before I knew anything about Zen, except for the fact that for the first time in my life I was confronted with the notion that religion *could mean* a different mode of experience and understanding. It was not simply, to quote that terrible definition of Matthew Arnold, 'Morality tinged with emotion'. And it was not simply repeating a series of propositions of a dogmatic kind which made absolutely no difference to one's daily life.

Religion had never been presented to me in this light before and it struck me with all the force of a revelation that it must be true. And if a method was taught which would help one to progress along this path, I wanted very much to learn it.

I was told that it was possible for a lay person to take part in what were called *sesshin*. These were retreats, held about seven or eight times a year in Zen temples or monasteries where there was a qualified teacher. During these periods the tempo of Zen practice was stepped up. The monks underwent longer periods of *zazen* than usual, and the critical confrontations with the Master, when one was questioned on one's progress with one's *kōan*, were more frequent, more intense and more ferocious. One was encouraged during these periods to fling oneself single-mindedly into the effort of breaking through the barrier and demolishing the 'silver mountain and iron wall' which lay between one and the enlightened world.

I think that rather than give you a plain chronological account of what happened to me, I would do better to group my remarks round certain headings if I am to pass on to you anything of interest.

The topics I propose are three: first, motive; second, method or discipline; and lastly, the teacher. All these three are essential elements in Zen practice. Drop one of them and you are outside the tradition, in a weak and rather helpless state.

First, the question of motive, on which the Japanese put such stress. Why does one decide to take up this hard and baffling discipline?

When I presented myself at my first *sesshin*, in the autumn of 1952 at the big monastery of Engakuji in Kamakura, the first question the Abbot asked me and the other four new aspirants to Zen practice was, what is your motive in coming here?

I replied on the lines I have just given you – that the idea of a religious discipline leading to another mode of experience and knowledge was quite new to me, and that I felt I must try to learn it.

The Japanese aspirants gave quite different reasons. One woman said that since her husband had died the world had held no meaning for her, and she was anxious to look for a new meaning through Zen training. Another girl said that she had recently had an appalling illness, and since recovering had felt the world to have no meaning. She had been tempted at times to commit suicide, such was her despair, but had resolved to find a way out of the impasse through *zazen*. There was a man too, I recall, who had a similar story; some tragedy had made his former way of life meaningless and purposeless, and he saw Zen discipline as a way out.

108

I subsequently learnt that my kind of motive was not usually regarded as very promising. There was not enough in my circumstances to rouse the tremendous spiritual energy needed to carry the discipline through to its conclusion. Without this driving force, it was only too easy to succumb to the temptation that ordinary life was better than all the pain and discomfort and boredom and depression one was going through in the monastery. A nice warm bed and no pain in one's legs and something nice to eat...

If one is to avoid these temptations, the motives which in Japan are regarded as promising are broadly three.

First, overwhelming personal tragedy, particularly the confrontation with death, which deprives life as we knew it before of meaning and purpose. Our jobs, family, hobbies, which we used to enjoy and which gave us a sense of fulfilment, seem now futile and purposeless and empty.

The same feeling can be induced by a sense of guilt or sin, for something the person has done and which he desperately wishes to expiate. They feel they are so hopelessly wrong as they stand that they cannot go on, and they come to *zazen* as a bridge whereby they can return to the sinless state they imagine was theirs before their fall

And third, and perhaps more typically Japanese, a sudden feeling assails a person overwhelmingly, that this world is transient and unreal. This feeling is called *mujōkan*, and it may be started off by something quite small – a glimpse of leaves falling in autumn or of blossoms scattering in spring may bring about a powerful conviction that the world as I see it is unreal. Again, Zen discipline appears as a means of discovering another real world behind it.

A few people are led into a religious discipline by a more dramatic form of calling; by a repeated vision, for example, of a divine figure such as a Bodhisattva commanding them to relinquish their present life and begin a new one involving the discipline. But though such initiations or 'vocations' are quite common in Japan, they usually lead the person to some discipline other than Zen – to the kind of ascetic life demanded by the shamanistic cults, for example. This may have something to do with the fact that imagery as such plays very little part in Zen training. If images arise in the mind, one is told not to take them seriously; they should be dismissed as hallucinations which tend to hinder the course

109

of training, and which have no relevance to one's final goal. It is rare that the Bodhisattva in the vision commands a Zen training.

Now what seems to be in common with all these valid and promising motives is that the person has suffered through seeing the world, and the life they took to be real, reduced to empty futility. And further, that they have the courage not to despair, but to turn this suffering into spiritual effort which brings them through the transforming discipline to the other side.

This point was put well by another Zen teacher I went to for instruction in later years, Yasutani Hakuun. He used to speak of the Three Essentials of Zen, without which you were unlikely to respond to the discipline. The first was absolute *faith* that fundamentally everything is well. I am Buddha, my nature is Buddha, the world is Buddha – awakened. But as I see it now it is all wrong. Nothing is Buddha. On the contrary, all is greed, hate and delusion. Why should this be, why am I in this wrong state? This is the second essential, great doubt. And this doubt gives rise to the third essential, a fierce determination to resolve this contradiction and see through the wrong view to the true one. This is great energy, *daifunshin*.

You will see at once how this formula applies to the people I have been talking about. And you will see too that all I have been saying is nothing but a restatement of the Buddha's Four Noble Truths.

This is briefly what I wanted to say about motive.

Now for method.

The method used by the Rinzai sect of Zen is different from that used by the other and less well known sect, the Sōtō. I will speak about it first because it is the only one of which I have any experience worth mentioning.

In a Rinzai temple the new aspirant is assigned, after a preliminary period on a breathing exercise called *sūsokkan*, the length of which varies from temple to temple, a *kōan* or Zen problem.

The *kōan* seems to be a unique method of spiritual discipline. There is nothing like it in the other sects of Buddhism, nothing so far as I know in Hinduism, and certainly nothing in Islam or Christianity.

In his recent book *Zen and the Ways*, Trevor Leggett described a *kōan* as a 'crystallisation of the life problem'. In

110

other words, the basic contradiction which I mentioned a moment ago can be focussed into a small space, and into certain statements. The *kōan* is a statement, in words, not comprehensible by the rational faculty, but if tackled in the right way can serve to help one across the barrier to the other side. This it does by bringing to life within us the state of consciousness from which the remarks were made.

Altogether there are about 1700 of these odd problems, but only a few of them are customarily used as 'openers' for beginners. One of these runs: What is my original face before my mother and father were born? And another, called *sekishu no koe*, goes: What is the sound of one hand? And another, called *muji*, recounts how a monk asked a particular Zen master: Does a dog also have the Buddha nature? The master first answered No, *mu*. But when asked the same question again a moment later he answered Yes, *U.*· You are told to find out what *mu* means, for it clearly does not mean No.

This latter *kōan* was the one assigned to me and the other new people in 1952, and we were told at once not to bother about the dog at all. We were to ignore the dog altogether, and concentrate entirely on *mu*. Just keep the mind focussed on *mu*, at the same time trying to question: What is this meaningless noise? You had to keep at this for about eight hours a day, in the half lotus posture, one foot on one knee, for periods of about 25 minutes at a time.

The régime was punctuated three times a day by the ceremonial confrontation with the Master, known as *sanzen* or *dokusan*. A bell rang, and you rushed to another room where you waited in a queue for your turn in this often terrifying event. (It was called a *shinken-shōbu* or a fight with real swords.) When your turn came, you prostrated yourself on the threshold of the Master's room, again just in front of him, with your forehead on the mat and your palms upwards as though to receive the feet of the Buddha.

In the strict Rinzai tradition you then stated the *kōan* you were working on, and the answer which seemed to you at that time to be the right one. The Master then simply rang a small bell, indicating that you were dismissed. He gave you no help, and no hint as to why and where you were wrong, but simply sent you away to try again.

The Master in Engakuji in 1952, Asahina Sōgen Rōshi, was not quite so strict as this, for he allowed you to say something more than the bare answer to the *kōan*. You could tell him how you were tackling the problem, and the difficulties you were having with *mōzō* or distractions, and the awful pain in your legs. But I have heard him criticised for laxness on this count; such modifications were considered to be a sign of the softness of the times and of lack of resolution in the disciples.

Perhaps I can best explain the system by an example. In 1963 when I was in Japan, I went to call on Dr Suzuki, whose name is familiar to most people nowadays as the first exponent in English of the enigmatic practices of Zen. He was then 93, so that his early training in Zen had taken place in the 1890s.

I asked him if he could not bring himself to write his memoirs, and tell us something of the training he himself had undergone in those days. He was at first reluctant; he was old and tired and had a great deal to do. 'Why not dictate them?' I then ventured. 'All right', he replied, 'we will start now!'

So I seized a pencil and paper, and for an hour every afternoon for the next ten days I wrote down what he told me of his practice in Zen up to the moment of what is called *kenshō*, the first 'seeing of your true nature', which coincides with your first penetration of your first *kōan*.

The first teacher to whom he went was Kōsen Rōshi, who prescribed for him the *kōan* called the sound of one hand. True to traditional practice, Kōsen Rōshi gave him no help at all. All he did during the *sanzen* interviews was to stretch out his left hand without saying a word. Dr Suzuki, then aged about 21, hazarded various explanations of the conundrum, only to be instantly ejected from the room.

Not long afterwards Kōsen Rōshi died, and his successor as head of the monastery, whose name was Shaku Sōen, changed Dr Suzuki's *kōan* to the one called *muji*. Again he gave no hint as to how to deal with the problem, and again Dr Suzuki in his early interviews hazarded various interpretations. He even read all the books he could find on Zen in the monastery archives. But always he was instantly ejected from the room without a word from the teacher, and soon he found that he had nothing whatever to say. For four years he struggled with *mu. Mu* was always nagging at the back of his mind, and he remembered sitting in a field one summer leaning against a rice stack and thinking that if he

112

could not understand *mu* he would rather die.

Eventually a crisis came when he found himself due to go to America to help Dr Paul Carus with his translation of the *Tao Te Ching*, and realized that his last opportunity for confronting the teacher was near at hand. It was then that he sank into a state of deep concentration, called *sammai*, on emerging from which the realization of *mu* burst upon him. *Mu* at once became luminously clear, and he was able to answer without hesitation all the supplementary questions called *sassho* – such as 'Cut *mu* in half', and 'Show me *mu* on a mountain' – which Shaku Sōen put to him.

So the method is to block any attempt by the disciple to find the meaning of the problem in rational terms, or for that matter in any terms associated with our familiar processes of thought. You try saying '*Mu* is emptiness', for example, or '*Mu* is the universe', and you are simply met with an iron wall. 'No, no, no, out!' is the only help that the disciple used to receive.

It is easy to see that so strict a method would prove too daunting for most people. *Mu* becomes utterly baffling and impenetrable, and they give up the task as hopeless.

But Dr Suzuki was one of those who responded perfectly to the intention of the *kōan* exercise. At the point of complete impasse, when all escape seems to be blocked, he was seized with a fierce energy and an overmastering determination to penetrate into the meaning of *mu*. He ceased to think about *mu*, but began to be absorbed in it in the manner which is described as that in which a lover is absorbed by his beloved or in which a hen sits on her eggs. From this state of absorption the truth suddenly burst upon him, and the meaning of the *kōan* became perfectly clear.

For most people of course, one *kōan* is not enough. A good many more are required to consolidate the new mode of awareness, in which the old 'I' ceases to function. Without this prolonged effort, so the teaching goes, it is only too easy for the glimpse we have had of the other shore to fade into a mere memory. And much as a dream does not alter our mode of living afterwards, neither does a single vision of the unconditioned. So more *kōans* are needed to enable us to see further and more clearly and to consolidate our habits of living in the new manner.

In my case, I have to confess that I never got anywhere near penetrating the meaning of *mu*, though I sat long hours in both freezing cold and boiling heat, in various *sesshin* over a number of years. It always remained baffling and impenetrable, and I was always told that I was not trying hard enough. I wasn't devoting myself utterly single-mindedly to the task, I was too interested in side issues, I was too easily put off and discouraged.

In 1958 I started to go to another teacher, called Yasutani Hakuun, who had no monastery, but a devoted band of lay pupils who gathered at his monthly *sesshins* in his private house. Yasutani Rōshi's methods were to give more help, so far as it was possible, in the initial stages. To spare the beginner a lot of preliminary floundering by clarifying such issues as the Five Kinds of Zen, the true function of *zazen* and the Three Essentials of Zen Practice. His *sanzen* interviews were apt to be much longer than those I was accustomed to; Dr Suzuki's had lasted about 30 seconds, Yasutani sometimes talked to a pupil for half an hour.

He could not of course convey the meaning of the *kōan* in words, but he felt he could help, by sympathetic discussion of the surrounding issues, to make the pupil fling himself into the effort with single-minded force.

He was the kindest and gentlest of men, but by an odd contradiction the conditions in his meditation hall were noisier and more violent than anything I had experienced in the Rinzai monastery. You have all heard of the use of the stick in Zen practice. If you find yourself dozing, or your concentration flagging, the monk patrolling the meditation hall will give you a few smart whacks on the shoulder muscles. This is held to have a stimulating and focussing effect on a flagging mind.

But in Yasutani's meditation hall the beating was really ferocious, especially as the *sesshin* began to rise to a climax on the fourth or fifth day. The man with the stick would go round the room systematically beating everyone, extremely hard, and at the same time shouting phrases equivalent to 'Stick to it' and 'Don't give up' and 'It doesn't matter whether you die'. The result was that the tension in the room rose to a terrific pitch, and most people responded by gasping and panting and giving strange groans and moans in their effort to hold on to *mu*.

There was no doubt that this treatment worked with most of the Japanese there, who responded in much the same way as a racehorse reacts to the jockey's whip during the last lap of the race. I know that many of Yasutani's pupils, when they came to write accounts of their experiences, were profuse in their thanks not only to the Rōshi but also to the man who had beaten them with the stick all night before their final breakthrough.

But I know that such methods were counter-productive with me, and in the end I found that every time I tried to sit, an appalling feeling of tension would grip me in the head, the last place where one is supposed to put any effort. This grew worse and worse until I realized that something was badly wrong.

It was certainly my fault that I did not respond properly to the instruction. My motive was clearly insufficient. But at the same time one should realize that this particular method is not suited to everyone. The Zen people themselves are the first to realize this. The Sōtō people of course disapprove of *kōans* altogether. The trouble about *kōans*, they say, is that they make you 'result oriented'. You want something and you are trying to reach it. But what is doing the trying? Simply the 'I' which it is my objective to see through and eliminate. Anything 'I' can want and strive for is bound to be only a picture I have made up for myself. It cannot be the real thing. Just as you cannot cure a sickness by the sickness itself, so you cannot make an image conjured up by 'I' lead to the elimination of 'I'.

The Sōtō people recommend 'quiet sitting' instead, in the faith that here and now I am the Buddha; not striving or trying, just sitting.

The danger with this method is perhaps the opposite – that you sink into a quiet pleasant day-dream in which there is no energy behind your practice. No energy, and hence nothing that can be transformed into the new kind of seeing. You never make the necessary leap.

The whole process is thus seen to be a truly narrow path between pitfalls. But one last important word on this subject is that neither method should ever be thought to be a technique. By which I mean something which will invariably produce the expected results if the necessary conditions are fulfilled. Do this and this, and inevitably the result will follow.

No spiritual method works in this way, though sometimes we are deluded by the mechanical models so prevalent these days into thinking that it is. There is always something

115

more which is beyond the causes and effects we understand, call it grace or a mystery, or what you will.

Finally a brief word about the Teacher. Nearly every spiritual method requires a teacher, and the relation between the teacher and pupil is bound to be a very special one. I think the Zen *Rōshi* stands in a different relation to his pupils from that of the Indian guru and his disciples. In Zen it is not a question of the guru taking upon himself the *karma* of his pupils, or the pupils regarding him as a living incarnation of the divine.

The *Rōshi* is someone who has made the journey you are starting out on. He has seen and experienced every step of the way himself. Now in this journey you cannot give the pupil a map, and say to him simply, follow this. Nor can you give him any photographs or sketches of the scenery he will pass through on his way. But the teacher, observing the pupil, can say, 'No, you have gone wrong there, try again.' Or, 'Yes, you are on the right road, carry on and step out with all the courage you have'. This is why the transmission is so important.

In Zen the presence of the teacher is absolutely necessary to prevent bogus and parrot-like imitation – of the kind so prevalent here about twenty years ago. The Zen form of expression is unfortunately subject to the humbug of imitation, and hence it is only a trained and proved teacher who is capable of distinguishing the genuine insight from the surface imitation of the words and actions which that insight may express. The chief trouble about all the rubbish that was talked twenty years ago in the name of Zen was that there was no one around capable of distinguishing the genuine from the bogus.

Many Zen teachers used to be extremely fierce, and even now some of them are still noted for their ferocious scolding. But there is a good reason for this behaviour, even though at the time it may cause shock and anger. In a sense the Zen teacher is helping the pupil to hatch out of an egg. There is a Zen phrase *settaku-dōki,* which means two beaks together at the same crucial moment. Just at the instant that the chicken inside begins to tap at the shell, the hen outside gives that very spot a good peck with her beak. This happy coincidence will cause the shell to crack and allow the chicken to emerge into the light of day.

116

Colin Wilson:

I'm going to say a couple of words to try to connect what we were saying this morning with the next speaker. What I want to do is to throw another idea at you.

The concept I want to put to you now presents, I think, a kind of paradigm into which we can fit some of these things we have been discussing, and it is briefly this: that we do not have what you might call one single self, we have a whole series of selves ascending like a ladder, one on top of the other, so to speak. I agree that sounds an arbitrary kind of idea. It occurred to me three or four years ago when I was overworked and came to the edge of a nervous breakdown. Suddenly, to my great surprise, I began to have panic attacks. I woke up in the middle of the night with a horrifying feeling of tension. My heart began to pound violently. I leapt out of bed and rushed to the lavatory, and sat there for half an hour until I'd calmed down. Then I got back into bed, and as soon as I lay down the panic started again, the same feeling of terror. And once this damn thing had started it was extremely difficult to stop – because, of course, you become afraid *of fear,* so the whole thing turns into a vicious circle. I discovered eventually, after quite a bit of struggling, that I could stop this very simply – by *waking myself up as fully as possible,* perhaps calling upon some of the kind of vital energy that Carmen Blacker was talking about. But it depended upon waking yourself up. And when I *was* wide awake, it was almost as if a school mistress came into a room of quarrelling children and rapped on the table; instantly there was a strange inner silence and peace; and it suddenly struck me that this school mistress was, so to speak, a higher level of me.

Now I had been doing a series of programmes for BBC Two on the paranormal, and I was particularly fascinated by a case of multiple personality which we dealt with – in fact, by a whole number of cases in which people become literally *several different people.* In the Christine Beauchamp case, a girl under hypnosis suddenly produced a totally different personality that had nothing whatsoever in common with her normal everyday personality. Even the brain patterns were different, which you know is physiologically almost impossible. Not only this, but she went on to develop into two more completely different personalities. I was baffled by this, and we couldn't get any answer from the experts on the programme as to what was happening. And then suddenly it began to dawn on me that we were in fact dealing with something very like a *series* of personalities inside us, one on top of the other. The only difference is that this 'ladder of selves', as I see it, is not shaped like an ordinary ladder with parallel sides; it is more like a triangle. The higher you go the more terrific the effort of compression that is required to get onto the next step up – whereas it is terribly easy to fall down a step to a lower level, which is what had happened with my panic attacks. So this was the concept that I began to work on, trying to see how many so called paranormal phenomena could be fitted into this framework. One thing that fascinates me about paranormal phenomena is that there seems to be, for example, a part of your being which knows what is going to happen in the future. And yet, as we also know, the future has not yet happened, so this is an impossibility. There seems to be a part of you that does not exist in time as we know it.

Now I'm basically a sort of scientist, so that I want to fit these phenomena into a kind of paradigm or framework. And it suddenly seemed to me that this notion does, in fact, not only take in religious experience but also paranormal experience. Anyway I throw that idea at you as a kind of parallel to what I was saying earlier about the left and right sides of the brain. I think there's obviously an interconnection here.

Now Dr. Morais, as you know, is going to talk on the subject of yoga. And I was rather curious, glancing at the titles of his books, to find that in fact the books listed here appear to have nothing whatever to do with yoga. There's a book about anti-semitism and a book about the emancipation of women. When I asked him about this, he said words to this effect: 'Ah, the reason is that any kind of prejudice shows people trapped within their concepts, and living rigidly by these concepts. But yoga is the ability to get back towards reality and into a more free-flowing sense of what really *is,* instead of being stuck in the rigidity of concepts and prejudices.' And suddenly I could see the whole matter that we are concerned with this week-end beginning to fit together into something much bigger than a discussion of the mechanisms of religious experience or mysticism.

118

The Contribution of Yoga to Modern Life

Vamberto Morais

Ramakrishna, the great Indian mystic and yogi, had a gift for striking similes and parables. More than once he compared spiritual awakening to a child who has become absorbed in his play or been cajoled by sweets, but at the end of the afternoon he becomes restless and says quite determinedly: 'Now I want my mother'. He will cry and scream at the top of his voice and no amount of adult persuasion will pacify him: he wants his mother and no substitute will do.

Many of us will no doubt be reminded of an obvious parallel, from that great master of parables, the story of the Prodigal Son. There too you have the engrossment with external distractions, the dissipation, and then the change of heart – the unshakeable decision to go home. Naturally, the awakening may take the form of leaving the family home, as Jesus himself did. In the case of the famous yogi of South India, Ramana Maharshi, a leaving-note to his family said: 'I go in search of my father.'

You may perhaps think this is a very timely parable for the modern world. Aren't we all dying to 'go home' in that sense? If you plunge deep enough, you may find in each one of us the crying child, longing for its mother and father, mourning somehow for a loss or dispossession that he does not understand: the child who is the heir to the spiritual kingdom, the prince in disguise, the son of God whose natural atmosphere is joy and bliss. And isn't the so-called consumer society the gigantic fraud, the Vanity Fair trying to cajole the child with sweets and toys and cheat him out of his inheritance?

In this image of the weeping or lost child, of the heart's hunger and need that can be appeased by one thing only, we probably find one of the great points of convergence of all religious traditions: in fact, what this seminar is trying to explore. Here at the core we can all understand each other, here we find the basis for the Interglossa, the common language of all religions, that some of us have been trying to

119

develop. It will not be a kind of synthetic Esperanto, but should grow unpredictably out of our own experience as we bring together all the various strands of the great spiritual traditions. In fact, towards the end of his life Thomas Merton was talking of 'a lingua franca of religious experience' and said, rather significantly, that 'we are well on our way to a workable inter-religious lexicon of key words, mostly rooted in Sanskrit' (*The Asian Journal of Thomas Merton*, published by his friends after his death in 1968, Sheldon Press, London 1974, p. 314).

It may surprise some of you that one should begin a talk about yoga in this way. I am not imagining that you hold the more naive popular image that yoga means just standing on your head or contorting your body into all sorts of ways. But there is a very widespread idea that yoga is essentially a system of mental and physical control, which has little or nothing to do with religious devotion or emotion. This idea is not altogether mistaken, for certainly methods of control are basic to yoga, nevertheless it underestimates enormously the bewildering wealth of approaches and paths of Indian spirituality. It also overlooks the undeniable fact that the path of love and devotion, bhakti yoga, has been for many centuries one of the most popular and rich in literature.

Perhaps another simile, this time a very direct one, will help me to underline this point. It is one of those many stories current in India, in which the disciple asks the master the traditional question: 'How can I learn to reach, to realize God?' The Guru does not say a word, but grabs the young man by the arm, takes him to a river nearby and plunges his head into the water. When the disciple is very near suffocation, the Guru lets him come up for air and asks: 'Well, what was that like?' The young man replies: 'Master, never have I felt such a need for air.' 'Now then,' says the Guru, 'when you feel like that about God, you will certainly reach him.'

The moral is close to Ramakrishna's simile, and the connection with breathing is a pointer to an important aspect of yogic practices. It is not irrelevant to remember, I think, that in a description of religious ecstasy quoted by Plutarch the subject felt as if he was breathing 'for the first time, after a long and painful oppression' (*De Genio Socratis*, 22).

The popularity of bhakti yoga is by no means limited to later periods, down to the time of Ramakrishna in the 19th

120

century; it goes back not only to the *Bhagavad Gita*, which has been described as the New Testament of Hinduism, but to the *Upanishads* themselves, which place the practice of yoga squarely in the heart of Hindu devotion. In fact, the oldest Sanskrit text giving precise instruction on yogic meditation seems to be the *Svetasvatara Upanishad*. It says that 'the wise man, with upright body, neck and heart, should make the senses and the mind enter into the heart' (II,8). Elsewhere in the *Upanishads* there are a number of references to 'the secret, hidden place in the heart'. This very formula, 'mind in the heart', is repeatedly prescribed in a traditional method of prayer followed in the Greek and Russian Orthodox Church. There are many parallels of this 'prayer of the heart' in the Catholic tradition, and among the Sufis with their idea of 'opening of the heart'.

So this is obviously a great highway in spiritual development. The story I told just now makes the point that until the heart is touched, vibrated, kindled into a steady fire, nothing great or important can happen. The old, lovely Greek word *enthousiasmos* means being fired from within by a divine fire, by the bliss or *Ananda* of the Hindu scriptures. Following the great Orphic tradition, Plato said that people can only do something great and beneficent when they are literally mad, out of themselves, inspired by the divine fire. And indeed the *Svetasvatara Upanishad* makes a striking comparison between yoga and the process of making fire by friction of wood. Yoga could then be described very briefly, as the art of setting fire to oneself: a steady, controlled fire, not something that overheats the furnace.

Even in Patanjali's *Yoga Sutras*, which is a highly condensed summary with no poetry at all, as dry as kitchen recipes, as terse as some of Aristotle's treatises, the element of devotion is by no means forgotten. Attention or 'surrender to God' (*Isvara Pranidhana*) appears prominently as a basic precept of yoga, and one that is easily translatable into Christian or Sufi language. Patanjali says in fact that surrender to God is one of the ways leading to the highest yogic state (*Samadhi*) and therefore to full liberation (*moksha*). It has been conclusively shown that the concept of Isvara or God is not a later accretion or a kind of second thought, to an originally agnostic yoga, as some scholars have supposed, but was there from the earliest beginnings.

So on reviewing yoga's contribution to modern life, it is

first of all, I think, to this basic spirit of devotion that we must return. In the ecumenical process of convergence that is taking place, yoga could very well play the part of an important linking element, for which it has two important qualifications. First, although it came out of Hinduism, it is not tied to any rigid system of beliefs, and in its tradition practice always comes first (the Hindu religion is perhaps the only one that allows a giving up of specific rituals at a further stage of development). Secondly, it offers a great variety of practical methods and devices which can be tested and used by people of many different beliefs or no special belief at all. It is hardly necessary to say that Buddhism developed out of yogic practices. Some Sufi schools have obviously been influenced by yoga, and a number of devout Christians are now talking of a Christian Yoga. One should not forget either that etymologically yoga (=yoke, *iugum*) means *connection, union, link*. Harnack once said that 'Christianity is not one religion among many; it is religion'. If this sounds a little arrogant, it might be compared with Vivekananda's breath-taking claim that yoga is the science and art of all religion.

We may not be prepared to go so far, but one cannot fail to be impressed by what I have described as the 'variety of approaches and paths in yoga' and by its armoury of subtle psychological and physical methods. The very fact that it can so easily be distorted or corrupted, say, into a cosmetic yoga for the wealthy, leisurely woman, or an adjunct of success for the business executive, shows its protean character. I think one should also admit that the label of 'yoga' covers a great deal of quackery, play-acting and exhibitionism.

People will find in yoga only what they are prepared or qualified to find, but even minor gains should not be underestimated. For many it is just a method among others for keeping fit and inducing relaxation, that will often strengthen the ego instead of making it wither away as is claimed in traditional yoga. But the practice of meditation is becoming very widespread, and much of it owes its inspiration to a yogic or Buddhist school.

In a recent booklet on meditation a Dutch Jesuit, Father de Rooy, says that until some time ago Christian meditation was going through a deep crisis. 'But today', he adds, 'as a result of contact with the religions of the East, we have been re-taught to use our senses and perceptions, and stress has been laid on the importance of the body in prayer. The elemental values present in classical spirituality and mysticism have been re-discovered and this has happened through a detour among the religious practices of the East' (Fr. De Rooy, *Tools for Meditation*, Grail Publications, 1976, p. 6). This is a revealing acknowledgement and shows an entirely different spirit from the narrow parochialism of the past. One should add that it is often reciprocated by many Hindus and Buddhists, who in fact were the first to take the initiative in this wider ecumenism. It is well to remember that Ramakrishna was the first modern prophet to proclaim the validity and truth of all religious paths, which his disciple Vivekananda preached in the West, particularly at the First Congress of Faiths (Chicago, 1893).

There is no doubt that the phenomenon described by Father De Rooy is indeed happening to many people who grew up as nominal Christians but had virtually no experience or understanding of Christian spirituality. In a number of cases it was through meditation and other practices under Hindu, Sufi or Buddhist guidance or inspiration that they have come to a better understanding of what Christianity – and indeed all religion – is about. There again you find the vital link being provided in the wide-ranging process of convergence and cross-fertilization that is taking place.

This is an important gain, but as we all know many people take up a given system of meditation, or join one of the innumerable sects that are now proliferating in all Western cities, mainly to relieve their distress or frustration: to seek peace of mind or to escape from the growing feeling of emptiness and barrenness that haunts contemporary society. Once again, it is the weary child, tired of its play, seeking its mother.

There is no guarantee, as in fact there has never been, that the search will be entirely successful. But a number of people have found that at least they have become more able to stand the growing pressures of contemporary life and gained precious insight into themselves and others. They find that the ultimate questions about man, God and the universe are not to be tackled by endless speculations or verbal arguments which solve nothing, but through the deepening of one's experience.

This deepening is a process of growth, as mysterious, as

full of wonder and unpredictable as life itself. Yoga can never be a mere application of set rules and techniques, as some people seem to imagine. One of the first things the student or disciple learns is that there is no dividing line between 'meditation' and 'life': interaction between the two is constant, both positively and negatively. The essence of the process is that meditation should continue throughout life and become a permanent, natural condition: just as the Christian ideal is to turn the whole of life into prayer ('one great continuous prayer', as Origen said). Or, as Theophan, a Russian Orthodox monk put it, 'If prayer is right, everything is right.'

After some progress, and usually many difficulties and setbacks, one comes to realize – in *practice*, not intellectually – that everything in one's life hangs together and that yoga 'works in a circle' and *aims at a circle*, the traditional symbol of perfection. There is the good cycle, that makes for growth and enhances one's energies, and there are all the vicious circles that poison and weaken life with whirlpools of fears, depression and aggressive impulses. For instance, any creative activities (work, sports, arts, service to others, etc.) can be drawn into the sphere of yoga and enrich its practice. As Sri Aurobindo said, the follower of integral yoga 'has no method and every method: in his yoga there is nothing too small to be used and nothing too great to be attempted.' How far we are here from some narrow conception of a mere set of techniques to keep fit or inducing relaxation, just aiming at making life a little more tolerable! Like the mustard seed, yoga begins in a very small and humble way, like someone practising stillness and peace, or reciting a Mantra in a corner of his room. It can grow until it pervades one's whole life. But the great test, as for every spiritual path, is whether it can really change people.

It is at this point that one faces the decisive problem, at once fascinating and exasperating, of human consciousness. It lies at the very heart of the human puzzle, of the sort of creatures we are. From this point of view, the psychology of yoga, both in theory and practice, has been almost unique in its definite, very explicit claim that there is another level of consciousness and life which is radically different from the one on which we normally live. Given the necessary conditions, this level can be attained not only in states of ecstasy which are experienced in all religious traditions and outside them, but as a permanent condition. In fact, the whole practice of yoga is based on the assumption that, once the mind is completely stilled and mental control achieved, the real Self (Ātman) emerges in its natural condition of unshakeable peace and bliss, to quote Prasad Shastri's beautiful description: 'Like a small child which strips off its clothes one by one to run naked in the sunlight, so we strip off the convictions "I am this body", "I am old, I am sick", "I am sad", "I am angry", "I am this mind", "I am so-and-so", and come naked into the sunlight of Infinity' (*Yoga*, Foyle, London, 1974, p. 43). Lovers of Blake will no doubt notice the similarity both in the imagery and the message.

So the contradictions of our ordinary mental level, what the poet called the 'wearisome condition of humanity', can only be solved on this higher level of integration, not by any logical formula or answer.

One of our major troubles seems to be that we would like to be coherent and unified, and know somehow we have to be, but this is practically impossible on our ordinary mental level of semi-organized confusion. There has to be a radical change, which is in fact envisaged in all higher religions, but perhaps given a more explicit psychological formulation in Hindu yoga and Buddhism.

Obviously, this is not the place to go into details of meditation practice and psychology of yoga, which I have dealt with in talks given elsewhere. But there are a few aspects I should like to mention as an important part of yoga's contribution to modern life.

The first is connected with the whole question of consciousness. Every twenty-four hours we go through at least three different states of consciousness, and yet we know very little about them, particularly about sleep. They were properly distinguished for the first time in the *Upanishads*, and it was only very recently, from 1953 onwards, that modern physiology came to recognize that distinction through research carried out in sleep laboratories. It is now admitted that dream sleep (called by physiologists REM sleep or 'paradoxical sleep') is associated with a considerable measure of body activity, especially with 'rapid eye movements'; while dreamless sleep ('orthodox sleep') is quite a different state, a much more relaxed one. Now it is significant that physiological research should confirm something that had been stated many centuries ago by the Indian masters of yoga. It is now clear that our life is a continuous cycle of states of consciousness whose succession, in most cases, is the only way of maintaining the harmony of the system.

But the *Upanishads* go farther than that, for they describe these changes as 'the four quarters' (*pāda*) of the Ātman or Inner Spirit. The first is the waking state, then come the states of dream and deep sleep, which are strictly distinguished in Sanskrit terminology. The Fourth Quarter (*Turiya*), the state of yogic bliss or *ananda*, remains as a latent condition during the other three and closes the whole cycle as it were, thus revealing its true nature. In really deep, peaceful sleep, the *Upanishads* say, we are in contact with our true blissful nature, but unconsciously, hence its refreshing and restful effect. On the other hand, once the Fourth State is attained, it is claimed that one can obtain all the peace and rest that are necessary.

These ideas find a very suggestive parallel in Christian books of devotion which often compare ecstasy to sleep. For instance, Richard of St Victor says that ecstasy of the mind, 'is rightly called sleep', and the *Epistle of Privy Council* (by the same author of the more famous *Cloud of Unknowing*) explains that in ecstasy, this 'spiritual sleep', 'the simple soul may softly sleep and rest in its loving regard of God as he is, so that man's spiritual nature may be fully nourished and restored' (see Richard of St Victor, 'Benjamin Major', in *Spiritual Writings on Contemplation*, Faber & Faber, London, 1957, pp. 176–7; *The Medieval Mystics of England*, John Murray, London, 1962, p. 176).

The theory of the Four Quarters of the Atman is an inspiring one and ought to be seriously considered by psychologists interested in the problem of consciousness. But yogic philosophy has gone yet further and postulated (with Shankara) the existence of three bodies: *the gross or material body*, which normally overshadows all awareness of the other two during the waking state; the *subtle body*, which is experienced during the dream state; and the *causal body*, which emerges in deep sleep. We have to admit that this theory, although suggestive, is very difficult to prove or disprove. But there is little doubt that during the state of dream some people may be particularly susceptible not only to spiritual visions but to clairvoyance and other extrasensory phenomena. I do not think that ancient traditional beliefs in these matters should be despised.

126

But there is a more immediately relevant fact. Recent physiological research has also shown that in deep meditation and states nearing ecstasy, the EEG pattern (brain waves), muscular relaxation and other bodily signs are similar to those of sleep. This has been found in both yogic and Zen meditation. Some physiologists are, therefore, inclined to accept that meditation 'performs some of the functions usually required of sleep' (Gay Gaer Luce and Julius Segal, *Sleep*, Heinemann, London, 1967, p. 215). For instance, an American housewife who meditated for five days without sleep at a Zen retreat did not show any of the usual signs of sleep deprivation: on the contrary, she appeared alert and refreshed. Such evidence fits in very well with traditional reports about yogis and saints who were said to stay for long periods without sleep.

The relation between sleep and dreams on the one hand and spiritual experiences on the other, far from being an academic study, is very relevant to modern conditions of life. We all know how the prevalence of insomnia nowadays has led to a staggering consumption of sleeping tablets of all kinds. This is yet another symptom of the imbalance of the modern world and its appalling lack of peace of mind. Here what yoga has to offer in methods of relaxation and breathing exercises (*Pranayama*) is proving very useful.

If in sleep breathing is deeper, slower and more rhythmic, nothing is more plausible than to use breathing techniques to induce the states that accompany sleep, and ultimately all modalities of consciousness. Again, in the states of ecstasy and deep absorption (usually called *Samādhi* in yoga) breathing is very slow and sometimes barely perceptible: that is why the *Upanishads* recommend diminished breathing as part of the method of meditation (*Svetasvatara Upanishad*, II, 9). Ramana Maharshi expressed this in neat psychosomatic terms when he said: 'By control of breath the mind gets controlled, and by stilling of the mind the breath gets controlled' (Ramana Maharshi, *Collected Works*, Rider, London, 1959, p. 34).

An identical observation was made by St Gregory Palamas, one of the masters of Hesychasm in the Greek Orthodox Church (see *Early Fathers from the Philokalia*, Faber & Faber, London, 1967, p. 405). It is now well known that the art of prayer practised by the monks of Mount Athos in Greece and later spread to Russia (and now to Western

Europe) includes the reciting of the Prayer of Jesus combined with rhythmic breathing (*The Art of Prayer: An Orthodox Anthology*, Faber & Faber, London, 1966, *passim*; see particularly pp. 96, 104 and 198). Again, the role of breathing has not escaped the attention of teachers of prayer either in the Catholic Church or in Islam in which the practice of *Dhikr* was developed, especially among the Sufi communities.

There are strong indications of a correlation between mental and spiritual development on the one hand and the type or pattern of breathing on the other. It is very likely that undeveloped, coarse individuals, prone to violence or to a disturbed emotional life, tend to have heavy, irregular breathing. It is almost certain that the pattern of respiration changes as people make progress in peace of mind and mental control, and this must happen in all religious traditions. In Western Christianity references to this are very sporadic, but all the more revealing because there is no record of the use of breathing techniques in Western monasteries. Joseph Surin, a French mystic of the 17th century whose case fascinated Aldous Huxley, gives a tantalizingly brief description of four types of breathing, all of which he says he experienced. He calls them breath of the devil, of nature, of grace and glory (see Aldous Huxley, *The Devils of Loudun*, Penguin Books, 1974. p. 298).

The subject of sleep disturbances leads me to the second point I wanted to deal with, which concerns the whole question of human health. The practice of yoga in the West, and indeed in the whole world, tends to be considered part of what is now called 'fringe medicine', together with acupuncture, faith healing and a hotchpotch of other practices which only recently have become a little more respectable. Some doctors have even taken to recommending meditation as a means of reducing nervous tension. But in general usage the word yoga is almost always equated with a simplified, and one might add distorted, hatha yoga, which means in practice the *Āsanas* or postures, relaxation and perhaps some breathing exercises. The spiritual side is usually more or less ignored. In fact, from the educational point of view – say, at classes run by local authorities – yoga is normally considered a branch of physical education, and teachers who try to persuade the authorities to accept a wider, more correct view of the matter have been having a very uphill task.

Admittedly, some teachers and writers on hatha yoga have made and do make vague and exaggerated claims about the benefits of the exercises and other practices, and this has not helped the reputation of yoga in more discriminating circles. Nevertheless, there is growing medical evidence that some advanced masters of hatha yoga do acquire remarkable control over their bodies, like the much publicised ability to stop the heart altogether or to stand intense cold. But more important than the question of any supernormal powers is the fact that yoga and other practices are helping to change our whole concept of health and restoring the broken link between medicine and spirituality. As the modern practitioner finds himself more and more helpless in the face of purely functional disorders, we seem to be on the eve of a medical revolution, which should restore the lost balance and do away, among other things, with excessive reliance on drugs.

For instance, many Christians nowadays tend to regard Christ's power of healing as something almost incidental and separate from his essential message. From a more integral, yogic point of view, physical and mental healing becomes more understandable, and is in fact recognized as an almost inevitable result of the emergence of a spiritual force. Spiritual union heals and reintegrates, and it has been rightly pointed out that from the linguistic point of view 'whole', 'holy', 'heal' and 'hale' are all related.

Here in Britain we are in the middle of an official 'Keep Fit' campaign whose motto is 'Look After Yourself.' But it is time we had a deeper and wider concept of health and recognized that spiritual exercises are as much part of health as running and swimming. We must look forward to a time when the meditation room or shrine are accepted as essential public places, like a gymnasium or swimming pool. A few decades ago, Evelyn Underhill was complaining of general ignorance about what she called 'the science of prayer' and 'the hygiene of the soul'. Apparently, she could not foresee that a more widespread knowledge of such things would come via the East.

On the other hand, physical exercises can be done in a religious spirit, and they are likely to have a stimulating effect on the mental and spiritual side. The fact that the early Christians compared themselves to athletes, and that the idea and practice of 'asceticism' is connected with Greek

129

athleticism is no coincidence. There again yoga provides a useful link, for the hatha yogi is supposed to do his exercises in a spirit of concentration and reverence, and some of the postures and *mudras* (ritual gestures) are acts of worship: a little like the medieval tumbler who dedicated his leaps and acrobatics to the Virgin Mary in the lovely story of the 'Jongleur de Notre Dame'. From this to the use of dance and rhythmic movements in spiritual training is only a step.

But there is a deeper significance in any sort of regular exercise, whether physical or mental, which is practised in a spirit of perseverance, 'religiously', as people often say, though without any explicit spiritual aim in view. It is not only the humanistic ideal of *mens sana in corpore sano*, nor is it just to keep up our self-respect, our image of active, hard-working people, that we cling to certain exercises or rituals. It is almost a tacit recognition that man as such is an unfinished product and needs to exert himself in order to change: it may be almost a distant glimpse of the profound metamorphosis we have to undergo in order 'to become what we really are'. In yoga, as one would expect, the concept of *abhyāsa* (devoted practice) is a very important one and figures prominently in the *Gita* and in Patanjali's *Yoga Sutras*.

Finally, we can ask ourselves whether such radical change is to be envisaged as an individual matter or whether it embraces the whole of society. Followers of yoga have sometimes been accused of being too concerned with individual salvation or liberation, and of alienating themselves from the collective problems of mankind. But if Hinduism has been to some extent world-denying, so has Christianity for long periods of its history. The main difference, in my view, does not lie there but in the prophetic or historical character of the Jewish-Christian tradition, which is one of its most original contributions. Here one should admit candidly that yoga, on the whole, has had little or no historical sense. And yet this is changing, no doubt through the cross-fertilization I have mentioned. The part played by the revival of Hinduism in the whole movement for Indian independence is a very significant one. The fact that leaders like Ghandi, Tilak, Sri Aurobindo and Vinoba Bhave have blended Hindu spiritual teaching with social and political reform is a very important one. Swami Viveka-nanda himself, the first Indian to teach yoga in the West, was passionately concerned with problems of poverty and social justice. But perhaps the best answer to the question I have just raised is the emergence of a philosophy of yoga which is both prophetic and evolutionary: that of Sri Aurobindo. Aurobindo has been rightly regarded as the counterpart of Teilhard de Chardin in the East. His concept of Integral Yoga (*Purna Yoga*) broadens this ancient tradition in a way that is extremely bold and breath-taking, and yet remains faithful to the spirit of the *Upanishads* and the *Gita*.

Like Teilhard, Aurobindo envisages a spiritual revolution, a radical new stage in which mankind will be entirely infused by the divine spirit. To him the evolution of life, and indeed of the whole universe, has been a kind of yoga. Could it be that we are all in a similar position to that of Molière's M. Jourdain, who said he had been making prose for forty years without being aware of it? Could it be that we are all unconscious yogis? Well, to some extent this is true. One is reminded of Tertullian's famous phrase *anima naturaliter Christiana*. The whole practice and theory of yoga is only the distillation, as it were, of something that is already taking place. After all, centration and concentration are part of all processes in the universe.

Indeed, the extension of the concept of yoga is in no way foreign to ancient Indian philosophy. A great passage of the *Upanishads*, for which there is a close parallel in Plotinus (III,8,1), says: 'The heavens contemplate as it were. The waters contemplate as it were. The mountains contemplate as it were.' (*Chandogya Upanishad*, VII, 6,1) The Sanskrit word used here is in fact the same as is normally applied to yogic meditation (*Dhyana* and cognates). The connection with nature mysticism and with the traditional impulse to seek wild places, the forest or the Himalayas in India, the wilderness in Ancient Israel, or the desert among Eastern Christians and Muslims, is obvious. And need I add that the asphalt jungle and the destruction of wild life are an attack on our spiritual life?

But prophetic visions of the future, however inspired and inspiring, should not be an excuse to escape from the present. As we look at the extraordinarily complex and bewildering picture of the modern world, it seems that two wide-ranging processes are occurring at the same time: one of dissolution, which horrifies so many people, making them

131

feel that everything is falling apart; and one of recreation, in which we are groping towards new patterns and forging new connections. This new creation is often difficult to discern, for it is obscured by all sorts of negative forces and conflicts. But it is there all the time, and certainly one of its clearest aspects is this wider ecumenical movement which is slowly breaking down sectarian barriers. As Teilhard de Chardin said, the temperature of the whole human mass is increasing. And if we want to tame Babel, connection must be one of our key words. 'Only connect.' As all paths seem to be converging, each can offer its own contribution as a free gift to that great spiritual revival which has been prophesied. The special contribution of yoga lies exactly in providing that linking function which I have been trying to illustrate throughout this talk: the connection of man with the universe and its Creator, the link between body and mind and the union in love of all paths that lead to the centre.

A short reading list

Most books seen in bookshops with 'Yoga' in the title are in fact practical handbooks of *hatha yoga,* variable in quality, but usually concentrating on the postures (*Āsanas*) and other physical practices, giving only perfunctory attention to meditation and the psychology of yoga. The list given here deals with yoga in the traditional sense: the practice and theory of spiritual development through meditation and other disciplines.

(1) *Introductory*

HARI PRASAD SHASTRI *Yoga* Foyle: London, 1974. An admirably succinct, practical guide (under 100 pages).

CHRISTOPHER ISHERWOOD (Ed.) *Vedanta for the Western World* Allen & Unwin: London, 1951. *Vedanta for Modern Man* Allen & Unwin: London, 1952. The articles by Swami Prabhavananda on yoga are specially recommended.

(2) *More Advanced Works*

SWAMI VIVEKANANDA *Raja Yoga* (with the Sanskrit text of Patanjali and an English translation) Advaita Ashrama: Calcutta, 1970.

Bhakti Yoga Advaita Ashrama: Calcutta, 1974.

SWAMI PRABHAVANANDA and CHRISTOPHER ISHERWOOD *How to Know God* (Translation of Patanjali, with commentary) Vedanta Press: California, 1970.

Meditation by the Monks of the Ramakrishna Order: London, 1972.

SRI AUROBINDO *Synthesis of Yoga* Sri Aurobindo Library: New York, 1950.

ALAIN DANIÉLOU *Yoga: The Method of Reintegration* University
Books: New York, 1955.

HARIDAS CHAUDHURI *Integral Yoga* Allen & Unwin: London 1965.

MIRCEA ELIADE *Yoga: Immortality and Freedom* Panther Books: New
York, 1958.

JAMES HAUGHTON WOODS *The Yoga System of Patanjali* Harvard
Oriental Series: Cambridge, Mass. 3rd Edn., 1966. Invaluable for
the translation of Vyasa's commentary on the Yoga Sutras.

THEOS BERNARD *Hatha Yoga* Rider: London, 1970. Authoritative and
unpretentious, based on the original extracts.

J. M. DÉCHANET *Christian Yoga* Burns & Oates: London, 1960. A
'Christian adaptation' of yogic methods by a French Benedictine.

Bhagavad Gita and *Upanishads* There are several good translations
available, including those of Juan Mascaro (a little too free in
places), published by Penguin Books. Those wanting an edition with
the Sanskrit text and a scholarly commentary with many quo-
tations and parallels with Christian works should read the translations by Radhakrishnan: *The Gita and a Selection of the
Upanishads* Allen & Unwin: London, 1948.

Discussion

Q. Can Dr Morais expand on what he said about yoga's
potential role as a link through practice between religions
rooted in very different cultures?

A. I tried to explain in my very first example of the experience of love and devotion that in fact, if people can understand through their own practice, what is experienced is
very much the same although it can be expressed in different ways; I think this is one of the important connecting
links. For instance, I could give you a concrete example
which may sound somewhat odd but Ramakrishna himself
went through a period in his life when he fell totally in love
with the Christian religion; he had visions of Jesus and the
Virgin Mary, and so he came to understand, and he said
'Now I understand that the Christian religion is true
because I have seen this truth in love.' Then he went
through another stage when he began to pray to Allah as a
Moslem. Of course, the Moslem religion was well known for
many centuries in India and there had been a lot of contact
and cross fertilization between Islam and Hinduism so that
there was nothing very new in that, but this is the experience of a great mystic, who may be compared to, say, St
Francis on the Christian side. Now while St Francis was

really immersed in the Christian tradition, which was the only one he had contact with, Ramakrishna was a man of another era, a modern era, he had contact with several religions, and he could see. He was not an intellectual; he lived totally through love; love almost on a childish level. He behaved as a child in fact, a bit like St Francis. He could as it were, fall in love with the whole story of Jesus and the Virgin Mary and love it on that level. I think that this is one way in which the purely practical element can lead people to see that the basis is the same although expressions might be different. If you study, then the deeper you go, the greater the convergence is; it is as if you have a centre, you see the image of the spokes of a wheel, and the deeper you go towards the centre, the more similar things get, the deeper the experience is. For instance, in the comparative study of mystical experience, you can see sometimes that even the similes used by mystics of very different traditions are in fact the same.

Now yoga helps in the sense that you look at experience in a very detached sort of way. This began very early even in Patanjali's *Yoga Sutras* which give, if you like, a prescription for meditation and progress in meditation. If you read a book of, say, Christian meditation in the middle ages, it is thoroughly involved in Christian beliefs. For instance, you are asked to meditate on the Passion, you are asked to meditate on the Trinity and so on. So the themes for meditation are all there within the Christian tradition and Christian theology. But if you look at the *Yoga Sutras* which are usually dated about two or three centuries before Christ, you will see that Patanjali in a very pragmatic sort of way gives a few subjects for meditation and then adds 'You can meditate on anything that strikes you as perfect' which is really: meditate on anything you like really provided you concentrate, provided you love that thing. This is like one of the famous stories current in Indian circles about a boy who was trying to do yogic meditation but he loved a goat of his and he could only think of that goat. Then the guru said, 'Well, concentrate on your goat. If you concentrate enough on your goat you will make progress.' From the beginning you get this pragmatic, this very open way of yoga in the whole Indian culture. This is one of the ways in which the people can approach each other, can communicate with each other. I am thinking of the inter-religious lexicon which

Thomas Merton talked about. Now Thomas Merton was a monk who had lived in the great discipline of the Trappist order of silence and so on, and he had a lot of spiritual experience. When he went to the East he could see that the experiences that a Buddhist monk would have or a Hindu monk would have were at some point something similar to his. So in experience, without discussing dogma, you can actually find points of contact.

Q. Another technical question on yoga: can you please comment on the value of mere correctness of posture as in the Alexander techniques or Moshe Feldenkrais's exercises?

A. Posture, of course, is one of the bases of the ancient yogic discipline. Patanjali's yoga, which is the basic tradition, gives you what they call the eight limbed yoga, astanga yoga, which starts with the moral precepts, negative precepts, then the positive precepts, which I'm not going to waste time on now. The third limb is posture, which says when going into meditation, the first thing you have to do is to adopt a correct posture which is, according to the classical tradition, both firm and pleasant. This is the classical definition of posture. Posture should be both pleasant and firm, the middle way, neither slopping about nor tense. The experience of many people who practise meditation is that once they become aware of it in meditation they tend to carry that awareness throughout the rest of the day; if they find that they are adopting an incorrect posture, there is an almost automatic device of correction. It is interesting – and I have this experience and I've found people have a similar experience to me – you don't like chairs because they must have an upright back; in meditation you must keep your back upright; so you no longer like those, to me, horrible chairs. This has happened to many people and it even leads to new ideas about the design of furniture, or acquiring new habits like sitting on the floor. I think with many other people that sometimes it becomes an affectation with Western followers of yoga that they want to sit on the floor just because the Indians sit on the floor. But the Indians sit on the floor because they are used to it, it comes naturally to them, while we in the West normally sit on chairs; so some teachers of meditation, Eastern teachers of meditation, tell Western people, 'If it costs you such effort and is such a strain, don't sit just on the floor; you can do your meditation on a chair. The important thing is not that you should adopt

135

a certain posture but that you should do your meditation in a posture that is natural to you.' This is very practical advice and sensible, unless of course you can sit on the floor as a natural posture. I have not myself studied the techniques of Alexander and Feldenkrais, but I know something about them and I'm sure that a practical connection could be made between these and the yogic traditions of posture.

Q. Does Dr Morais envisage spiritual experience as having a correlate in neurological activity within the brain?

A. A very interesting question, very difficult to answer. I would say that I don't think that in the present stage, you can correlate neurologically the more subtle distinctions of psychological states, or of spiritual states. For instance, if you look at the yogic terminology, there is a very complicated distinction between states of Samadhi; there is a sort of hierarchy of states. Samadhi is the highest state of which you are capable, usually translated as absorption or ecstasy or union, but between the lowest Samadhi and the highest Samadhi there is quite a difference. Now I very much doubt whether you could distinguish them through the EEG brain-wave pattern or any other physiological data. So far the studies that have been done are really of the EEG pattern and states of relaxation and sometimes also the blood content in people who were in deep states of meditation, usually very advanced yogis, and I don't think they have revealed any great distinction between shall we say more superficial states and the deeper states.

Colin Wilson: Could I add a footnote to that and explain that, when I spoke about the left and right sides of the brain, I didn't mean either that there should be some sort of neurological correlation. What I was saying was much simpler than that: that the ego, the 'you' that is now listening to me, and the 'me' that is now talking to you, is basically a *rational* ego which tends to be identified with the left side of the brain, while mystical and religious experiences seem to be identified with the right side of the brain. Now the problem is that the more rational you are, the more anxious and tense you are, the more you're stuck, so to speak, in the left side of your brain with a rational ego. Graham Greene tells in his autobiography how when he was in a state of almost permanent depression he played Russian roulette, putting one single bullet into the chambers of a revolver, pointing it at his head and pulling the trigger. And he says that when there was just a click, and he looked down the barrel and saw that the bullet had come into position, he got a terrific sense of relief. He said 'Suddenly I saw that the world was an incredibly beautiful place.' In the same way Ramakrishna was about to kill himself with a sword because he felt separate from the Divine Mother, when quite suddenly, he said, the vision burst upon him, and he was swept away by sheer ecstasy. Now this seems to me to be the hard way of doing it. The ego, the rational ego is wound around you like the Old Man of the Sea around Sinbad the Sailor's neck. What Graham Greene and Ramakrishna did was to scare him off by pointing a gun at him. All mystical disciplines are an attempt to do it more gently and gradually and less dangerously. The next question follows logically from that. Basically do you really see any evidence for spiritual evolution? Isn't it rather a matter that societies have changed?

A. You can't prove of course that there is any spiritual evolution, but I think there is evidence of a great change in the area of religion. There is no doubt that religions have been converging. Some people say, 'Ah well yes, they have been converging because they are frightened of extinction, they are so much threatened by the materialist or whatever it is view of life which is now predominating that they are all getting together because of this fright.' I don't think that this is quite right. In spite of all intolerance and people going on killing each other and all that kind of thing, people on the religious side are getting to understand each other more, and that I think is a sign of progress. For instance, look at the change in the religion in which I was brought up. For some time I was very violently anti-Catholic. I couldn't really enter into any dialogue with a priest. Now I see the priests as people who have changed tremendously. The whole Catholic church has changed; especially in Latin America where I come from, there has been a tremendous revolution. This is a sign of progress to me. I do believe in progress. I do believe in change, no matter how discouraged and how depressed and how close to despair we are sometimes. That's where the yogic discipline should come, or the discipline of any spiritual path, because I remember what St John of the Cross said: 'Even if the world were coming to an end tomorrow there would be no sense in worrying and being upset about it.' I think this is perfectly true; is there any

137

sense at all ever in being in the throes of despair or worrying about anything? There is no sense. This is the part of what I think Mr Wilson was saying about this part of the brain that keeps you in a vice, in a sort of vicious circle of worry and depression. It leads to no good whatsoever. But I do think that there are objective signs of progress, although the picture is extremely mixed – one of great conflict as well as of this apparent progress.

Q. Here's a rather technical question again: do yogis and you in particular draw from Sufic sources in the acquisition of particular breathing exercises, or is it the other way around or both?

A. I should make quite clear that I'm no guru. I'm just somebody who tries to follow the yogic disciplines with varying success but I think that if you look at this historically, you have to admit that obviously yoga is the oldest spiritual discipline that we know of in religious and spiritual terms: there is nothing older; the Sufi school came much later. I know of course that the Sufis developed some breathing techniques and methods. Whether this was under the influence of yoga or not one just doesn't know. It is the same with the technique I mentioned in my talk which is now quite well known, the prayer of Jesus done with the same rhythm of breathing; there is no proof that this was due to the influence of yoga. It may have been an independent discovery. It may have been a sort of a happy discovery of the monks of Mount Athos in Greece and nothing to do with yoga, so you can't postulate any sort of influence or any derivation of one from the other, but in terms of history there is no doubt that yoga came earlier. So if you were able to trace one to the other, which I don't think you can, then of course yoga would be the earliest breathing technique that we know of.

Colin Wilson: I'd like to add a footnote to that comment: I started off this morning talking about Raskolnikov standing on his narrow ledge and feeling that he could stand there forever without getting bored if he knew that he had to die at once. One might say, I think, not only about yogic disciplines but of all kinds of spiritual disciplines, that there is a very simple formula: if you were convinced that as soon as you allowed your eyes to glaze and become blank – the moment you allowed yourself to drift into boredom – *if* you were convinced that you would have to pay for it in terms of misery and inconvenience, I think you would be capable of staying almost permanently in a non-bored state of pulling yourself together and refusing to drift. This tendency to drift seems to be the basic problem.

I have noticed already one rather fascinating contradiction in the two talks we've heard so far. This morning, Carmen Blacker talked about the necessity for a precise posture in Japanese Zen Yoga while Dr Morais has said this afternoon that posture doesn't really matter provided you're comfortable. Again I noticed in Dr Carmen Blacker's talk that she talked about the two different schools of Zen Buddhism, and said that one method depends upon giving the mind a kind of shock – the necessity for energy, as though you were pulling back a bow, and were hurled forward into some kind of intensity. The other insists upon relaxation and contemplation, and the trouble is that you can just sit cross-legged and allow your mind to drift off. A rather interesting question this, I think. I suspect that the answer lies in a build up of what you might call a *feedback effect* between the two sides. This feedback effect explains also the whole problem of neurosis, which is basically a kind of negative feedback. Your unconscious mind, as Freud realized, has enormous power which 'you' do not consciously possess, but the relation between your conscious and your subconscious mind is rather a peculiar one, somewhat like the relation between Stan and Ollie in the old Laurel and Hardy films. If you remember, Stan is always glancing at Ollie's face to see what he thinks about what's happening. If they are in an awful situation and Ollie looks rather miserable, Stan is plunged into the depths of gloom, whereas if Ollie looks rather cheerful Stan sort of jumps around wagging his tail like a dog. He always *over-reacts*. Now *this* is the unconscious mind. You get up in the morning; your conscious mind says; 'Oh God, Monday,' and your unconscious mind, noticing this effect of gloom on the face of your consciousness, immediately says 'Oh God, Monday,' and fails to provide any energy. The unconscious mind appears to be in charge of our energy supply. If, on the other hand, something nice happens and the conscious mind smiles, this once again is transmitted to the unconscious, and ten minutes later for no particular reason you suddenly find yourself feeling that funny little fizz of vitality coming up from your depths. In neurosis there is a feedback effect between the two – that is to say that the conscious mind allows itself to be depressed by problems, the unconscious mind groans and fails to send up energy: this in turn makes the conscious mind lower and more miserable still, and it faces reality as it were with an even more pessimistic expression. The unconscious reacts once again to this and plunges lower still, and unless something intervenes from the outside world to interrupt this awful vicious spiral downwards, you would actually plunge into total psychosis. It is lucky that the physical world is always making these little interventions, like the sunlight coming in through the window, or a cheque arriving in the post that suddenly jerk you out of your moods of pessimism. *That* is negative feedback, and it seems to me that it explains the whole process of neurosis completely, without need for Freudian sexual hypotheses or any of the others. On the other hand what is far more interesting than negative feedback is positive feedback: that is, when quite deliberately you maintain an inner drive and you succeed in transmitting that optimism to the unconscious – because the unconscious undoubtedly works on optimism. As Carmen Blacker said this morning: 'To feel that I am the Buddha – that all is well – this is the first step.' And if you can actually get that feedback going between the conscious and the unconscious mind, the build up suddenly begins, and there comes an interesting point *when you can't do a thing wrong*. You're in such a state of happy intensity that everything you see looks positive. You can see no negative aspects anywhere, and suddenly your mind as it were mushrooms into a state of bubbling happiness which I am sure could actually develop into the Hindu *Samadhi*. This, I think, is the basic process of mystical awareness.

When I was talking about this to dom Silvester this morning, he remarked that it was the first time that he had heard this concept of the left and right side of the brain, apart from a mention by a rather interesting 3rd century mystic.

dom Silvester: Evagrius Ponticus, 4th century actually.
Colin Wilson: I then tried to persuade him to explain to me something about the way that he relates poetry to mysticism and contemplation, and I got absolutely no change. So I've nothing whatever to tell you about him except that he con-

140

tributed to the *Oxford English Dictionary* and there's a poem of his in the current issue of the magazine *Words Worth*. He is going to talk to us about the tradition we have already mentioned, that is to say, basically the tradition of Christmas contemplation, the withdrawal into inner silence rather, I take it, than the need for inner shock.

d-r-a-w-n-I-n-w-a-r-d

Silvester Houédard

INTRODUCTION

Since our Western tradition of union with God, (*henosis* in Greek, *yoga* in Sanskrit) has been so largely influenced by Benedict I want, as a monk of the West, ie a benedictine, to look first at what he said and then at the writers he cites as sources and recommends to disciples. This I shall preface with an outline of the rational skeleton that gives coherence to the christian idea of *theosis,* or divinisation: the spiritual path of perfecting the human image of God into the likeness of God. You will have noticed that the title of the paper is a one-word visual poem: a palindrome, which at first glance is about 'withdrawal' from any direction to the inner, central 'I', the ego or self, which if the poem is completed in two or three dimensions is the centre of a mandala composed of five circles or five spheres.

Yet in the teaching of Christ this ego centre is a hollow filled with the non-ego, with the Other. A cup of which the inside is to be cleansed, the heart that is to be pure, our *tameion* or inner room in which, with closed door, we pray in secret and in silence to the one, who as Father shares with us his divine nature and has his kingdom in that closed centre where he hears in secret.

The logic of this paradox is an insight (into the nature of reality) on which both the *Old Testament* and *New Testament* are based: the universe of everything subject to change and available to mind as the data of science is itself the primary revelation of God, revealing him as its opposite, as not it. On this basis catholic theologians say we can know *that* God is but not *what* God is, that only *negative* terms are adequate when talking about God so that if we say things exist and are real, then we must say that God is not real and does not exist, or if we say God is real and does exist, then we have to say the universe has no existence and is unreal. And yet as visible creation reveals the invisible creator, it is his image in the same way that every poem is the image of the

142

poet speaking in his poem, and is our only means of access to him as poet. Of all the images of God that make up the Universe the human being is inevitably the one we are going to find most like him, and the human image available to our closest scrutiny is ourself.

But since we are part of creation, of the world, turning the mind inward to the image of God that we are, is not turning away from creation but turning to it, to that part of it which is not just nearest to us but which actually is us, hence flight to God, our search for him, is not flight *from* the world but *through* the world. As Alan Watts said, the human mind is the means by which the cosmos observes itself. And the point at which we observe the likeness of the inner mind to God is the sound of the one-hand clap, the insight into the ungraspableness of our invisible, inner, nothing centre as the image of the invisibility and ungraspability of God. This is why dom Augustin Baker can say that union with God (henosis or yoga) is the union of nothing and nothing. It is one point at which Catholic theology is in total agreement with the Wu (Mu) of Taoism and Zen, where the *nada nada* of John of the Cross is identical with the *neti neti* of hinduism, and the only barrier to this union or yoga is egotism or *pathē*; and the degree to which we reach the self-lessness of the non-self is the degree to which we have reached apatheia (egolessness) and the degree to which we suffer from egotism is the degree to which the human image of God has failed to become like him.

S. Paul says the one perfect human image (icon) of God is Christ, so becoming like God is also becoming like Christ, ie becoming sons of the divine father sharing the divine nature of the father. This is the process called *theosis* or divinisation: as the Father and Son are one, we become one with the Father and the Son. This is rebirth (or regeneration, as Christ calls it) through sharing the same Holy Spirit with him and with the Father, ie through the presence of the Holy Spirit in our own spirit or nothing centre. Hence, as egotism is eliminated in the divinised saints, the deifying light shines through them, and, being branches of the vine which is Christ, their deeds (or fruit) are visible manifestations or revelations of God present in them. In the classical tag of catholic and orthodox theology, Christ was hominised that we might be divinised; the *logos* became man that man might become God. Not by becoming the *person* of the

143

Father but by coming to share his *nature*.

BENEDICT

On that sketch map of the spiritual life, the path indicated is not only common to the Greek Syriac and Latin doctors of the church, it is the path all christians are called to follow. I want to begin with this tradition as it was inherited and taught by S. Benedict, the patriarch of western monasticism and patron of Europe. 1980 was the 1,500th anniversary of his birth. Within 50 years of his death, one of his monks, Augustine or Austen came to this country when the pagan saxons were completing the conquest of the british (the welsh) whose monastic tradition was that of S. Martin, to whom Benedict dedicated one of the oratories he built on Montecassino, so the contemplative tradition introduced by Augustine, first at S. Martin's oratory in Canterbury, then at Canterbury Cathedral, Rochester Cathedral and S. Paul's Cathedral, London, was not different from that of the celts. (1)

In his rule for beginners, the reader is referred for teaching on contemplation to Scripture, its commentaries, the works of John Cassian, the Lives of the Desert fathers, (ie the book by Palladius, and the anonymous lives translated by Rufinus) and to the works of our Holy Father, S. Basil of Cappadocia. Cassian (born 360), Palladius (born 363) were contemporaries in the desert, disciples of Evagrius (born 345), the friend of Rufinus (born 345) and of Basil (born 330). It was this small creative intellectual group indicated by Benedict that interpreted the apophatic contemplative tradition of Alexandria and transmitted it to both the greek and latin halves of the Great Church inside the Empire and to the persian church outside. Translated into syriac, armenian, persian and arabic, they (and especially Evagrius) inspired the creation of Sufism and, as the texts on which monks of the Chaldaean rite were formed, they were taught for 207 years (till 845 AD) in the Monastery of Luminous Religion, founded by Emperor T'ai Tsung in 638 (the year Hui Neng, the 6th Patriarch of Ch'an/Zen, was born). In China these texts were to influence Taoism, Buddhism, Ch'an/Zen and the Golden Flower. It is the tradition of the Jewish Philo and IV Maccabees, of the christians, Clement and Ammonius, and of the two disciples of Ammonius, the christian Origen and the pagan Plotinus,

144

and (through Plotinus, but distorted by his fear of matter), it flavours neo-platonism. The value of this approach for the Wider Ecumenism and for a Conference on the Nature of Religious Man is obvious, particularly if seen as a harmony of jiriki/tariki, of jnana/bhakti, of atheism/theism, of science and mysticism.

SUMMARY OF THE REGULA BENEDICTI

The Rule begins: 'Obsculta, o fili, precepta magistri et inclina aurem cordis tui' – Listen to the precepts of the Master and listen to them with the ear of the heart ie open the inner (third) ear and listen. The 'Master' (as in the Rule of the Master) is God and Benedict adds: Listen to the vox divina, the voice of God who before we invoke him replies 'Adsum', the voice that invites us to follow Christ to his glory, to the tent of God on the holy mountain, where human eyes are opened to the lumen deificum (where the eye of our mind, the third eye, is opened to the deifying light). This inner journey (*poreia*) or ascent (*anabasis*) to deification begins then in the heart (*leb* in hebrew; best translated in greek as *nous*). Heart or nous is that which knows, that which 'grasps' the knowledge we have, ie what flows in; it is also the source of thoughts and acts, of what flows out. Nous can be intuited but, by its nature, is invisible to and ungraspable by our own introspection. As the unchanging centre of change, the experience of its ungraspability is the sound of the one hand clap, is the answer to the Wu/Mu koan and is the 'who' that asks in the hua tu. Hence says Benedict the road begins narrow but along it the heart and mind, by serving God with the good things he gives us, become dilated and enlarged, the essential condition for enjoying the unwordable in the Kingdom.

This road as leading to the Kingdom and to our divinisation in it as the offspring of God (sharing the divine nature) is our life. If considered as Jacob's ladder then it is climbed by our deeds, since deeds link mind and body as rungs link the ladder-sides. This (Dante calls it the gold ladder of Benedict) begins like the road in the heart but is a ladder we climb down in order to reach the top which is 'the glory that is our inheritance'. Progress on it is thus measured by *humiliatio cordis* and this humiliatio, which is what sometimes appears narrow at first, is the same as the *dilatio cordis*, the expansion of mind. Two Victorian commenta-

145

tors, abbot Delatte and dom Francis Doyle, call this humiliatio cordis (the basis of the whole rule), the 'descent to our
inner nothingness' and 'self-knowledge of our own nothingness.' In the 17th century it inspired dom Augustin Baker's
dictum: Contemplation is the union of nothing and nothing.

This road or ladder is our life of contemplation spent
searching for God through *oratio*, through prayer defined
(eg in the old penny catechism) as 'raising the heart and
mind to God' or better perhaps as 'turning the mind to the
presence of God in the heart.' This oratio is to be frequent
but *pura* and *brevis* and never to be said with a *clamosa vox*
or *multi loquia* but with *puritas* and *intensio cordis* – it is
the oratio of the monk who always says in his heart the
prayer of the publican.

All these images are scriptural: turning the mind in the
search for God; the inner ear and eye of the heart and mind;
the invitation to the holy mountain and deification by the
lumen deificum; the dilation of heart and enlargement of
mind; becoming royal heirs of the kingdom; the ladder to
heaven; the humiliatio, puritas and intensio of the heart;
the avoidance of multiloquium and the vox clamosa; incessant prayer of the heart and specifically the mantra of the
publican (Lk 18.10) Lord be merciful to me a sinner.

Turning the mind, *metanoia,* was preached by the Baptist,
by Christ, by Peter in his first three sermons and was taught
by Paul and by John: Turn your minds for the kingdom is at
hand (ie within); produce fruit worthy of mind-turning; the
disciples preached mind-turning in all the towns and
villages; the joy in heaven if one person turns the mind is
greater than if ninety nine don't need to; He opened their
minds to understand scripture which says Christ would
suffer, die and rise, and that mind-turning would be
preached to all the world beginning with Jerusalem.

That prayer should be secret and silent comes from Mt 6.5:
'Avoid hypocrisy by praying where you can't be seen. Go into
your *tameion* (your storeroom, treasury or cellar, an inner
chamber with a door) close the door and pray in hiding to
your father who, since he can see into your secret place,
needs no *polylogia,* none of the *battalogia* pagans imagine
necessary to attract God's attention.' That prayer should be
frequent and ceaseless is taught by James, Luke and Paul:
He told them the parable to teach that they should pray
always; He told them to watch and pray without ceasing;

The continual prayer of the just man avails much; Pray without ceasing; Continue in incessant prayer; Pray always; Continue in prayer.

The dilation of mind and expansion of heart is explained in the biography of Benedict by Pope Gregory (written 593 and so 30 years after the death of Benedict when Gregory was 53: his list of informants does not include Benedict himself). On the night of the 30th October, 540 (the year Gregory was born, and the night Bishop Germanus of Capua died) Benedict, leaning out of his window, had the vision that inspired Dante's Paradiso. He saw the whole cosmos compressed in a single beam of light. Gregory comments: All things are NOTHING to the mind that has even a glimpse of the divine light of the creator. By that light the capacity of the 'inner soul' (the heart or *nous*) is inwardly enlarged and extended in God so as to be above itself and above the cosmos. Thus, snatched up in the light of his nous, Benedict was out of this world. To say the cosmos was 'compressed in his sight' means not that the earth and outer space were reduced but that his mind was enlarged. Thus in the outer light seen by the eyes of Benedict, the inner light of nous carried his mind to heavenly things.

Dante's gold-ladder is a ray of light: stretching from sphere 7 up to sphere 10 (the Empyrean) it balances in 7–8–9 the earth's shadow-cone in 1–2–3. Down it came the contemplative splendori like ravens, and Dante looking at them makes his two eyes mirrors of the two sided ladder (body/mind: image-using and image-rejecting contemplation). His mind following his eyes, the ladder comes to rest in it and the ravens perform the three dances of prayer; direct (study of creation, God's poem), oblique (study of God the poet as reflected in his poem), circular (the mindstilling return to God of negative theology by introspection of one's own nothing centre). By the time of Benedict, the scriptural images had become technical terms; to understand them Benedict suggests a daily reading of Cassian. (2)

CASSIAN

Of the fifteen Abbots reported by Cassian, I want to quote Abraham who concludes the teachings he received in the Delta, and Isaac who concludes the teachings received in Scete. However, I want to glance at the two first Abbots he heard in the Delta. Both were coptic and needed interpreters, both spoke of the stages of contemplation.

Abbot Chaeremon

Aged over 100, he could move about his cell only by crawling like a child. His teaching is on Perfection of Heart which God gives in three stages. By inciting us he gives the desire for good, by protecting he gives the chance of acquiring good through doing it, by strengthening he gives the help we need to 'hold on' to goodness acquired, but (and this is the characteristic Alexandrian note) at no stage does he interfere with our freedom. What Augustin Baker defined as the union of nothing and nothing, Alexandria (from at least Origen on) called the union of freedom and freedom.

Nestir

He spoke on the sequence of active and contemplative in the spiritual life. *Praktikē,* the active, has a single two-sided aim – expelling vice and attaining virtue. This on the one hand means knowing the nature of faults and the method of cure, on the other, it means knowing how virtues are interrelated so we can form our mind to delight in them. *Theoretikē,* the contemplative life, aims at knowing the divine and invisible – and progress in this gnosis is by deepening our knowledge of the created and visible.

A few remarks on Nestir. Here we have what distinguishes the jewish/christian from the dualist. There are two 'texts' we are to read: Cosmos and Scripture (Creation and Revelation); the visible, veiling the invisible, leads to it, (is 'finger pointing at moon'). Flight to the uncreated is not from but through the created – mind can only approach God by seeing his presence in creation and supremely in the ungraspable nous. Philo found the ideal of these two ways (and of their sequence) in the Essenes and Therapeutae: 'Having mentioned the Essenes who follow the practical or active life in my treatise *That the Virtuous Man is Also Free* (again the Alexandrian note, freedom), the order of the subject demands that I now talk about the Therapeutae, contemplatives who, being continually taught to see with the sight of the mind (which alone can distinguish true and false), aim at seeing the living God; they apply themselves to this kind of worship because they are carried away by a certain heavenly *agapē.*' Of the Essenes he had said 'they study to preserve their minds in a state of holiness and purity by frugal-life, hard-work and common-property'.

Philo explains the name Therapeutae (3) as either curing minds (not only their own) of the passions and their consequences, or serving the living God, 'better than the good, more simple than the one.'

Nestir is the first to propose as a method of reading the two texts (Cosmos and Scripture) and penetrating from the surface and visible to the deepest and invisible, the fourfold discipline of the literal, tropical, allegorical and anagogical that was to dominate European thought, art and culture. In Nestir as in Dante they are the four stages of the interior journey, and derive from Origen's three levels: the literal, allegorical and spiritual which he compares to body, mind and spirit. Since we are part of the Cosmos, this journey from the surface of things to their centre, to the meaning of nature, is at the same time a journey to our own centre. So *praktikē* and *theoretikē,* as the double path or road or ladder of Tao reflects the distinction in Tao between *ming* (sympathy, creativity) and *ching* (self-realization). The four-fold sense passed into Jewish thought (I'm not quite sure when) as the method of P-R-D-S (PaRaDiSe): *Peshat* – explanation, *Remez* – hint, *Darush* – homily, *Sod* – mystery. The balance of God-gift and free-search in Nestir is the harmony of jiriki/tariki (self-help/other-help). He himself is remembered in the desert sayings as the guru of silence: They called him 'the bronze serpent of Moses' since he healed all through spiritual excellence but above all by keeping silence. Abba Joseph came to be cured and said 'I have a problem – I can't stop talking'. Abba Nestir said 'To begin with, why not stop talking about the problem'.

The Fish-Dome Sermon of Abba Abraham c.392 AD
The ease
   with which concentration of thought scatters to the four
   winds means guarding vision one-pointedly.
To keep the target in view
   sit motionless on the high rock of your mind:
   a mystical fisherman
   eager to catch food by the apostolic art
eyes sharpened at the swarm of thoughts
   swimming below in the calm depths of your heart
   watching, selecting, rejecting.
The name we give this art of watching
   is 'Guard of the heart'

we use it in stilling thought-storms
　　on our mental lake.

The method of fixing attention one-pointedly
　　we call 'the remembrance of God'.
As thoughts rise
　　lead them to circle round this one point
　　like an architect building a dome;
he measures the rope
　　ties it to an unchanging centre
　　and at that distance
　　exactly fits each stone.
Kept unceasingly
　　by these mystical compasses of love
　　whatever swims into mind
　　the centre tells us if it fits
　　or needs to be thrown away
Easily lost
　　recover it with accuracy:
　　guesswork is blindness
　　to what spoils the beauty of true roundness.

Lost
　　there is nothing can determine the one right point at
　　which the dome must finish:
so establish the centre
　　and keep it unceasingly
　　for the one right point
　　round which mind is to work without ceasing is God.

And the building we dome
　　the spiritual edifice described by Paul
　　is that house desired by David
　　the beautiful palace where glory dwells.

Built by pointed-mind
　　the dwelling is worthy of spirit
built otherwise it collapses
　　ruined
　　before any glory
　　is received from the blessed inhabitant.

In this sermon by Abba Abraham, you will notice two
points of similarity with Sufism. *Dhikr,* (the remembrance),
and turning. You may have noticed also the Taoist concern

to learn 'holding on' after 'finding the centre'. Abraham was the last of the Delta abbots. Isaac was the last of all the fifteen whose teaching is recorded. As the first part of Cassian culminates in Abraham on the Guard of the Heart and perpetual Remembrance of God, so the whole of Cassian culminates in Isaac on continuous prayer.

Abbot Isaac begins (399 AD)

Isaac said: continuous prayer is the top of the lofty tower in Luke (14.28). It takes time to build but first we pre-estimate the cost by knowing what to reject and what to keep (again the 'discretion' of watching and selecting between mind-fish). In turning inward we discover the mind is a feather often blown about, but often bedraggled, heavy and sodden by the egotism of cares and desires which are diseases of the mind. Oratio must be pura and the mind angelic, ie the heart must be free and intent on the highest good (the *puritas* and *intensio* of Benedict: puritas is freedom from all that interferes with intensio – it is freedom from egotism).

The aim of oratio is attaining *agapē* (the non-selfish perfect love of all others as the father loves them which is 'being perfect as the father is perfect'). We contemplate the good by turning to God in the heart for the sake of all and not for the sake of self – since agapē is the exclusion of eros or self-love. Yet oratio varies from intense and fiery to silent. It is often sparked off by something accidental: a word in a psalm – a phrase in the music – something read to us, or the way it is read (like autumn *satori* induced by the falling leaf). Mostly we forget what caused a particular sort of prayer – all we know is that we have contemplated with joy or silence or tears or all three and that it was not contrived but spontaneous. This is what Antony meant by his more than human saying: Prayer isn't perfect if you know you are praying. What we can practise consciously is attention of mind in the inner cell of the heart without din of thought, with closed lips and in secret praying *frequenter* and *breviter* ...

Abbot Isaac interrupted

At this moment the conference was interrupted by the arrival of the Pascal letter for 399, sent out by the Patriarch of Alexandria every year after Epiphany, 6th January, and before Ash Wednesday. It announced the dates of Lent and Easter and took the occasion to mention points of doctrine, appointments of bishops etc. This 399 letter from Theophilus declared that God did not have a body. The next letter, 400, declared that he had, hence the Patriarch's nickname of Amphallax, the spiritual see-saw, merited, too, by the way he turned against his old friends, Paphnut, Isaac, Palladius, Cassian and the rest of the three hundred that he exiled. Evagrius died on the feast of the Epiphany, 399; Isaac as priest of Cells can only just have buried him when the 399 letter arrived. The funeral may have been the occasion for his conference with Cassian.

Genesis says we are made in the image and likeness of God. Origen said this means we are visible images of the invisible God (the jewish interpretation since Aristobulos, the royal counsellor who taught philosophy c.150 BC at Alexandria University. The letter in 2 Maccabees, 1.10 is addressed to him and he was quoted on this point by Clement and Eusebius). In 399 the theology of idolatry was in the air. For 7 years Theophilus had been using an Imperial Permit to destroy temples and their idols. The 3 biggest destroyed were: Osiris-Dionysius, the Mithraeum and that most beautiful building of the Mediterranean, the Serapeum (the library and temple of Serapis, a composite divinity invented as patron of Alexandria: the statue was by Bryaxis).

Some monks like Audius (condemned 325, died 372), held that Genesis meant God had a body: his schismatic Audian church (5) existed in Damascus, Antioch, Mesopotamia, Edessa and Egypt. Other monks like Pathomius in Scete said Genesis authorised mental images of God in prayer. Evagrius on this problem talked of temptations from left and right. The left ones tempt us to envisage God as having form; the right ones tempt us to think of 'nothing' as a special sort of 'something'. The formlessness of God and of his image in us thus become a special sort of form, and instead of having 'no-thought', we have 'a thought of no thought'. Mind nature is unattainable. Any attainment is just the old subject/object mind-split.

In Genesis P-text, (redacted during the exile), God created Adam in his own image and likeness, in the J-text (500 years earlier in the time of Solomon), God created Adam of clay, breathed in the breath of life and put him in Paradise, with the Good Tree of Immortal Life and the Forbidden Tree of Knowledge of good and evil; one tree is Adam learning what God calls good and the other is Adam deciding for himself. They are trees of union with God and split from God; trees of contemplation and egotism; of *agapē* and *eros*; of yoga and non-yoga. As part of his polemic against the sex rites of Canaan, J is teaching that to know and do God's will is the immortality that Adam lost, not (as in the older myth) by a whim of God or the snake eating it accidentally, but by his own will. In the exegesis of P and J together, the clay golem becomes the image and likeness when spirit is breathed into it by God. Adam lost the likeness but remained the image; hence Seth was born in the image and likeness of Adam. Thus the return to Paradise (to original face and the Tree of Life) is by perfecting the likeness which (to quote the penny catechism again) resides chiefly in the spirit, in the heart, the leb or nous. Hence the two patrons of contemplation are Enoch who walked with God and was not, because God 'snatched' him (the word lqh is the technical word for ecstasy) and Elijah who was taken up in the chariot (the same merkabah Ezekiel saw 250 years later). Hence the Jewish division of contemplation into *ma'aseh bereshit* (creation, that is from God) and *ma'aseh merkebah* (the chariot, that is return to God).

Hence too the fundamental split between those two pupils of Ammon Saccas: Plotinus holding the greek view that likeness is a condition of knowledge, Origen holding the jewish scriptural view that knowledge produces likeness. Hence the logic of the essential concept of divinisation: knowledge of love (gnosis of agapē) makes us like God, sharing as sons the divine nature, and converting eros (self-love, egotism) into agapē (love of all others). The path to this gnosis is contemplation of God (the uncreated nothing reflected in the things of creation which are God's image) but especially contemplation of the divine nothing in the ungraspable mirror or nous, in that inner nothing womb which of all created things is the nearest to us and the most creative known component of the cosmos, as well as being a perfect image of the divine nothing since it is invisible to its own act of introspection. Hence our nothing-centre is both the bank of inflowing data and the cradle of outflowing agapē, and as such is 'original face' and centre of the cosmic mandala. This is the background to the interruption.

Abbot Isaac continues

Having an image of God in prayer is to 'change the glory of God for an idol' (Ro.1.23). Simple minded christians think it justified because Genesis says we are the image and likeness of God, but anthropomorphists teach God really has got a human shape. Our catholic tradition is to reject this notion and so arrive at ORATIO PURA and this is: prayer with no figure of God, no memory of a name, no least appearance of divine action, no hint of character. With the Heart Eye we can look at Jesus in the forms of his first or second comings, but with the pure Mind Eye we can look only at the glory seen on Sinai, Carmel and Tabor by Moses, by Elijah and by Peter, James and John. Jesus too retired into a mountain alone to teach us oratio pura and retirement from crowds.

By oratio pura and retirement we adapt ourselves to (and learn to anticipate) the future bliss by the union (yoga, henosis) described in Jn.17: the Father loving us as he loves his son that we might be oned to the Father in the way the Father and the Son are one: May they all be one as you Father in me and I in you – may they also thus be one in us.

There are 2 effects of this prayer: (1) the perfect love with which the Father already loves us (1 Jn.4.16) passes into our heart so we love the whole of creation and everyone else and (2) we are united to God in heart love and desire, with effort, thought, life, words and breath and thus, whatever we breathe, think or say is God. By it pure mind is raised daily to the spirit and the whole of our life deeds and thoughts are one continuous prayer. Germanus and Cassian asked two questions: (a) How one begins in order to reach such towering heights of contemplation; what equivalent is there to learning the ABC and rules of grammar? (b) Having grasped God in contemplation, how do we 'hold on', and how do we 'recover the grasp', so easily lost?

Isaac answers (a).

To ask that shows you are inside the hall of true prayer. What I am going to say will allow you to roam through its inner recesses. The equivalent of the ABC is reciting a mantra, which every monk progressing to continual recollection of God recites unceasingly in his heart. One formula handed down by some of the oldest fathers is the Deus in adiutorium.(6) This covers two opposite needs of a spiritual state: acquiring one (when mind is barren and can't give

154

birth to its child) and not lingering in one (as whenever, aware of the Holy Spirit in us, we think mind has achieved its purpose through one-pointed sharpness because we understand truths we never realised before). Said ceaselessly, whatever you are doing, both at the door and in the recesses of the hall (with the mouth and with mind-in-the-heart) it leads to invisible, heavenly contemplation as mind becomes pure enough in spirit to do without the riches of other thoughts (Pss.39 and 73: The poor and needy praise him and he helps them).

Rocks for the Hedgehog, Mountains for Stags.

Illumined by God as we climb the mountain of knowing him, we feed on higher and more sacred mysteries. The Spiritual Hedgehog, 'a feeble folk living in rocks', shelters in the rock of the gospel and ceaseless mantra. The Spiritual Stag keeps a hedgehog simplicity but with the virtue of discretion can stamp on snakes (thoughts) and escape them through keenness of one-pointed mind. When psalms become records of our experience and their meaning comes from us and not from what we have been told, mind is moving to wordless, incorruptible, and imageless prayer; it becomes 'fire' and texts become mirrors reflecting our insight into the nature of things (cf. Zen and Tao). Germanus now sees how we escape by mantra from the limitations of the visible.

Isaac answers (b).

The shifting heart is anchored and distractions cured with meditatio, watching (*nepsis*) and oratio. Cassian and Germanus are 'astonished' at this mantra teaching (Benedict: With astonished ears). It sounds short and easy but is deeper and harder than their old meditatio on Scripture. It shows that illiteracy is no bar to oratio pura.(7)

EVAGRIUS

To understand the snake and stag in mountain contemplation we must look at the teaching of Evagrius (the friend of Isaac, the disciple of Gregory of Nyssa and the Doctor of Introspection) quoted by Benedict on 'dashing incipient thoughts to nothing.'(8)

He links the 3 stages of contemplation to faith, hope and charity as the three elements of what Paul calls the

'Mysterium of Christ' ie the divinisation of the cosmos, the pleroma. The nature of mind is to know truth but for nous to reach reality and approach the immaterial immaterially, we must go on from eros (self-love) and pathē, (egotism) to apatheia (the imperturbable calm of egolessness) and agapē (the ungrasping love of all, as in karuna, compassion for the least blade of grass). Nous (pure mind) is thus emptied of thought and concept and, from love of truth being overshadowed by the Holy Spirit, God enters as the formless into the formless and from there (nous) spreads knowledge to mind (pysche) and peace to body (soma).(9) By this gnosis of trinity every form of ignorance except one is destroyed, for the infinite essence of God being inaccessible, ascent to it can never cease. As the nature of *nous* is to go ceaselessly forward, nothing impedes its ascent if we guard its deep calm; upset its balance with body and you will mistake smoke for the light that ends the conflict of opposites. The lives of the desert Fathers constantly tell us to enter our cell and weep. Evagrius explains that, as the journey is endless (not because God recedes, but because he is endlessly approaching) we 'weep always' at the distance that always remains. This endlessness that continues after death means, not that the goal is never reached, but that the path itself is the goal. Technically this endlessness is called 'Epectasy'. Beware of visions: demons attack mind in pairs, so you call on one (formlessness) to repel the other (form). They are powerless only against the total nothingness of humility. Let me end this look at Evagrius, by giving his list of the seven macarisms (beatitudes) of epectasy. Perfect formlessness; perpetual advance; freedom of nous stripped naked; anaisthesia (Antony's: If you know you are praying, you aren't); awareness of nothingness; viewing the welfare of others with more joy than your own; and regarding people as all equally good. He adds: Keep to the one joy of contemplation in contemplation, attain the evangelical promises, and reign as King: a hint at what in sanskrit thought is the Cakravartin reigning at the centre of the cosmic mandala.

Conclusion

In this paper I have kept to 3 essentials of the apophatic path we travel when d-r-a-w-n-I-n-w-a-r-d from any direction whatsoever: (1) attaining the emptiness of the ego or I at the nothing centre, (2) seeing that as the image of God, of the Divine Nothing beyond each and every something and (3) seeing the lumen deificum shining through that image. The path thus begins with erotic desire for personal sanctification. Since it starts from the nothingness and changeableness (contingency) of all phenomena, it links the nothingness of *samsara* with the nothingness of *nirvana,* and progress depends on the conversion of eros into agapē (self-love into other-love): a conversion we can't achieve either by effort or desire, since desire is the return to eros, to the split between subject and object. I have tried to hint how, as in Taoism, this path of contemplation linking the outer to the inner, is the same path as that of creativity linking the inner to the outer. In its document on art, (10) Vatican II says: Artists ... should ever bear in mind that they are engaged in a kind of sacred imitation of God the Creator. This inner harmony of *ching* and *ming* was neatly reflected in the 13th c. benedictine/cistercian formula: Ora et labora, often quoted as Orare et laborare. I have concentrated on one small 4th c. group because (a) they are recommended by Benedict since (b) they summarise the authentic jewish/ christian tradition of prayer evolved in and near Alexandria and (c) they are the group that both created the syriac-greek-latin christian tradition and, through Evagrius, influenced Taoism and Buddhism and Zen as well as Sufism.

Appendix on the Mantra

Having introduced Evagrius to explain the Spiritual Stag trampling on the mental snakes of distracting thoughts in mountain contemplation, I would like to end with a few notes on the christian mantra, behind which the Spiritual Hedgehog shelters at the foot of the mountain.

In christian writers the *monologistos* or one-phrase prayer is defined as *meletē kryptē. Meletē* is a classical term for repeating (aloud or mentally) a speech being learned by heart: *kryptē,* hidden, means saying it mentally.

Isaac was teaching mantrayana (with a touch of prana-yana in 'so all we breathe is God') in 399: the earliest reference to the method in the desert is 345 when BESSARION gave the harlot Thais a mantra 'without the name': Be merciful creator to what you created. This implies name-mantras were already in use.

MACARIUS SENIOR (died 391), visited c.383 by Evagrius (tormented by pathē of mind and body and asking a 'word to live by') said: Tie the ship's anchor-rope to rock, then safe from every storm of our empty world, it will sail in the dark over demon waves in the illusory sea. He explained: the boat is heart (guard it), the rope is nous and the rock is Logos – tie it with the knot of mantra, saying with every breath 'Iēsou, mercy, thank you, help me'. Macarius also suggested to others 'Lord, you know and desire mercy' or simply 'Rescue me' (from the same psalms as Deus in adiutorium). He also said: to be purified like Adam in paradise (the 'return to original face') say: 'Iēsou mercy' attending to the name in the heart and as your lips move draw the name into your mind and in repose you will see the divine reposing on you.

BASIL (330–379): Pneuma (prana), when neither scattered among outer things nor split through lack of sense-control, returns and climbs up itself to the divine. He also said: The apostles thought of God without ceasing and their spiritual state, their lives, were thus their ceaseless prayer.

APPA JOHN (4th c.): went from Syria to Appa Poemen and asked about hardness of heart and was told in greek: Like water and drop by drop the stone is worn away. In prison John always made mention of God and so was fulfilled 'I was in prison and you visited me'. (He used the 3rd person, I assume he refers to himself.)

GREGORY OF NAZIENZEN (329–389): As often as you breathe, remember the name of God.

EVAGRIUS (383–399): When tempted by visions and sounds use short ones intensely like 'you are with me' (Ps.22.4).

THE OTHER ISAAC (4th c.): To your inner chamber and to the chamber of heaven there is a single door. Enter with mantra. Done intensely with measureless heat in heart, there are flaming thoughts. Intensify it and mind, refined by heat, acquires eyes. As heat gives birth to tears the mind is stilled and with still mind you see the pure vision of divine mysteries – the Lord in yourself.

THE PSEUDO-MACARIUS (post 390): The inner life is continual mantra with Guard of Heart and attention to God, in *nepsis* (no-thought) and *hesychia* (quiet) and *aisthesia* (awareness) and *plerophoria* (experience) of the light living in us, transforming us. He also said: In hesychia (quiet place) with katastasis (inner quiet) without confused cries (with mantra) applying attention to the Lord with ponos (effort) of heart and nepsis (soberness of no-thought). He also said: The laws of spirit and the heavenly mystery are Scriptures of Light engraved on the heart – observe them like Scriptures of Ink. For body is ruled by heart, and heart is nous. When thought-sheep feed on heart-grass, grace enters nous to rule the body. He also said: The human remains wholly human in mind and body though becoming wholly god in body and mind. The later practice of fixing eyes during mantra on a body-spot (nose, navel etc) was to be called 'The Macarian Method'.

MARTIAL OF CALAMUS a pagan official of Africa converted after the discovery 415 of Stephen's relics recited as a mantra till he died c.425 the last words of Stephen: Lord receive my spirit.

NICEPHORUS OF PHOTIKE (5th c.): By remembrance of God close the exits of nous but nous needing work give it the Name for occupation. With it increasingly in heart-depth you see the light of your nous for, kept with care in the heart by thought, it burns up dust on mind's outer skin. It is name-in-the-mind and heat-in-the-heart, planting the seed of loving the good we call it pearl-of-great-price. He also said: Begin by shooting dragons in the heart and shoot until you feel the wound then limit doing to remembrance of God; ceaselessly, soberly, as heart-heat evaporates evil, your mind will shine.

ABBOT ISAIAS THE HERMIT OF GAZA (trained in Scete, died 488): Devoting your energy to kryptē meletē your 'heart grows not and kindles meditation' (Ps.38.4LXX) for 'God is fire' (Hb.12.29) melting thought-wax and drying pathē-mud to give light to mind and warmth to heart. By it angels make us castles of inner peace, it is the mirror for mind, the lamp of conscience, the mother of tenderness which warms the mind, melts it to tears and makes you the place of God.

BARSANUPHIUS The Egyptian of Gaza and recluse of Seridos (died 540): You can practise it even with psalmody; it makes the passions or 'demons' flee for mantra is safer than anti-rrhesis (suppressing thoughts by thought).

JOHN MOSCHUS quoting a Senex '108 miles from Alexandria' (in Scete) who said (between 578 and 594): Sedete in cella ubi vultis, sobrie et vigilante, quietem et silentium servantes et sine intermissione orantes et spem habeo in deum, filli, quod mittet vobis scientiam suam ad illuminandas animas vestras.

ABBOT PHILEMON of Egypt (6–7th cc.) told a monk who said his mind was distracted and wandered: It is the external sickness that is cured as the warmth of knowing and loving God increases through the practice of kryptē mēletē, saying with neptic mind and heart 'Lord Iēsou mercy'. The monk did but it came and went. Philemon said: Keep it always in heart – eating, drinking, talking, relieving yourself and everywhere; let it do the praying in secret.

JOHN CLIMACUS The ladder of Sinai (born 6th c.; died 7th c.): Enclose the sea of mind in yourself, and the incorporeal in your body by banishing variation of thought with the monologistos. Unite it with your breathing and understand the meaning of hesychia, for prayer is estrangement from both worlds. Heart-free resurrects it and, as it ascends, God-fire descends to your middle chamber. The eye of your heart sees the sun of your mind filling you with light.

THE PSEUDO-HESYCHIUS (an anthology by monks of Batos, the burning bush monastery of Sinai 7th–10th c.) says: By the Epiklesis Iēsou (1st use of this term for the Jesus Mantra) mind is purified, and unified; thoughts become playful fish, dolphins leaping in a calm sea. First the name is a lamp in the dark, and next a full-moon in your heart-sky, then it is sun-rise in our mind and lastly, with the ceaseless breathing of mantra as sun, it is broad day with luminous thoughts. Say it till it becomes your own name (till you are divinised). Our aim is not the silence but the aim of silence, hearing the Logos. It is not the monologistos that banishes logismoi (thoughts) and dispassionates the mind, but saying it with nepsis (the soberness of no-thought), prosochē (attention) and tapeinōsis (humility or nothingness). Never *seek* light: it manifests when mind is empty, and when it does, neither accept nor reject it. The mantra in mind is like air in the lung, like a wick in the flame. Daylight from the sun, sun-thoughts from the name.

SIMEON THE NEW THEOLOGIAN (955–1032): Filled in prayer with joy and burning tears he cried in amazement at the revelation of light that gave him power to see in his mind-sky the formless cloud of unwordable glory.

ABBOT ISAIAH (c.1200) to the Princess-Nun Theodora: For the words I recommend Kyrie Eleison.

NICEPHORUS THE LATIN HAGIORITE of Athos (late 13th and

early 14th). He wrote the Guard of the Heart and probably wrote the method of prayer (attributed to Simeon the new Theologian) two major works on progress from words through mantra to the wordless. His directions to beginners are: Sit on low stool, lower chin to chest, establish calm within by concentration, gazing at body-centre, slowing the breath, and making mind descend to heart, repeating from morning to night: Lord Jesus Christ son of God have mercy on me.

FRANCIS OF ASSISI (c.1208) in lay dress still and living as the 'Fool of God', was heard to pray all night: My God my God my God (cf. Eli, Eli).

FRA MASSEO (2nd disciple of Francis of Assisi) having c.1220 offered God his eyes in return for yoga was told to keep his sight and have union too; thereafter he prayed like a dove saying Hu Hu Hu.(11).

WALTER HILTON (d.1396); setting heart-thought on the cease-less mantra Jesu Jesu it becomes your joy and sings itself. This is soul-song singing to the rhythm of the church and not this one only but any other one-word name of God.

ANON (possibly Hilton) in the Mantra Appendix added (1350–1400) to the Benjamin Minor: To see God and be reborn as Benjamin the Sight-of-God collect your mind, make your heart a church then enter and stay there learning the one-word mantra Jesu. Think it lovingly and ceaselessly till mind is taken above itself and fed with angel-food and you become Benjamin in mentis excessu.

ANON (possibly Hilton or some other disciple of Rolle d.1349) from The Cloud: If in words then short words and one syllable rather than two and without speaking it or thinking it but meaning it in the heart and only if it rises spontaneously. An example of a one-word mantra is 'God' and if I knew a shorter I'd give it, but never use examples you read instead of what rises spontaneously.

ANON (the author of The Cloud in his Epistle of Discretion): You ask me whether to go in for silence or speaking, fasting or eating, being alone or with others and my answer is that none of these, even when 'done for God' can do much good since the only place you find God is the heart and to find him there is to know how it is. So speak silently and be silent with words; eat fastingly, but fast with food. If you are in company be so alone, but if alone then be so in company. The only target is God and the sharpest eye of the mind can't see it, but, even if you blindfold your heart, every shot of love will hit it. Reason can't see the power, goodness and wisdom of God, but the heart without reason can love and learn and live and pray, feeling God, finding God, and hitting the target every time. With the point of your heart set on the one thing only it couldn't matter less if you speak or stay silent, if you eat or fast, if others are with you or leave you alone. Speaking, silence, fasting, eating, being alone or in company, none of that reaches the one thing only that can only be learnt from God within by leaning toward him with silent mind and empty imagination and it teaches you without any strain whether to speak and eat or not, whether to go out or stay home. This is the discretion you learn from Prayer of the Heart and when you learn it you find yourself never just copying what others do.

MAXIMUS KAPSAKALIVITUS the hut-burning hermit who fled from the tourists on Athos (14th c.). He was the first to unite in the monologistos the memories of Jesus and the Theotokos, His words are not known but inspired the form: Jesus Christ son and word of the living God, for the sake of the Holy Theotokos have mercy on me a sinner.

GREGORY OF SINAI (and later of Athos where he died 1346). The gift received at baptism (the Seed of Grace) is a buried treasure found by either the powerful long path of keeping commandments or the even more powerful short path of Remembering God: practise it till the mind bursts into flames with love of him and of the whole human race. In his book *On How a Hesychast Should Sit Down to Pray and not Get Up too Soon* he said: Any text will do but don't change it frequently, at the most have two to alternate when tired. Say it with lips or mind or both, but don't let the words interfere with attention of mind, just leave them to say themselves since it nourishes like the Eucharist if said like Paul: I live yet Christ, not I, lives in me! As it warms your heart and scorches rising thoughts, pure prayer with stripped mind becomes spiritual sabbath, so ignore rising thoughts for as Isaiah the Hermit said mind is unrestrainable – restrain it.

THEOLEPTUS (died 1315) disciple of Nicephorus and master of Gregory Palamas: Sit and remember God speechlessly; draw the mind inward then let the divine magnet attract and illuminate it imagelessly, and you will truly know he alone who is (cf. the Sufis). We don't name everything we happen to see and that is the way to let mind see God. Collect it within, then let it return to itself and it will ascend till thought becomes pure and acts become worthy. As God made Adam and then breathed into him, so mind (remade by virtue through the monologistos) undergoes a divine change.

GREGORY PALAMAS (1296 to 1359). The stilling of thought purifies nothing but mind, but by longing for God we purify all our powers (body and soul) till pure mind endures and makes the human receptive of deification. As the incorporeal *logos* entered the virgin womb so mind enters heart and thus the divine unites with the human. As fire needs fuel, the divine needs you to manifest itself to others (cf. *contemplata aliis tradere*: to hand on to others what we have contemplated). Teach beginners to look at themselves and by breath-control, to send the mind back inside. As the hardest thing to contemplate is mind (it flies away because of its great mobility) the point of breath-holding is to teach mind-holding. Gregory repeats the following in 3 different books: When the morning star rises in our heart at dawn (2 Peter 1.19) true self sets out for true work; guided by its light we reach the mountain top and view the miracle of extra-cosmic reality. Not on imaginary wings of reason divorced from matter but through power of spirit we become angels on earth, messengers sent by God and drawing to him every created thing (*karuna* for the least blade of grass).

Two 14th c. monks of Athos, CALLISTUS of the Pantocrator and (1397) patriarch of Constantinople, and IGNATIUS of Xanthopoulos were co-authors of *The Centuries*, the last of the medieval rules for hesychasts, and the most complete. It is the first to suggest breathing out during the up and outward movement of mind to God (Lord Jesus Christ, son of God) and breathing in during the inward movement of mind to self (have mercy on me). Sit in seclusion and lead collected mind into the path of the entering breath, so that mind follows the breath into your heart. Leave them there and give mind the mantra. Though they get lonely, don't let them out too soon, because the moment that mind is about to descend within is when it becomes single, naked and free, though it comes out distracted, varied, dispersed. Never confuse method with the prayer itself.

The monologistos is first mentioned in Russia (15th c.) at the Trinity monastery near Obnora, and S. Nilus Sorsky (1433–1508) introduced it to monks of Transvolga.

SIMEON OF THESALONICA died 1429: The Jesus mantra gives the Spirit and his gifts. By it the Logos living in us, expels demons, and shining in us, heals psyche, and remits our sins. NICODEMUS THE HAGIORITE and MACARIUS OF CORINTH published the *Philokalia* (love of beauty) as an anthology of the divine neptic fathers in 1782. Nicodemus says: Teach novices how we collect spirit, and return it to heart, with chin on chest and breath holding. Two hours in the quiet dark each evening saying the mantra with words and will. Explaining his terms Nicodemus says: We distinguish the essence of a thing from the energy that gives it existence. It is only when energy and essence unite that a thing can actually exist. You must force the energy of your pneuma (prana) from external things (by guarding your heart and imagination) and let it return to its essence, in other words, to the centre of the heart. By its return you become free to contemplate your inner being. The 'return' is what Denis calls the circular movement of mind (cf. Dante's third dance); Basil calls it pneuma climbing up itself to the divine. To locate your inner mind turn its eye and ear to the words of the mantra without any mental pictures, words or ideas. Since God is outside anything that exists, outside anything we think, union with him is impossible till pneuma is detached from both matter and thought. Fix your will on the mantra till pneuma and inner mind merge into one, when they do you will appreciate beauty in a new way; have a new tenderness; see your 'self' in the 'mirror'; have pure perception; experience unwordable joy; and discover that God is hidden inside you.

PAISSY VELITCHKOVSKY 1722–1794 published his translation of extracts from the Philokalia in 1793 with the title DOBROTULUBIE (Love of the Good) and a fuller edition came out 1857 and even fuller (5 volumes) 1877.

S. SERAPHIM OF SAROV 1759–1833 inspired his biographer in 1855 to add an 80-page supplement on The Return of Spirit to Heart in which the Jesus mantra is reduced to the 'simple cry' Iissoussé moi (My Jesus).

IGNATII BRIANCHANINOV 1807–1867 published the 1857 Dobrotulubie and his own book 'On the Prayer of Jesus' the year he died. Say it slowly with quiet breathing enclosing the mind in the words. Just seek the union of heart and mind: technique will appear by itself – don't let it distract you.

STARETZ PARTHENIUS of the Pechersky Lavra at Kiev (1790–1855) said: It is a small murmuring stream inside you.

ANON The peasant of Orel who wrote The Pilgrim. He probably learnt the Jesus Prayer when it was being taught in the 1830's by the hieroskhimnik Basil in Kursk and Orel and by the Skhimnik Athanasius (disciple of staretz Basil Kishkin of Athos) who lived at the monastery of Bryansk in Orel and died 1844 in the monastery of Beloberezhsky. A latin priest from Wilna told the Pilgrim that greek monks learnt the monologistos from hindus in Bokhara, but his staretz said indian monks took their teaching from the neptic saints. Many copies of The Pilgrim circulated in Russia before it was printed at Kazan in 1884. The first translation into English was made at Prinknash.

THEOPHAN GOVOROV, the recluse, 1815–1894. Mantra lets God into the heart: he is the spark, it merely fans the flames. Words and posture have no importance, the essential is holding ready the inner hollow of heart. The one thought is the thought of one – it stills your mind.

THE ONOMOLATORS or IMENOSLAVTI grew from the teaching (just before and after 1900) of Januarius a Russian skhimnik of Athos and a hermit later in the Naked Mountains of Caucasus who thought the name and the essence were one and spoke of Christ incarnate in the mantra. Of the 1,000 disciples on Athos in 1913, 500 were deported when the Russian government sent a warship the following year. Even in 1932 a talk at the Russian Institute of Orthodox Theology in Paris said it was still a problem to know if the name of God contained his essence or was just a means to help us godward.

FR CASSIAN KARG the capuchin of Altoetting published The Little Secret in 1923 (1926 the 7th USA edition of 140,000): The art is taking breath by means of the prayer and is our key to the inner treasure-chamber of God. Each should have his own secret thought and the shorter the better, by it we co-operate with the Logos in saving all beings. Taught to children from the age of 12 he found it prevented them growing up stunted by the use of words in prayer.

Conclusion

The primary purpose of the monologistos is absorbing thoughts like blotting-paper so its meaning is unimportant and 'cabbage' might do except that irrelevant meanings tend to scatter rather than assemble the mind and if mind turns back for support to the sound it needs a conventional depth even if (as in OM) the meaning is symbolic. Given the importance in Jewish thought of The Name, then Yahweh, Iesous, God etc. are appropriately inevitable. The concepts of Mantra and Monologistos overlap enough to make the terms interchangeable but Mantra, more heavily conventionalised, has developed a logic and science of sacred sound (a bit like assigning greek vowels to the 7 directions and 7 spheres) which opens avenues the West mostly ignores (in spite of the 'elements' in Paul, the 22 Paths of Tarot and various symbolisms of the tetragrammaton) and which lead away from the simple aim of mind-stilling. A detailed study of mantra and monologistos would include a comparative history of, not only the rosaries they generate, but of all the aids that, relative to the union of nothing and nothing (freedom and freedom) are totally trivial but which, relative to the fruit of that union (handing on the things that are contemplated), are creative of culture, art, play and every means of communication.

Notes

1. About 500 A.D. Benedict left university to join a community at Enfide 50 miles from Rome, then became a hermit near Nero's villa at Subiaco and, as disciples joined him, founded twelve small communities in and around the villa and wrote (or adopted) what is called the Rule of the Master. About 530 (the year Bodhidharma went to China) he founded the Abbey of Montecassino in buildings that comprised the castle of Cassino, the Temple of Jupiter and the oracle of Apollo. Here he wrote 'for beginners' the abridgement of the Rule of the Master known as the Regula Obsculta or the Rule of Benedict. He died about 563.
2. Born just over 100 years before Benedict (c.360) Cassian joined the old monastery of Bethlehem a few years before Jerome (in 386) founded the new one. He and Germanus his syncellus (cell-mate) spent eight years in the monastery of Abraham in the Egyptian Delta (385–392) visiting spiritual masters nearby and taking notes on the teachings of eight of them. After a brief return to Bethlehem (392) they spent another eight years under Abbot Paphnut in the Abbey of Baramus (Pa-Romaios, the greek-speaker house) in Scete, the third Alexandrian desert. Here they took notes on seven spiritual masters. Expelled with 300 others in 401 by the Spiritual Seesaw, the patriarch Theophilus, they were

among the fifty offered asylum in Constantinople by John Chrysostom who lodged them in the Anastasis (a villa owned by friends of
Gregory, Basil and Evagrius) and who ordained Palladius bishop,
Germanus priest, Cassian deacon, and sent them to Rome with
letters in his defence. They arrived there 405 but Rome was
sacked 410 and Cassian went to Marseilles where he founded the
Abbeys of S. Saviour for women and of S. Victor for men. He spent
the ten years 419 to 428 writing up his notes on the fifteen
Egyptian masters and died at the age of seventy-two just four
years after their publication. We can't say how far he worked his
own experience into the notes; final publication was forty-three
years after his first arrival in Egypt.

3. Philo says the Therapeutae c.50 AD lived 'just past' lake Mareotis,
   presumably in the direction away from Alexandria. The map in
   James Willard *Desert Pilgrimage* shows that Lake Mareotis, now
   much reduced in size, once extended to within 5 miles of Nitria (el
   Barnugi on the canal to Naukratis). If accurate for the first
   century, it means Ammon and Antony chose a site that answers
   perfectly to the jewish monastery of Philo's Therapeutae. It would
   also be the site where abbot Fronto and his 70 companions lived c.
   150 AD. At the time of Cassian, however, as well as the 5,000
   monks of Nitria, Cells and Scete, there were 2,000 'near Alexandria'. Some of these may have occupied the Therapeutae site and
   all 7,000 were influenced by Philo (so often quoted by Clement,
   Ammonius and Origen) since Jerome, Eusebius and others (mis-
   takenly) thought Philo was describing the jewish-christian contemplative converts of S. Mark.

4. Born 351, Isaac was nine years older than Cassian. At the age of
   seven he joined Macarius junior, then sixty-five, a priest and
   Abbot in charge of Cells who spoke greek, knew the whole bible by
   heart and had responsibility for the group or synodia of three
   hundred (later expelled) which included Isaac, Cassian, Palladius, Evagrius, the Long brothers etc. By then Isaac himself had
   become Priest of Cells, also knew Scripture by heart and gave his
   teaching on prayer in 399 when he was 48 and Cassian 37.

5. *The Schismatic Audian Church*
   Epiphanius says Audius never denied the faith but failed to
   conform to tradition. This is less than adequate. He not only
   asserted God had a body, he founded his own church with bishops
   and deacons. From 400–500 his disciples were an important group
   in Edessa and between 770 and 800 they had either been refound-
   ed or they started to come into prominence again and this time as
   heretical gnostics and claiming Audius had written:
   The Apocalypse of Abraham
   The Apocalypse of John
   The Book of Strangers (or Allogenous Book)
   The Book of Requests
   The Apocalypse of Strangers
   though actually all of these, except the Book of Strangers, are

older than Audius.

6. Deus in adiutorium meum intende, domine ad adiuvandum me festina: From Pss.40 and 70: Run O Yahweh to rescue me, make haste to help me. May all who seek you and love you as Saviour rejoice and ceaselessly say 'great is Yahweh' (cf. Allah akbar). I am afflicted and poor, Lord remember me, help me, set me free. Here, as in later Sufism, Dhikr, Fana, seeking, remembrance, ceaselessness and poverty are all combined.

7. A dig at abbot Pakhom who allowed only literates into his monasteries. Antony, though of a well-to-do family with 300 acres, had never been to school because he was frail as a child. During the interruption, caused by the Paschal letter, an old coptic monk, Serapion, already 50 years in the desert, became upset. He 'used to set the image of God before him in prayer' and this image being now banished from his heart he complained 'They have stolen my God. I have nothing to lay hold of'. Though Photinus, a deacon visiting from Cappadocia, convinced him intellectually that the letter taught what the whole church believed, Serapion found he could no longer pray. The incident shows that the Synodia (group) of Evagrius and Ammon never excluded the simpler coptic monks and never forced oratio pura on them.

8. Born 345 at Iveronü (Ibora) near Anessi, the family home of Basil and Gregory Nyssa in Pontus, he was ten years younger than Gregory, who at 15 became his tutor. Ordained Deacon at 34 by Gregory Nazienzen, who wanted a secretary in Constantinople when invited there to restore the faith, they turned the villa of a friend into a basilica, called it the Anastasis and here 25 years later, the Long brothers, Cassian, Palladius and the rest of the fifty were lodged (401). After three years the second Ecumenical council, (381) under Gregory as President, elected Nectarius as the new archbishop and he made Evagrius his archdeacon. For a year he lived with the smart set, fell in love with the wife of a senator, dreamed the husband attacked him and decided to go for advice to Melania and Rufinus in Jerusalem. She clothed him as a monk and sent him to Pambo, Isaac, the Long brothers and the other monks she had once looked after when they were exiled to Sepphoris. After two years as novice in Nitria he went on (385) to the Long brothers in Cells, where eight years later he was joined by Cassian and Palladius. He died on the Epiphany, 6th January, 399, just before the Easter letter. For the last 14 years of his life he was co-leader with Ammon of the intellectual group (or synodia) formed by Macarius junior. He was often sent to Alexandria 'to confute the philosophers' who may have been neo-platonist pagans, audians, or gnostics. He wrote 16 works (of which I take the 'speculative' books to be a pioneer attempt at ecumenical dialogue with gnostics) and was the first (Westerner) to make a systematic and zen analysis of events in the brain and mind during thought and the suppression of thoughts.

9. On this 'trichotomy' cf. 1 Th.5.23: May the God of peace make the

whole of yourself wholly holy: pneuma, psychē and sōma. In taoism these 3 'elements' (the san chia) are what function through the '3 treasures' (san pao): shen – ch'i – ching.

10. Chapter 7 of the constitution on the Sacred Liturgy (6.127) promulgated 1963 dec.4.

11. Cf. the Sufi use of HU as the ismu 'l azam (exalted name) or the ismu 'z zat (name of the Essence) or, in its extended form, he who is is he who is he whom no one knows what he himself is but he (ya hu ya hu ya man la ya'ramu ma hu illa hu). This excludes the error of the onomolators who confuse the name and the essence.

Short Bibliography

1963 (1960 french) Louis Bouyer: The Spirituality of the NT & Fathers 2 vols (London)

1970 M. Lot-Borodine (intro by cardinal Danielou): La déification de l'homme (Paris)

1970 John Bamberger (tr & ed): The Praktikos of Evagrius Ponticus (Cistercian Publications, Spencer, Massachusetts, USA)

1974 John Meyendorff: Byzantine theology (London)

1977 Sergius Bolshakoff: Russian Mystics (London)

Discussion

Colin Wilson: While dom Silvester was talking, I was reminded about the interesting story of Aleister Crowley, who had a film star called Elizabeth Fox to stay at the monastery that he was running at the time on Cephalu. He was hoping that she would be beautiful so that he would be able to seduce her, but she wasn't, so he decided instead that he would teach her contemplation. He told her that she should go and sit on top of a cliff in a makeshift hut that had been built there. She went to the top of the cliff, sat there for two or three days, and became so excruciatingly bored that she determined that she would leave on the next boat. However when she enquired about the next boat she found that it didn't come until the end of the month anyway, and that left another twenty seven days to go. So she sat there still bored and miserable until, during the second week, she became absolutely furious and angry. In the third week this turned into sheer apathy. And then suddenly in the fourth week went into a beautiful floating condition of pure happiness, so that she did not want to get up and go away. She said that quite suddenly she saw what Crowley meant when he said she'd got the sky and the sea to contemplate – what else did she want? I think it's an important recognition that when you are trying to achieve inner calm, the 'you' who is trying to contemplate is a you that doesn't really want to contemplate at all. What you have got to do is somehow shift sideways into the you who does.

Q. Has your form of contemplation a place outside of the monastery setting?

dom Silvester: I was trying to explain that this form of contemplation has been going on since 3000 BC. I was asked recently to give a talk on the Eastern churches and I was pointing out how in the West, even though children are taught in the catechism that prayer is raising the mind and the heart and that you are an image in the likeness of God, the idea doesn't get very much further; children leave school without realizing that prayer is something wordless, silent and imageless and that God is better described as nothing rather than something; indeed if you use the word nothing, you already have a concept. Some people think *oratio pura* refers to Madame Guyon and others link spiritual prayer with the *devotio moderna* of the Brothers of the Devout Life in the 14/15th century. Père Bouyer, who is still the best introduction to the early spirituality of the church, in his *History of Christian Spirituality,* devotes Volume One to the New Testament and the Fathers, that is the Neptic Fathers, the spiritual writers in the desert. He traces present Byzantine awareness of the old Christian classical contemplative spirituality among ordinary people to the invasion by the Turks. Gregory Palamas and his friends were expelled from Athos and, rather like the Tibetans, they went round teaching mantra prayer to the people, and so it became very widespread in the Balkans, in Greece and the Byzantine tradition; in the West this withered and tended to be kept inside the monastery. The real culprit was the conception, which is still popular, of mysticism as exalted states, bi-location, levitation, all the *sidhis* that make 'mysticism' something exceptional, something rare, something just for a few people perhaps, but not for ordinary people, whereas of course the Christian tradition is that contemplation is ordinary prayer; it begins with the visible and moves to the invisible but it is all one thing. This misconception of prayer was certainly never shared by even the late writers of the 16th century like Teresa of Avila, and John of the Cross; it

170

only goes back to the introduction of meditation in the sense of having pictures in your mind, which is the very thing that the fathers teach how to eliminate. One of the earliest people to correct this misconception was Père Lamballe whose little book *Mystical Contemplation* (1913) shows that contemplation, 'mysticism', is in fact the ordinary prayer of ordinary people and has nothing to do with special states which may come, but have nothing to do with the normal way of the true mystical contemplative tradition. The *word* 'mysticism' came in with Denis the Areopagite about the 6th century. I try to avoid it always. The old joke has gone on for 50 years or more, about mysticism beginning in mist and ending in schism because it is centred on the 'I'. In this country it is a bit different because of the Reformation but in the Latin rite generally there *was* this tendency to cultivate pictures in the mind. But my quotation from dom Augustin Baker shows that at any rate in this country there was the tradition of the ordinary lay person having the ordinary 'mystical experience' of prayer.

Colin Wilson: Can I throw in a question which seems to be related to it? How far do your views agree with my suggestion that there are two religious natures of man? What I am referring to is the suggestion that there are two ways of contemplation: the *shock,* requiring tremendous effort, and the way of deep relaxation.
A. It can be a shock to some people to discover 'the sound of the one hand clap', to discover that nothing, Mu (or Wu in Chinese), is the true nature of God, perhaps even more of a shock to discover that this Wu is the most perfect image we have of God. In the *hua tu* technique in China (asking 'Who am "I", What is this original face?' very much as in Christian tradition) you get back to the pure *oratio pura* of the *puritas cordis,* which is what prayer is all about; all that can be a shock to people, but I doubt if people come to realize it *through* a shock. Shocks do odd things but that would be an exceptional way, like other exceptional things in prayer, levitation and bi-location and things like that.
Q. But would not for example the sort of monks who flogged themselves be an example of trying to shock oneself into the experience?
A. I have no evidence that anyone who flogged himself ever got anywhere. That is the very first thing in the 14th

century *Epistle of Discretion:* it does not matter whether you flog yourself or not, it won't get you anywhere unless you have the awareness of the Mu, of the nothing.

Q. Could you explain a little more about the mystics of the Alexandrian desert? Did they contribute to the Alexandria library that was burnt?

A. The great Antony was a frail child and so he never went to school and never learned to read. But he came from a rather well-off family. In Egypt he went to the desert in 300 AD and he began as people often did, he lived in what in Russia is called a pustinya, he became a pustinik, living in a village as a recluse, a hermit, or anchorite. Anchorite means withdrawn so that is the best word. These village hermits or pustiniks were common in Egypt and all over the Middle East. In the first, second and third century they were called monazontes and other names which suggested just retirement or recollection, very like the Taoist living on his mountain. Antony then went a little further off and lived by himself in one of these rather luxurious tombs for five years, 305 to 310 AD. In 310 he started taking disciples and by 370 AD there were 3,000 monks in Nitria and 20 years later there were 5,000, plus another 2,000 living in Alexandria city itself or round the lake. The desert of Nitria is fifty miles from Alexandria. Amon, a balm grower, had been married for eighteen years, and had lived as a contemplative with his wife; when she wanted to join a convent, this persuaded him to go off to the desert at Nitria, near where the Therapeutae lived that Philo talks about. When it became crowded, Antony suggested moving to another place. Lunch was always at 3 o'clock in those days in monasteries, the 9th hour, so they walked from the 9th hour to sunset and that became the 'inner desert' of Cells where Evagrius later lived with the Greek speaking monks. A little later the 3rd or 'innermost desert' was founded. It takes a whole day to walk there from Cells. The four earliest monasteries there are all flourishing today. Most monks were Coptic speaking and the Greek speakers tended to live together; they came under two abbots, Macarius the Senior and Macarius the Junior, the two Macarii were the great gurus, the staretsi of Cells where Palladius and Cassian both lived. Athanasius, a great friend of Antony, a great encourager of the monks, often visited them. Desert 'mysticism' was simply the teaching of Philo, of Clement, of Origen and Ammonias

Saccas. One of the things that helped the diffusion of this spirituality was the upheaval under Theophilus, the successor to Athanasius. He began as a great supporter but he was a very odd person. (His nephew, Cyril, was even odder because he was the one who got Hypatia murdered by Coptic monks: they chopped her to pieces in the Basilica.) Theophilus, the uncle, who may have been responsible for destroying one of the two libraries in Alexandria, sent out a circular letter in 399 AD which said it was Catholic teaching that God does not have a body, and he wrote it because of a fuss caused by the anthropomorphists who contemplated God with form rather than without form. The letter only caused further riots and when some Coptic monks marched to the Bishop's Palace, he changed sides (and so was always known afterwards as the spiritual see-saw – Amphallax) and expelled 300 monks from Nitria, including Cassian and Palladius. Evagrius died on the Epiphany, 6th of January, a week or two before the letter arrived in the spring of 399; the expulsion was in the summer of 401 AD. Everybody got involved in the affair: all the patriarchs, the Emperor, Jerome, Augustine, the Pope and his successor; it went on after the fall of Rome in 410. The exiled monks went first to Palestine and fifty ended up in Constantinople where John Chrysostom had been elected archbishop. Theophilus the spiritual see-saw had in fact nominated a friend from the desert, Isidore, to be archbishop and when he was not appointed, had John Chrysostom exiled.

To expel the three hundred monks, Theophilus persuaded the two emperors, Arcadius and Honorius to issue decrees forbidding people to read books which taught that God had no form, specially the works of Origen, so he was able to apply to the governor of Alexandria to enforce the decrees. One gets the impression from some books that a great army arrived to expel them, but actually one soldier turned up with the order and they went; they picked up their *melotes,* (their sheepskin which was what monks wore for travelling then) and went off. Theophilus himself invaded Nitria one night and burnt all the cells including one with a child who was burnt to death. Marrou in his *History of Education,* begins the Christian section with the schools in the desert; for example, S. Isaac went to Nitria at the age of seven and died at the age of 98, exiled in Constantinople.

Q.   There has been a great recrudescence of interest in the old religion, shamanism, etc. Is this in your opinion retrograde or merely a return full circle?

A. It depends whether the interest is academic, or an attempt at ecumenical understanding. What is known as the *logos spermatikos*, the presence of Christ in all truths, is the presence of truth in all religions. I have always said and I think it is quite true, though it sounds a bit glib and facile, that there is no point in asking about anything whether it is true or not. The only valid, useful, fruitful thing is to discover what truth is in it and having done that, to see how this helps your own understanding of truth. On shamanism, we have comparatively few documents. There are modern ones, such as the study of shamanism about 1850 in the Medicine Society at Manitoba. 'Medicine' (as with the therapeutae) means curing the mind, the soul. As Indians in reservations tended to stop being nomadic, the shaman just died out and the medicine man took his place. It happened almost overnight, so that what we know about the American shaman has been collected by writers in this century and the last. We know a little more about shaman meditation, by ascending the inner channel to the mind which is perhaps a little bit different from the concept of going to the centre and grasping the centre and holding onto the centre and finding it the image of God. Nevertheless it is the inner journey to the head and so in Christian art the halo of light is the presence of God shining out through his image. In many ways the shaman is the earliest type of the pre-Christian monk, and relates to the prophet and the sons of the prophets who lived together like monks in the old testament. For Elijah and the community that lived with him on Mount Carmel, as for the ecstatic prophets, the important thing was the interior awareness of God. I think you can say that the more we know about the shaman, the more we understand about the nature of religious man. One must use every means to understand the two books of Cosmos and Revelation, to understand their deeper meaning, and the shaman is part of that.

Colin Wilson: Angela Tilby is going to talk to you about the problem of testing religious experience. She made an interesting comment to me a few minutes ago that she felt that one of the essentials of religious experience was the element of conflict that goes into it. It is not entirely a matter of bliss and sweetness. Which brings me back to what I was saying yesterday, about the effort, the energy actually required to catapult you, so to speak, from one rung of the ladder up to the next. Because this is what we are really talking about. If the ladder inside you, what I call the ladder of selves, is shaped roughly like a triangle, and there is what you might call a different 'you' on each step of the ladder, then your real problem is to generate a sudden violent and intense energy, enough to catapult you literally to the next rung. One implication – and this is a different form of what I was saying about the left and right sides of the brain – is that the 'you' who is listening to me is essentially the you in the left side of the brain and not the other one. In the same way, the 'you' who is now listening to me is not you at all; it is simply one level of a number of beings who call themselves you. In some of the cases of multiple personality that I have written about in my book *Mysteries*, it is absolutely baffling to see the personalities taking over the bodies of people who have had a breakdown, moving in and out like different drivers of the same car. And yet I believe that these so called personalities are not genuinely different entities. Which brings me to the core of the matter. In the nineteenth century the French psychologist, Pierre Janet was also fascinated by the activities of hysterics and he noted that the hysteric's field of vision actually becomes narrower – tunnel vision. They only notice what is directly under their noses. Hysteria, of course, was a late 19th century phenomenon, and does not occur nearly so often nowadays. The hysteric subjects become so over-tense that they notice nothing except for what is literally under their noses. They have actually narrowed the field of vision. What Janet discovered was that he could go up to a hysteric who was staring intently at something in front of her and whisper 'Raise your arm' and she would raise her arm. Then he would say in a normal voice 'Why have you got your arm in the air?' and she would look up startled, and realize that she *had*. He was addressing another part of the personality, which raised the arm.

In one of Janet's most famous cases, a commercial traveller suddenly went into a state of depression in which he was convinced he was in hell. In this state, the devil – or what sounded like the devil – spoke out of his mouth in a completely different voice from his own, in a sort of deep baritone voice. Whenever Janet tried to hypnotise the patient, a man called Achille, the devil, would say, 'Ah no, you're not catching me like that' and decline to co-operate. Then he discovered the solution: that he could hold a conversation with the devil by putting a pencil into Achille's right hand and addressing him in a low voice. The Devil would then write down the answers on a piece of paper, while Achille himelf carried on a conversation with whoever happened to be in the room, not in the least aware of what his hand was writing. At some point Janet asked 'Who are you?' and the pencil wrote: 'The Devil'. Janet then said 'What do you want?' and the pencil replied: 'To drag his soul down to hell'. Janet then asked 'Are you really all-powerful?' The Devil replied: 'Of course!': Janet asked: 'Is it possible for you to put him into hypnotic trance?'; the Devil said 'Of course'. So Janet said: 'Let me see you do it', and the Devil promptly sent Achille into hypnotic trance. In this state, Achille's mental problems became perfectly accessible. He had been with a prostitute on one of his trips, and become so consumed with guilt that he first of all became psychosomatically dumb, and then became convinced he was in hell. Janet staged a big reconciliation scene with his wife, who said 'I forgive you', and the Devil instantly and promptly disappeared.

Now Janet's observations amount to this: that the complete mind, the whole mind, could be compared to the full moon, but that our normal everyday self is in fact only a very small segment of that complete mind. You remember that poem of Yeats called 'Under Ben Bulben', in which he says:

> 'Know that when all words are said
> And a man is fighting mad
> Something drops from eyes long blind,
> He completes his partial mind,
> For an instant stands at ease,
> Laughs aloud, his heart at peace.'

This phrase 'he completes his partial mind' suggests we *are* only partial minds, a small slice of the moon. In your normal state you are a fairly large slice. When you get hysterical and anxious, you get smaller. And when you get into a state of real illness and hysteria, you are such a tiny slice that it is only a fragment of the 'essential you'. Your problem is to relax into the bigger 'you'. And yet the 'bigger you' always remains there as a kind of penumbra. This was the area that Janet could talk to by putting a pencil into Achille's hand.

What is equally important to grasp is that when you relax, you relax into *other you's,* not just into a bigger area of you. We are all used to the fact that when we relax and enjoy ourselves, we as it were feel bigger, we feel more in contact with nature and the universe. But the idea that it is actually a different *personality,* and that as you narrow, you cut out succeeding layers of you, is absolutely strange to psychology. And yet I am convinced that this is the truth. This is what we are speaking about when we talk about the ladder of selves, about the difference between the two cerebral hemispheres. The ultimate religious experience would be to somehow get to the apex of the ladder. Then the moon would be absolutely complete. What could happen then I cannot imagine. (Although Edmund Husserl would say that the apex of the ladder is what he calls the transcendental ego.) I think that religious people say the apex of the ladder is God, and that this is the meaning of the saying that man is ultimately God, that Atman is identical with Brahman.

But how do we widen the slice of the cheese? This is the central question of religious experience. Angela Tilby was doing a series of programmes last year for the BBC, *The Long Search Continues,* and in doing this had to fly all over the world, and talk to an enormous number of people of different religions. This is how she became fascinated by this particular problem: of the religious experience in completely different religions.

Testing the Spirits

Angela Tilby

Cosmic Visitors

During the 1950's two elderly women started to meet
regularly on Saturday evenings in a flat near Bognor Regis.
One of them had psychic gifts. I have some notes describing
their sessions which they wrote up regularly and circulated
among a small group of friends. These notes describe how
they were visited over a number of years by over eighty
spiritual beings: Jesus, John, the Beloved Disciple, the
Spirit of Buddha, Poseidon, Ajax, a number of cosmic over-
lords with names like Nocturnas and Lumina, and a
recently deceased Anglican clergyman. All these dropped in,
as it were, on Saturday evenings, and gave teaching and
counsel. One of the ladies was my grandmother. She was a
very sane and practical person with Lancashire wit, and a
healthy enjoyment of material comfort. I was not present
when the visitations took place, and I have not the slightest
idea what actually happened. All I have is the testimony.
And there is no doubt that to my grandmother what was
going on was revelation. The beings were sent from God,
from the divine spirit, and their message was of the deepest
significance for the human race. My grandmother never
doubted that she was a practising Christian, and she frequently wrote to the newspapers on religious matters and
signed herself, 'A Christian'. Not surprisingly, she was extremely upset when members of a rather aggressive local
Pentecostal church came round to rid her of her demons. The
Pentecostals, were, of course, exercising the ancient
ministry of testing the spirits, but for my money they misin-
terpreted the situation rather sadly. They thought of
demons and witchcraft, but my grandmother's spirits were
not dangerous – they were dull. They were dull with the
dullness that all uncriticized testimony possesses. They
were dull because they spoke the language of the Authorised
Version. They attacked the decline of morality with relish;
they launched into diatribes against the ignorant scientists
who were interfering with the universe by trying to send

rockets to the moon. The visitants clearly inhabited the same region as those who reappear to their loved ones bringing reassurance and consolation, and get written about in *Psychic News*. It has always amazed me that having died and gone through death, the dissolution of the body, the flight through whatever lies beyond, Fred should only want to communicate to Mabel about her backache, her financial worries, and the green pastures and still waters of the other world. Uninterpreted, uncriticized experience has a flat dullness about it, which I find, as a religious journalist, I recognize again and again. And it doesn't matter whether it's a ley line hunter or an evangelical Christian, a Jungian or a crypto-Buddhist or a yoga-freak, there is to me a boredom, a staleness about those who no longer believe, but *know*.

Theology and Experience

And yet we assume a distinction, even a contradiction between institutional religion and religion of direct experience. On the one side are the traditions with their dogmas, systems of authority, laws, rituals, patterns of devotion or meditation; on the other side is revelation, direct, unmediated, the experience of God in the soul – the kingdom within, for those who are within, the cognoscenti, the elect: 'O world invisible, *we* view thee.'

And I think it is sometimes assumed that these two different sorts of religion relate to each other historically. The prophet experiences God. It is hot experience. His revelation burns with divine fire; it is like molten gold, all who touch it share the original glory. The new teaching is revolutionary. It changes all who hear it. And then we assume that the prophet dies, stories get built around his memory, the stories turn into scriptures, his followers become a church, his teachings become law, within a few generations theologians and law makers have taken this hot golden, fluid experience and poured it into hard cold moulds, the categories of doctrine and of tradition and then it gradually loses its heat and glow and goes rigid.

Search for Religious Experience as Therapy.

This picture is common and it is comforting. It tells us what we want to hear at the moment about religion. We want to know that true religion is knowledge, not intellectual knowledge, not knowledge of facts, but hot knowledge,

179

the knowledge of those who have heard and seen for themselves, and so have no need of doctrine. Relgion is a kind of therapy. We want it to save us. To heal the split between mind and body, thought and feeling, to heal the division between us and the animals and the stones and trees. Whole food, holistic medicine: this is the way of holiness that is manifesting itself as an alternative to our old truncated English Hymnal version of Christianity. Surely it is at least a more attractive alternative! I have gone to sleep in lectures on Christian theology as boring as those of the legendary Dr Torpedo, whose course was hailed as a cure for the severest cases of insomnia. And I have winced as a cathedral dean has stared venomously into the camera to give the blessing on 'Songs of Praise'.

Preaching and Experience

And yet the search for authentic, hot experience is as real inside the Christian churches as elsewhere. 'I don't know whether Christian doctrines are true,' a colleague said to me recently, 'but for myself, being a Christian *works*.' Metaphysical questions are improper questions. They are widely regarded as rather distasteful: 'So shut the Bible up and tell me how the Christ you talk about is living now' wrote Sydney Carter in a song. Evangelical preaching to students concentrates on the appeal to new life, resurrection now, authentic human existence. No longer the detailed discussion of the classical arguments for the existence of God, or the logical necessity of an atoning death to pay for the sins of the world. I think of an evangelical student who brought a discussion on some point of doctrine to an abrupt end with the remark: 'God wrote the Bible, man invented theology.' The funny thing was, I don't think he was really at all interested in the verbal inspiration of the Bible as it had come to be expressed in Calvinist theology; he certainly had no interest in defending that doctrine to me, an unbeliever. Interpreting his comment with as much charity as possible, I think he was telling me, that the God who spoke to him through Scripture did so so clearly and unambiguously that he had no need of an interpreter. He was one of those who did not believe. He *knew*.

Testing of Spirits and Therapy

And no doubt that student got from his religion some

therapy, some brighter, less depressed sense of himself than he had had before he saw the light. How do you test the spirits of those who know they are saved? For some, there is a real theological virtue in vagueness. But if I have a dream of the Buddha, or of Christ or the Virgin Mary I want to know what the dream meant. I want also to ask metaphysical questions. Did the vision come from here, or there, from inside or outside? If I knew the answer would it make any difference? Can God speak in dreams? Or is the vision thrown up by the subconscious mind? Or are they the same thing? And if they are the same thing what is the criterion for judging the dream and testing the spirits? The new religious orthodoxy would say 'take it as revelation'. The true self is not deceived. And yet how do I know that? The religions also speak of self-deception, of sin and darkness and ignorance. Are these merely, as some would say, conditions of the conscious mind, which get swept away in sleep or meditation, or are they, in fact, conditions of our being in all its depths, so that at the most basic level we are really threatened by death and unreality? The religions give different answers, which is why the questions matter. And those who test the spirits must explore the different answers. Doctrine is unavoidable.

The Politics of Religious Experience

Doctrine is suspect for political reasons. Experiences without doctrine cannot contradict each other. They can only be more or less helpful and relevant. But when you bring doctrine into the picture there are clashes. We all know that there is no way that the great religious systems can be reconciled intellectually. The Burmese Buddhist and the Nigerian Muslim conceive the world differently. The Russian Orthodox Christian and the American Zionist live in different universes. Realizing this is, I find, a profoundly uncomfortable experience. It is not surprising that some of those who are involved in the dialogue of religions are searching for a vantage point as far away as possible from this draughty region of the spirit: the goal is one, the ways are many. All religions are true, but none of them is completely true. What alienates religions from religions is precisely what is taken to be *secondary* – the theologies, the dogmas, the institutions; and what unites religions is man's experience of the divine.

As I understand it, in much of Indian religion this assumption about the nature of religion has the virtual status of doctrine itself. We can understand this by considering the way Hindu religion has developed it is an organic religion, spreading out like a great tree in many directions, without a known beginning, or a founder, or a single revelation. It is, more than one religion, a cluster of religions, with sharp divisions of doctrine and practice. These divisions have not often led to wars or to heresy hunts, because there is no historic point of divergence, but that is not to say there are no distinctions. Doctrine and theology are worked out with a passion that is foreign to most Westerners. I think of the classic division between the religion of Shankara and Ramanuja, and how their spiritual descendants have kept the division alive. For Shankara reality was one and impersonal; Ramanuja was more of a theist really, and stressed the way of love and devotion to God. Now one way out of this unfortunate clash is to roll one's eyes, look up to heaven, and say 'Ah, but it's all the same thing, really. It's all one.' Such remarks have been made to one more often by Westerners than Indians as it happens, but that is not the point. The point is that it does matter very much whether Shankara or Ramanuja was right. The followers of each will in time develop their own spirituality, their own awareness. Their experience gives rise to doctrine and their doctrine deepens their experience. And if I was looking for criteria by which to judge a religious experience by a man who claims to be a follower of Shankara or Ramanuja, I could only begin by asking him about doctrine. What does he believe to be true?

When what has been called the Hindu ideology of religions gets transferred to a Western context it leads, not to a sharpening of this debate, but a flight from it. Comparative religion is the booming subject in some of the West coast universities of America. It is taken for granted by many who study it, and some who teach it, that comparative religion is not an intellectual discipline, but an initiation into a personal quest. One academic I spoke to a year ago said that as he saw it, the faculties of religion were providing a smörgasbord of religious delicacies from which students concocted the ingredients for their own personalised casserole. Today I am into Zen and tomorrow Vedanta. Ecology is a spiritual science. Meat eating makes you violent. I have experienced the Cloud of Unknowing. No need any more to go to and fro upon the earth like the unfortunate messengers of God. Eternity is here, now; reach out and take it. But don't ask questions about it. Questions only prove your ignorance, your alienation, your lack of spirituality. While you question you cannot be saved. And where is the testing of the spirits in this? Without doctrine, or rather, with too many doctrines there can be no tests. I sniffed, with my all too fallible religious nose, and had the same sense of weary flatness, the repeated clichés of the new gnosticism. If these are the saved I would rather be among the damned. But that wasn't all. I repeat I have no personal authority as a tester of spirits, but I was moved, sometimes. I did now and then find myself thinking, 'Yes, this is it, or this is something like it.' And usually when I felt that, it was because there was an awareness that a struggle had taken place. That on the spiritual journey *this* disciple had fallen over and got muddy; he had wrestled with light and darkness, with the false and the true. The scriptures to him were not travel brochures; he wrestled with them to find their authority, and so with the difficult sentences, the creeds, the execrations, the antique laws. He accepts the reproach of joining the church or whatever community claims to link itself to the tradition he is struggling with. In accepting the struggle and the suffering, this disciple is being a witness, a martyr. He is making himself the meeting point of tradition with hot experience. When the tradition is abandoned or denied because it has become politically dangerous – and that is usually why religions fade out – the martyr insists that the tradition lives on in him. Martyrs do not die for what is helpful or relevant; they do not die because they've had a therapeutic experience, or have come to believe that all religious experience is equally valid. Martyrs die for what they believe is true. And they are an offence to the world, and to the religions of personal therapy, which are also and always religions of political expediency, whose adherents are to be found mouthing clichés about love and progress and the spiritualization of matter while the neutron bomb is tested and the cries of the earth intensify.

But even martyrs can be self-deceived. They can be sick and deluded. How to test the spirits?

The Implicit Claims of Experience

I want to suggest at this point that religious experience contains implicit theological claims. It is theology that makes an experience religious, and not aesthetic or sexual. It simply isn't clear that experience comes first and is of primary importance, and theology comes second and is irrelevant. What of those who: 'had the experience but missed the meaning?'

In many cases theology precedes experience and gives it its shape and colour. 'Jesus, son of God, have mercy upon me' – this is a phenomenon which needs explaining. Such cries are a new language of man to the divine; they are already a new doctrine and all that later formulations do is struggle to find words that will not mislead. And why do Christians have visions of the Virgin Mary, and not, on the whole, of Kali? Theology colours experience. Now while I think this is true and could be substantiated in more detail, the problem always arises over the question of the new prophet, the new doctrine. Many feel that the Christian church has a particularly shameful record in this respect. It has declared Jesus the last word of God to man. It has said Holy Scripture ends with the Book of Revelation, and that the church contains within itself the criteria for interpreting the tradition. Every new claim to revelation has to be measured against the tradition, and the mystic or the prophet has to risk the martyrdom of being judged wrong. In retrospect we can see that the church has acted outrageously. It has often got it wrong. It has condemned saints, and exalted dry theological Yes-men. Yet through a longer process it does seem that a new balance emerges. Luther is reconciled to Rome through the theology of Hans Kung. Charles Wesley's hymns, backbone of the Methodist hymn-book, are discovered to be stuffed with theology that the catholic and orthodox can recognize as their own. In the end, though the struggle goes on, the church accepts Lady Julian of Norwich but rejects Mary Baker Eddy. And if we were to ask why, I think it could be shown that the marks of struggle, questioning, wrestling with a tradition, are present. Yes, Luther was right to cut across the dead weight of merit doctrines and proclaim the doctrine of justification by faith. He saw it in the scriptures, in Abraham, David, Paul, Peter. It was there in the tradition, but the tradition has got out of balance. Yet, where to

184

draw the line? Which side of Mrs Eddy or *The Book of Mormon*? One could point out that Mrs Eddy in fact did rediscover part of the tradition; she wrestled with the tradition of the new Testament healing miracles. She became the place where that tradition and live experience met. She suffered an emotional martyrdom from orthodox religious leaders. And yet, in asserting the reality of healing, she developed doctrines that contradicted the tradition. She spoke of the innate purity and divinity of the soul, of the ultimate unreality of evil, of salvation as release from ignorance. At that point the church started to get nervous. And when she went on to say that the Christ was a creation of God the mind, and was distinct from the human Jesus, the church had to hand a number of alternative heretical labels to condemn her with. But were they right or wrong? They applied the criteria of creed and doctrine, but what if the tradition itself had gone wrong? This is the testing point – the point of tension. I think the reason why this question is so urgent is that those of us who do our religious searching in the Western tradition have inherited a kind of schizophrenia. In this, theology has become a detached science, an exercise of the reason. Academic theology is applied to experience rather in the same way that a dentist looks for cavities with a selection of nasty, steely instruments. Today in the churches, the theologian is alternately regarded as a dry-as-dust figure, endlessly pouring over ancient Syriac texts or as the very embodiment of rationalist disbelief. The theologian comes across as the one who believes less than the historian or the anthropologist, or the scientist, whose answer to every question of truth or falsehood begins 'It depends what you mean...'

Yet in Eastern orthodoxy, the theologian is firstly a man of prayer. Doctrine precedes his prayer and arises out of it. He prays 'with the mind in the heart'. I contrast that with the tendency in modern theology to split serious study from the emotional and experiential side of religion. In a lecture last year, John Hick who is the Edmund Cadbury Professor of Theology at Birmingham University suggested that as a result of the debate between religions, Christians would gradually grow out of their attachment to such doctrines as the Trinity and the Incarnation. In time, these would be seen: 'Not so much as precise, metaphysical truths, but as imaginative constructions, giving expression, in the religious and philosophical language of the ancient world, to the Christian's devotion to Jesus.' He adds: 'I would suggest that this is the kind of development which the more intellectual part of the Christian mind (appropriately, in the human brain, the left hemisphere!) is likely to undergo, whilst its more emotional half perhaps continues to use the traditional language of Christian mythology, without raising troublesome questions about its meaning.'

So Professor Hick suggests a new programme in which Christians accept the Jesus of St Mark and not the Jesus of St John, except perhaps as giving rise to cloudy images in the right hemisphere of the brain. And Christians are to enter the debate between religions not as 'adherents of historical Christianity', but 'simply as disciples of Jesus.' This splitting of the mind and the heart, of experience and tradition is, to me, a rejection of martyrdom; it is refusing to stand in the draughty place, in the uncomfortable place where I am both and inevitably a disciple of Jesus and an adherent of historical Christianity. Perhaps the two loyalties will tear me apart. Perhaps then I will know resurrection. But as far as I can see even theologians of the Western tradition have tried to pray and study 'with the mind in the heart'.

Thomas Merton writes of the Lady Julian of Norwich: 'She experienced, then thought, and the thoughtful deepening of experience worked it back into her life, deeper and deeper.' Karl Barth, after writing thirteen volumes with the unpromising title *Church Dogmatics* confessed that the most momentous discovery of his long theological life was that: 'Jesus loves me, this I know, for the Bible tells me so.'

These theologians seek discernment. They do not just accept the testimony of the intellect, or the emotions, or the senses. They tested the spirits with very basic questions. Did an experience lead to greater charity, or a deeper love for others, to greater humility in the service of the church? Did it lead to a fuller realization of the Trinity and the Incarnation? Think of Lady Julian struggling with the revelation that forced her to speak of the femininity of God, God as mother as well as father. She is still criticized for that, but on the whole the tradition vindicates her. And yet, the real struggle was in her, and it came out in various forms of illness, neurotically based perhaps; she thought she was dying. That taken with the sanity and wisdom of her

186

teaching and its theological integrity marks her as a martyr, someone who speaks with the ring of truth. She got no instant therapy out of her revelations. They were revelations of suffering, and they caused her more suffering. The martyr prays with Charles Wesley that his wounds will be made deeper. And he doesn't know at the time either whether he is a true martyr or a sick masochist, or whether he can be both at the same time.

Buddhist Doctrine and Experience

I have used Christian examples so far because they are more familiar to me. But as far as I can see there is the same pattern of struggle between tradition and experience in other religions too. The Buddhist way, as I understand it, involves at least in the early teachings, a cure for suffering and impermanence through mindfulness. Through mindfulness, taking continual note of the changes and fluxes outside and inside oneself, one comes to the realization that there is no substantial self, no permanent subject for all these varied experiences. Now the doctrine of non-self is a real doctrine. It is not just a commendation of unselfishness; it is a radical and metaphysical denial. There is no self. And when we look at the advice given to those who seek to take up meditation practice we remember the basis of doctrine. There are warnings against those who take up meditation in order to increase their mental and persuasive powers and so gain influence over others. There is no self. So the desire to use meditation in this way is proof of falsity. There are some who have experiences in meditation of light and sound. There is no self. So a manifestation of light is not proof that you have made progress. It is irrelevant. Even to desire to make progress can suggest that the doctrine of non-self has not been properly understood. So the doctrine which is at the core of Buddha becomes the critique of claims to experience. All claims to revelation, to progress, to mastery, must be tested against the tradition.

It seems to be the character of authentic theology to be critical. It insists on interpreting, analysing and evaluating. It accepts neither arid academicism nor uninterpreted experience, nor will it settle for a hopeless split between the left and right hemispheres of the human brain. It is the task of theology to test the spirits and it requires experience and study, prayer and thought, contemplation and analysis.

187

Charles Williams, the poet and novelist, was fascinated by the occult. He made studies of various kinds of esoteric religion; he was, as we might say, 'into' astrology and mysticism. Yet he never doubted that, even if these things were permissible, they had to be ruthlessly tested by the Christian tradition. He wrote a cycle of poems about King Arthur, and in it he struggles with what he sees as the peculiarly materialisitic nature of Christianity, its concern for flesh and spirit, law and theology, doctrine as well as experience and love marked with accuracy. Off the coast of Cornwall lies a wood, which is at the same time, a sea. It's called Broceliande. Sometimes it appears as water and seaweed, sometimes as tangled trees. It is a magic, enchanted place, and somewhere beyond it is the Castle Carbonek, the home of the Holy Grail. C. S. Lewis, in a commentary on the poems, wrote about the sea or wood of Broceliande: 'It is what most romantics are enamoured of; into it good mystics and bad mystics go: it is what you find when you step out of your ordinary mode of consciousness ... Saint, sorcerer, lunatic and romantic lover, all alike are drawn to Broceliande, but Carbonek is beyond a certain part of it only. It is by no means the absolute. It is rather ... the unlimited, the formless origin of forms. Dante and D. H. Lawrence, Boehme and Hitler, Lady Julian and the Surrealists, had all been there. It is the home of immense dangers and immense possibilities.'

It seems to me that what passes for the dialogue between religions is in fact a gentle swopping of stories of what goes on round the edges of Broceliande. And, as we should expect, much the same sort of stories occur again and again. Many seekers have transcended the ordinary limits of day-to-day consciousness. Many have experienced the sense of oneness, of unity and identification with all forms. Many have sensed the timeless moment, for that wood or sea is eternally present. Out of it, some would say, come our dreams and fantasies. Broceliande is the unconscious, and over it hangs an enormous question. Beyond the trees and the seas, the darkness and the light is there a true castle of Carbonek? And if there is, surely what matters about it is its location. The wood itself is ambiguous. Now the religions offer maps through Broceliande, through the forms into the formless. The maps differ from each other quite radically. Professor Hick feels that the only hope for honest dialogue is to leave

188

the maps behind: 'As long as they all stand firmly within their respective circles of faith, dialogue will consist basically in the display and comparison of these incompatible beliefs.' Of course, once one leaves the circle of faith, once one leaves the map, everything does look remarkably, and deceptively the same. 'Haven't we been here before?' we ask, when lost in a wood, passing the same thicket (or is it the same thicket?) as we passed twenty minutes ago. Yet if you stand on your path and tell me what you see, and I stand on my path and tell you what I see, we will probably see different things, and yet it is likely that we will be passing on real information. Once I leave the path I can tell you nothing. Religion as the media and the churches present it, is hung up on experience. Our religion, Christian and otherwise, shows signs of decline into a series of loosely-linked, gnostic, salvation cults, which take you on the journey into the wood and leave you there. In abandoning tradition they have abandoned the ability to be self-critical. They are religions of wholeness, certainly; that is what they offer, but it rings of the cheap grace that Bonhoeffer criticised so stringently. They can offer no coherent theology, because they are not wrestling, they are not offering martyrdom, but techniques of spiritual masturbation.

The option of being a witness or martyr raises real problems which cannot be evaded. I think one of the hardest of these is the realization of competing claims to truth from the religions. For if we have moved from the unthinking universalism which declares that all religions are really the same, are we merely to retreat behind the barrages of our own traditions, at best to leave each other politely alone, and, at worst, to hurl insults at each other?

I hope there is a third way, and if there is, it will involve bringing together experience and tradition. Now much of Christian tradition offers me a rather negative assessment of other religions. If I look at the tradition critically and bring my own experience into play, it is clear that a lot of the negative approach came, not from theology, but from cultural isolationism, which we now cannot share. Alongside the negative estimates which provided the missionaries with their conversion theology, there are also the Christian doctrines of man made in the image of God, and of the incarnation, that God in Christ lived a human life and died a human death. Now this is about all I have, and as someone

189

who identifies with the Christian tradition, it is all I have to
work with in making sense of the non-Christian religions. It
is the implication of incarnation doctrine that the human
life of Jesus was universal as well as particular. The early
fathers speak of Jesus *recapitulating* humanity. This is a development of Paul's notion of Christ as the second Adam.
Jesus goes over the ground of human experience again –
birth, growth, adulthood, suffering, death. But as this
human life comes from God, and is lived by God, it has significance for all human life. Nothing that is human is left
out. And that includes all that one may find in the sea-wood
of Broceliande, and, also, all that may be encountered along
the different religious paths. It also includes, I believe, the
protest of atheism, and the experience of meaninglessness.
There are hints that Christ experienced radical isolation,
separation from the ground of being. Also he knew what it
felt like to be unforgiven and without hope. Nothing that is
human is lost. It has always been a peculiarly Christian
emphasis that even the dark, recalcitrant, hopeless aspects
of human life are included into God's experience. So, as a
Christian, I find myself trying to see all the religions in God.
Every adherent shows a different face of the divine image,
and it is his responsibility to refine it, to suffer in bringing
the image of God to birth, to suffer between tradition and experience. I may find, in conversation with a Buddhist, an
aspect of the image of God which I do not recognize. Perhaps
from my part of the wood it can't be recognized. Yet I must
accept it as valid, though I cannot say what it means; I must
accept it as valid because the whole image of God is in
Christ, and I deny Christ if I deny the image of God. I think
it is becoming true that to accept the validity of Christian
worship means accepting the validity of all worship, in its
particularity, in its concrete, historic and cultural forms.
The incarnation doctrine drives me to consider these, not to
try and separate flesh from spirit, or essence from manifestation.

On Easter Sunday last year I explained that theory, such
as it is, to a Japanese Buddhist, a member of the modern sect
of Rissho Kosei Kai. He was starting a mission to Europe,
and we were, I suppose, discussing tactics. He had spent a
year in an Anglican theological college in England, and
knew very much more about Christian theology than I did
about modern Buddhism. Anyway I explained my theory

which he listened to with great patience. At the end of it he said, 'My only problem with Christianity is the word God.' He then explained *his* theory of the relation between the religions. He started from the doctrine that at his enlightenment Gautama had become one with the universal principle or *dharma*, which existed before his birth on earth. The Buddha had become the teaching as well as the Teacher. Flesh had become Word. Then he explained that according to the doctrines of Rissho Kosei Kai, enlightenment was when a person realized his own Buddhahood – and thus transcended all alienation to become one with universal reality. As we spoke about this, I realized that I felt as though I was looking into a mirror. There were extraordinary reflections, but the images were all backwards. Or mine were. He spoke of the Buddha at the centre of the universe. I thought of Christ as the universal logos, as he is portrayed in the icons of the Eastern church. We spoke of the compassion of the Buddha as shown in the later Buddhist scriptures, and in particular, in the much-loved *Lotus Sutra*, where his compassion is described in parables, like but unlike the parables of the *New Testament*. We knew, both of us, that the basic question between us, the question of God, would never be settled. And it would be a mistake to try and settle it. On this issue, Chosan Nagamoto is convinced he's right, and I'm convinced I'm right. I accept the fact that he thinks he's right and must therefore accept the responsibility for the fact that I think he's wrong. The difference between us is absolutely crucial, and we would not be being true to our respective traditions if we did not admit it. We tried exploring what we meant by God and not-God. I tried phrases like the ground of being, Chosan tried phrases like universal *dharma*. The religious politician and ecumaniac would say that we were only arguing about words. There was no substantial difference between us. Yet I don't agree. Again, as in the wood of Broceliande, our languages have echoes of each other, but we cannot reduce the differences to mere semantics. They are differences which reflect a different way of conceiving the whole of reality, a different way of experiencing reality. We only had to look at the different images of faith, the standing Buddha, hand raised in blessing, and the crucified Christ – and there was the gulf between us.

Yet this did not diminish our fellowship; candid disagreement brought us closer than politeness could have done. We came close to each other by theology and experience. I understood his rejection of God as a valid human response to reality, which now and forever is included in God. He said he understood what it was like to live in a theocentric universe, because he lives in the universe of the Buddha. I don't think we could have gone further in honesty. We both found our positions were clearer, to each other and ourselves. That, to me, makes the dialogue worthwhile. The key question, of course, is beyond the scope of dialogue. I suppose it can only be answered by the future, when in heaven or Nirvana, we find Christians learning to live without God, or Buddhists discovering that they have been in God all the time. But:

'These are only hints and guesses.
Hints followed by guesses; and the rest
Is prayer, observance, discipline, thought and action.'

So I find myself compelled to suggest to religious friends who have a puritan horror of the church and its evils that there may indeed be 'no salvation outside the church', though I should have to add to that that there is no salvation outside the mosque, temple and synagogue also. What I am arguing for is an attitude of seriousness about religion, and a refusal to accept the current cliché that hot experience is the antithesis of creed, form and dogma. It has been said that Love requires a body. And for myself, in the Christian tradition: 'The hint half guessed, the gift half understood is Incarnation.'

Discussion

Q. Whoever tests anything must have first-hand experience of it. What is the way most likely in your view to lead to such experience?

A. I think that there is only one way and that is to join the tradition. In this country, for somebody born in these islands under our particular cultural tradition, I would imagine it would mean joining the Church, reading the scriptures and becoming a member of that community. I think the alternative is, if one feels strongly drawn to another tradition, to try and join that. Dr Blacker explained some of the immense cultural problems that that can cause, but it is a possibility, and I think there is no other way.

192

Q. It is noticeable that you mention struggle as a feature of the development of truth but no hint of purpose or meaning. Would you comment on how you test the validity of an expression of purpose?

A. It seems to me that the people who have struggled, as I understand it, have not very often had very much sense of purpose. It has been something which they have had to do; very often the future, the hope, has got quite quenched, and it has been quite difficult to see through it. In the *Old Testament*, the conflicts between true and false prophecy make interesting reading in the sense that often the true prophet had no sense of being true. In fact even Jeremiah felt that God had deceived him quite deliberately. He had a total lack of security that he was doing the right thing. Whereas often the false prophets were quite sure they were right. So I am not very sure about how one is certain of purpose or meaning. Theology would say to me that one can only test it continually against the tradition, against the reality of one's own experience and somehow suffer within that tension, and I think the tension is very real because they do sometimes contradict each other. Purpose is in the future and it is something that is experienced in hope rather than in the present.

Colin Wilson: If I may add a comment on that. This is a point which is of great interest to me because it is the thesis of my first book *The Outsider*. What I was trying to say there was that there are certain people who find themselves totally alone in a modern society, stuck in a corner or a little room feeling themselves alienated, seeing no way out of the problem. And somehow there's no way to reassure them. There is no way of saying to them 'Don't worry, you're just an outsider.' I am not sure that even writing a book called *The Outsider* was not a bad thing in a way. Because there is no way in which they can gain a certain kind of inner strength except by *standing totally alone*. The ultimate test is the courage that they bring to the task of standing totally alone. All you can do to help is to persuade them to go one step further when they are completely exhausted. All you can do is to persuade them that it is worthwhile to go on. But there is absolutely nothing else you can do that would not somehow remove the validity of this basic outsider experience. In short, I was treating the basic outsider experi-

193

ence as the experience of standing totally alone and struggling. In other words, it is the basic religious experience.

Q. Do you regard political persecution as helpful to religions?

A. This is something which every tradition has a different line on, as we might perhaps expect. The Jewish line is 'No – survive at all costs, even at the cost of apostasising from the faith', and this is a real tradition which has real authenticity, so that one gets Sabbatai sevi, the false messiah, in fact converting to Islam, and this led to all sorts of interesting theological speculations about him. The messiah had to go through sin, it was a kind of working out of further ramifications of an incarnation doctrine, but it depends what kind of tradition it is and I do think they vary over this. The Christian tradition is a martyr tradition; of course it is, because its founder was a martyr to the *n*th degree. But it is not the case in other traditions, and I think that is where one has to take religions in their cultural particularity. It is the nature of Christianity to be a persecuted religion and also, sadly, a persecuting one, which is part of the scandal of it.

Q Why should the future provide an answer to doubts not now decidable?

A. This is like one of those philosophical conundrums given of two people going on a long distance, the atheist and the believer: the believer believed that they would end up at the city of God, the atheist didn't; they were both on the same road. They would only know when they arrived or didn't arrive. I don't know when they arrived or didn't arrive. I don't know that the future will provide an answer; it is part of the tradition of belief that it will, but there is the risk, the scandal of living in faith at the moment when one does not have that kind of assurance.

Colin Wilson: T. E. Hulme, who was killed in the First World War, was in the process of writing a book to support the statement he made somewhere in *Speculations*: that people say that they can accept the sentiment of religion but not the dogma. 'Personally' he said 'it is not that I put up with the dogma for the sake of the sentiment, but that I might swallow the sentiment for the sake of the dogma.' That seemed to me the sensible attitude when I wrote *The Outsider*. But for various reasons I think I would now take a

194

view much closer to that of Angela's Buddhist friend, simply because I feel that eventually one *must* be allowed to use reason to some extent. It is true that science tends to confuse the issue by using reason in the wrong ways. And yet there is something deep down inside me that says if we abandon reason – the attempt to use our human power to shed light on things through reason, through analysis – then we have abandoned everything.

Panel Discussion

Colin Wilson: John Bennett tells in his autobiography, *Witness,* how he was at the Gurdjieff Institute of the Harmonious Development of Man at Fontainebleau, where they did extremely complex physical exercises in an attempt to wake people up – the simplest one being to rub your tummy with one hand and pat your head with the other. In some Gurdjieff exercises you have to do four different things with your hands and your feet and your head as well. One morning Bennett woke up feeling absolutely dreadful, having had dysentery and feeling so weak that he could not get out of bed. However something made him force himself out of bed and later on that morning a whole group of them started doing Gurdjieff exercises. Gurdjieff introduced a new and particularly difficult exercise and soon Bennett was completely exhausted and felt that he just could not go on with it. One by one the other disciples dropped out until Bennett felt that there was no point in carrying on. And at this point he felt Gurdjieff's eyes on him, watching him with a peculiar intensity. He drove himself on, and he said that quite abruptly he became filled with an enormous sense of power and strength. When this session was over he went out into the garden and asked himself whether this feeling was an illusion, so he seized a spade and began to dig at a pace that he could not normally maintain for more than thirty seconds. He continued to dig at this pace for half an hour. He said he then walked out into the forest, and met Gurdjieff who said something mysterious to the effect that there is an enormous reservoir of energy which is accessible to all people, but sometimes if you cannot get to it, someone else can act as an intermediary. Bennett went on into the forest and suddenly remembered something that Ouspensky had once said: that if you wish to prove to yourself that you are not really free, meditate on the fact that you can say to yourself 'I feel miserable' and actually induce a sense of misery, or 'I feel cheerful' and induce a sense of cheerfulness

196

but you cannot say to yourself 'Be surprised'. So Bennett said to himself, 'Be surprised' and said he was instantly overwhelmed with amazement. He said that as he looked around at the scenery everything seemed tremendous, amazing. Then the thought of fear entered his head, and he said that instantly he seemed to be surrounded by misery and horror. Next he thought about love, and as soon as he thought of it, he suddenly felt overwhelmed by love and saw that love is infinite in its shades and varieties. After about a quarter of an hour of being able to switch to any feeling he wanted, and being able to enter into it with a depth and totality that he had never before experienced, he felt exhausted, and said: 'I wish this would go away.' Instantly it vanished. This is an example of what could be done by the peculiar kind of effort that Gurdjieff induced. I also suspect that Gurdjieff himself gave the final sort of push that carried him over the top.

The first question which I am going to put to the whole panel is rather an interesting one.

Q.   It has been implied several times in this seminar that it is necessary to feel desperate before one can experience God directly. Most people in this room appear reasonably contented with their lot. Does this really mean that religion is not for them?

Dr Morais: I would first of all say 'No' to the idea that you have to be desperate to have an experience of God. The experience comes under very varied circumstances and if you look at the records of human experience, you find that it is by no means only negative experiences taken to the utmost that lead to God, but also the opposite. Spontaneous so-called mystical or religious experiences sometimes come after a very intense feeling of well-being. There is a classical experience, beautifully described by Dr Bucke, author of *Cosmic Consciousness*. He had a spontaneous mystical experience in London, funnily enough inside a hansom cab, when he thought he was enveloped by red fire and the red fire was inside himself. This came after a very happy evening of consorting with friends, reading poetry, talking about poetry, and a feeling of exaltation seemed to trigger off this experience. I would definitely say 'No' to the idea that it comes only from despair. Intense suffering can lead to finding the way, but it is just one path. There are many

197

paths. The other assumption is that people in this hall are all very contented. The idea that people as a whole are contented or happy is a very dangerous generalization. A few months ago I came across some figures on how happy the British as a whole were, or how happy the Finns were; these statistics are rather suspect. I would take them with a great deal of salt.

dom Silvester: I suppose one ought to allow the possibility that some people are contented with their state of desperation. Certainly desperation is what Evagrius would call one of the manifestations of pathē, of egotism, and one would have to eliminate this before one could have any sort of experience of God. At the same time he would say you must eliminate the opposite, which is a state of elation. Jerome's objection was that that makes you simply a block of stone. But the experience of God does not lead to desperation or to elation, though it can come through or after those states. Everybody in fact suffers from egotism; it is the human condition one has to rise above in order to have the experience of God. But as to it being necessary, you could say it is a condition that can lead to experience, but hardly an essential condition.

Angela Tilby: I want to raise the question as to what religious experience is for, which the question seems to be partly asking. There is a difference between seeking religious experience in order to expand one's own consciousness, in order to raise one's own power or experience, and finding salvation in religion. It may be that salvation includes of necessity a state of desperation, or it may not. But it seems to me that there is a distinction to be made between religions which offer well-being, harmony, peace now, and religions which offer no such thing and possibly a way of faith, possibly a way of suffering which may lead to salvation.

Colin Wilson: It seems to me that religious experience is basically a method of getting the fog out of your head. I think we are all in a state in which we do not see even ordinary reality around us. It struck me the other day on a country walk that I wasn't *seeing* the reality of the cliffs of Cornwall; I was seeing a sort of series of flat photographs of the cliffs

that were almost like ordinary two dimensional photographs of people; somehow I needed another part of my mind
to add that third dimension of meaning to it. This seems to
me to be essential, which raises the question: 'Is it possible
to add a third dimension of meaning step by step, or do you
have to do it with some wild, violent leap like Ramakrishna
seizing the sword?' I would say that it can be done in fact
step by step, provided you know precisely which step you are
taking. What you need is a sort of map of the inside of the
mind, a knowledge of where you are going.

Q.   Political aims, for world improvement, and the aims of
yoga, for spiritual development, operate on two totally different levels, do they not? Can they be combined?

Dr Morais: My answer would be that they do not operate
on totally different levels. The proof of that you can see in
actual cases of people who use the discipline of yoga for other
ends. The best known case is the Mahatma Ghandi. We do
not usually consider Ghandi a great teacher of yoga; most
Europeans would consider him a great politician or a great
reformer. But in fact he did practise yoga and he followed
the discipline of one of the great branches of yoga, karma
yoga, the yoga of detached action. There is no contradiction
between the two things; this is a false dichotomy, a false
conflict between contemplation and action. This kind of
argument has been going on for centuries. In Christianity
you have the way of Martha and the way of Mary and so on,
the active way and the contemplative way. To go back to a
very authoritative text on karma yoga, the Gita tells you to
engage in action with all your strength but detached from
results. That is the lesson, and I think it agrees fundamentally with what Buddhism tells you, and all the great spiritual paths. If you look at the people who are now engaged in
any sort of action, in social reform or political action, from
the religious side, they are at the same time engaged either
in prayer or meditation or in fact in strengthening their own
mind and spirit by maintained contact with the spiritual
level. As long as that contact is maintained, then I think the
action can be conducted on the right lines. It is when they
fail somehow in the contact that they are fascinated by some
of the attractions of action, they succumb to one of the temptations, political power itself and so on. The story that occurs
to me as an illustration of detachment is a famous one about

St Ignatius of Loyola. At one time he was very concerned that the Pope might dissolve the recently founded Jesuit order, which of course was his life's work. One close friend and associate asked him 'Now what would you do if this new Pope really dissolved the order?' He paused according to the story, and said 'Give me fifteen minutes prayer and all would be as before.' This is a good example of detachment. It does not mean that he could not care less whether the Pope dissolved the order or not, of course he cared. We make all sorts of verbal confusions between worry and concern. One should be concerned with one's problems but one should not worry about them. It may sound a pedantic distinction, but there is in fact a very important psychological difference between being concerned with a problem and being really worried. Worry is fear and the fear is ultimately concerned with the ego. As dom Silvester was mentioning just now, all worries and all fears are fundamentally concerned with the ego and we should try and eliminate them. Yoga in the past has been a way of individual salvation, and not concerned with social or political reform. But this has changed, with the emergence of a philosophy such as that of Sri Aurobindo who was very much concerned with the development of mankind, of human society as it is now. One can see not only Hinduism, not only yoga but Buddhism also acquiring a social consciousness: several Buddhist movements are actually engaging in politics in the Far East and South East Asia, and the Roman Catholic church also has been acquiring a social consciousness; priests, monks, bishops and sometimes cardinals are taking an active part in something like politics. This is happening in several countries and especially in Latin America, so I do not think there is any contradiction, any essential separation between action, especially political action, and spiritual development.

Q. Your contention that martyrdom comprises the touchstone of genuine religious experience smacks of the 'Onward Christian Soldier' type of chauvinism, a kind of cultural myopia. Isn't there a risk that you are omitting options invisible to your own cultural heritage but equally if not more valid?

Angela Tilby: I have a lot of sympathy with that question. My cultural myopia may be your sort of open-minded vagueness. The cross cannot be loved, that is where my answer to this begins. There is a suspicion in this question of the scandal, the stumbling block aspect of human suffering. In Christianity it is very, very central; it has often been sentimentalised and made into something very different from what it actually is. The cross stands for negation, for judgment, for scandal and for all the things which to our common sense religiosity would seem appalling. I am not saying that Christianity alone has that insight, because the more I find out about other religions, the more I talk to people who belong to them, the more I see, as they say they see in Christianity, echoes and shadows of the same thing. Gandhi's favourite hymn was 'When I Survey the Wondrous Cross', and he had an extraordinary attachment to and depth of sympathy with the passion of Jesus. This is something which is not unique to Christianity. I find in the Zen notion of destroying the mind by the *koan,* by the shock, rather the same sort of thing. There is a scandal, a point of discontinuity between the natural religious-seeking self and what comes from outside, and the Christian symbol of the cross expresses that to me. There are two sides to the matter. First of all, I can't get out of my cultural myopia, any more than anybody else can. Yet the hints and echoes of his own faith that a Hindu will see in Christianity and a Christian will see of his in another religion seem to me to be real and genuine. If you are rejecting the notion of discontinuity and suffering and scandal and stumbling blocks, then you are rejecting something which is very central and crucial to all religious experience.

Q. Can you describe your own concept of God?

dom Silvester: The concept of God has to be in the concept of that which cannot be conceived. That is why I began talking about the devils to the left and to the right. The right-hand devil is the demon that deludes you into accepting a concept of nothing as the equivalent of not having a concept. If one defines God as the Nothing, one should remember the 4th council of Lateran, 1215, and its rather celebrated definition that you cannot assert anything of God without at the same time asserting the opposite; this is the fundamental of all theology, the distinction between cataphatic and apophatic, the cataphatic is what says God is this, he is that, he is the other – the apophatic says no, he's not that, he's not this, he's not the other: *netti, netti* in India *nada, nada* in Spain. Both have to be held at the same time. I think it was Bossuet talking about antinomies in religion (i.e., the yin and the yang, the positive and negative, the cataphatic and apophatic, mercy and justice) who says you have to hold "les deux bouts de la chaîne', both ends of the chain. You know it is one chain but you cannot see the links. Your concept of God is going to be the opposite of the non-concept that you have at the same time. I don't know whether one can go any further than to accept given 'definitions' of God, but if contemplation, the aim of human life, is the union of nothing and nothing, (to quote dom Augustin Baker again) or (to quote Origen) the union of freedom and freedom, then you have gone about as far as you can, short of reciting the whole *Summa Theologica.*

Dr Morais: The negative way is very well represented on the Eastern side in India; there is a beautiful passage in the Upanishads which says that Brahman, which is the impersonal side of God, is that from which both mind and words recoil. To me this is very well put because if you try to give me a concept of God, in fact you are trying to imprison something that cannot be imprisoned by its very nature in mental concepts. To define is to set limits to a thing, is to turn it into a thing and God is no thing, is nothing. It is only by this negation that you can actually reach something like a remote idea of what it is.

Colin Wilson: My image of the ladder earlier implies that whatever is at the top of the ladder, at the apex, would be the transcendental ego or God or whatever you want to call it. But it is important to realize that this does not really concern us. It would be nice to get up to the top of the ladder but since we have no chance whatsoever of doing that at the present stage of evolution, let us think about getting to the next rung – which is the really interesting question and to me a thoroughly practical question. I can lift this jug of water because there is enough strength in my arm. If it were four times as big I would not be able to lift it. This means that there is a particular kind of strength that can be developed. This strength you can use or call upon in a sudden frenzy. My friend Ronald Duncan, the poet, studied under Gandhi. When he was leaving India he had the most atrocious cold – he could hardly breathe – so Gandhi said

'Call on a doctor friend of mine in Northern Bombay and he'll get rid of it.' So Ronnie went along to see the doctor, who strapped him to a sort of cast iron bedstead that stood upright, put his hands behind his head, then pulled a lever. The bedstead went down backwards with an appalling crash. The doctor then released Ronnie, who was furious and felt as if every bone in his body had been broken. He staggered to his feet swearing and cursing and then realized the cold had gone. This is the way of doing it in one single jump, and you can see that this applies to everything, not just reaching God but to getting rid of a cold. *This* is the sort of strength that needs to be developed. What interests me is how we can actually develop it in a thoroughly practical, down-to-earth way.

Q. How would you reconcile the evolution of man in a practical sense from the point of view of right action, with meditation as a process of slowing down, that is sleep-inducing?

Dr Morais: The states that are attained, whatever they are and however different they may be in different spiritual traditions – you can always ask whether samadhi is different from what the Christians have called rapture or ecstasy or satori in the Zen Buddhist tradition – to use the psychological jargon, they are all altered states of consciousness. These altered states of consciousness seem to have one thing in common, that they are relaxed states; in these states tension just vanishes. The questioner used the term sleep-inducing, but in these states, there is no sleep. You get some of the characteristics of sleep, with, in fact, tremendous and very sharp alertness, often with a sense of revelation that you are in fact learning something tremendously important about reality, that you are piercing the veils that normally exist between you and these levels, these hidden levels of reality. So they are states of alertness and the people who have written about contemplation and meditation all say that in these states there is in a way tremendous action. There is action in inaction, and this is again the conception of Tao; if you reach the Tao, by doing nothing you can do everything. This is the paradox, by being immobile you go everywhere; that again is the description of the Atman. It is a completely paradoxical description, but that is where you go beyond the opposites, action and inaction. People who have really reached very high stages of consciousness, by just being there can act on other people. When one reads the Gospels, one is absolutely sure that Jesus by his very presence was acting, by just being there, and so have some of the great sages and yogis. This is very much against our Western way of living and our present philosophy that we must always be doing something; if you are not actually up and doing, you are being lazy. This is a terribly superficial and a terribly wrong conception. The busy executive who must be rushing around, answering telephones and giving orders, if he is not doing that, then he is not being active, he is not fulfilling his picture and image of a hard-working, active man, the man who can command millions. Yet this is quite the opposite of the wiser picture of the man who can in fact act by doing nothing. The aim of spiritual development is not to reach a state of anaesthesia, where you give up and evade life, but to reach a stage of high alertness, where you are in fact alert and aware of levels in reality which you are not aware of in your normal condition, because we delude ourselves by thinking that in our normal waking state we are very efficient and active. We go through intermittent periods of action and laziness, but we always try to convince ourselves that we are being active by doing many things; this doing many things may be just a sort of expression of restlessness and sometimes of not having a proper aim in our mind. Once you begin a path in spiritual development then you become aware how inefficient you are in your ordinary life. Everybody who has tried meditation has made some appalling discoveries about themselves, not only how selfish they are, but how wasteful in their minds, how inefficient.

dom Silvester: What Dante calls Benedict's golden ladder, Benedict says begins in the heart and ends in heaven, because progress up the ladder is the dilation of the heart as it becomes the boundless centre. One does not *have* to use the word 'heart', but it is difficult to think of a word which everybody accepts immediately. From the heart come the actions you do; all action starts from the contemplative centre and so there is no contradiction between them because they are the two ends of the same thing. In the gospel it says 'by their fruits ye shall know them', which is in fact what the discernment of spirits is, you can only test them by the fruit, you cannot get at the centre because it is invisible. But the results, what is manifested, is what you can examine and judge. If the root is holy so is the trunk. If the trunk, the branch and if the branch, the fruit. But certainly in the West and also in the Eastern tradition, whatever ladder you are climbing, though we talk about ascending it rung by rung, we are always on all the rungs at once in varying degrees. You have the two data: scripture or revelation (whether it is through self or through written scriptures) and the cosmos. You have to read the cosmos at various levels, the four levels of interpretation from the literal down to the anagogical, the anagogical being the one that leads you to God. And you can progress in that reading. Frequently you can read the same thing twice (whether it is the cliff in Cornwall that we were talking about or a book), once as a child, and again when older and find you have got to a deeper understanding of it. Through what is manifest and visible you reach what is invisible and as this has no extension, it can be called either immensely large or immensely small, either nothing or everything. This is the ordinary progress which everybody makes. But we are at every point of that progress in varying degrees, at different times. In the morning you may be more obviously on one level and in the evening less obviously on another, but the reconciliation of the two is certainly not a problem; it is only a false problem which results from the fact that we put it into words and discuss two sides of the same coin at different times. You cannot see two sides at the same time but you know they are there.

The medical word *anaesthesia,* happens also to be a technical term of Western spirituality. It comes from St Antony who said 'If you know you are praying, you aren't.' If you are conscious that 'this is where I am' on the ladder then you quite certainly aren't. Pure Prayer is not awareness of what you are doing, but is the actual doing of it. Anaesthesia *can* be a misleading term, as it misled Jerome who assumed the monks in Nitria were trying to get everybody to 'live like a log or a stone'.

Q. Can one not test the spirits inspiring an individual by comparing the individual's personal conduct to other people after the religious experience and before it?

Angela Tilby: This is a question of 'by their fruits ye shall know them'. Standards of holiness vary; I think it is true there are a very few great and saintly people about whom one would know, one would feel, there would be a consensus perhaps, as to their having arrived, having got there, having understood something of the reality of the divine. Apart from such examples, the varying standards are rather difficult to cope with. What is holiness to a family of evangelical Christians, their behaviour towards each other and their behaviour towards the outside world, will not actually be the same as that of the Zen master teaching meditation technique. Their actual attitudes towards people, their actions, will be very, very different and I find it difficult to say therefore exactly how it is that one makes criteria, unless one remains within a culture which has a common set of agreed standards. St John Chrysostom was apparently a great saint. He did some very awful things in persecuting the Jews and nobody at the time seemed to think this was odd at all. St Augustine is allowed to lose his temper and be a saint. One can see on the one hand that there are certain advantages in the negative side. I mean the Zen master who hits you over the shoulder rather hard to keep you awake, that is an act of violence, it is not a very nice thing to do to anybody really, and yet one could within that tradition interpret this as a perfectly helpful, loving and good thing to do, to encourage the other person's spiritual development. What are your criteria? The other thing, it seems to me, is that there does seem to be a real risk in religion for some people. When as an adolescent, I decided I would become a Christian, I think I was absolutely awful for a long time. I went through a great decline in actual moral standards of behaviour. This probably came from my own misreading of what Christianity was about, but also alongside that went a very clear sense of the grace of God and the love of God which was quite new to me. This is a continual problem; how do you judge from your own point of view? I am sure they thought I had suddenly, or perhaps not suddenly, become unreasonably intolerant and unpleasant and aggressive towards them. Yet that was part of the inevitable fruit of a kind of religious experience which I think was genuine. On later reflection, one began to see its neurotic roots perhaps, or its extraordinariness, or the fact that it did not tie up, and one started to think through it again. But I know people about whom one would say their holiness perhaps springs from their neurosis; one knows of the holy alcoholic, the holy sinner, there are real people that one encounters in experience. One also knows of the other kind of person who is very adept at manipulating consciousness, who has journeyed a great way into the self and who uses it for making a very great deal of money out of other people who are gullible.

dom Silvester: This is the problem of the 'sainte courtisane', the holy harlot, of which there were so many examples again in the desert. But surely when one talks about fruit, one says you can't gather figs from thistles. There is only one fruit that is being thought of here and that is love, *agape*, which is universal love. You can judge the extent to which, even if they behave misguidedly perhaps, they are attempting some sort of universal love. The Zen master particularly has this for the least blade of grass; the Calvinist may perhaps feel that only certain blades of grass have been elected for salvation and certain others haven't – the lawn-mower approach to theology. But at least they are trying, within that little slice of cheese, to see through to what they feel is, what they understand to be *agape*, love, universal love, non-egotistical love. To that extent you can have some sort of criterion for judging between the Zen master and the Calvinist; whether it is up to us to make the judgment, I don't know. One only makes judgments for one's own benefit perhaps; the Calvinist, even though he thinks that three blades of grass have been destined for salvation, at least he looks after them very well. So he is manifesting universal love in a rather particular way. But then we all manifest universal love in particular ways. This is again the nature of temporal existence, that you can't do it all at once; we have to do it from morning to evening.

Angela Tilby: The problem for me is that if you are going on someone's behaviour, on their actions, the only way you have to interpret them is through your own cultural myopia. You don't really have any other way in the end, though you can learn about other people's expectations from talking to them. You can observe a great deal but how do you know in the end that what the Zen master conceives as universal love and the Calvinist, are really the same thing. I find it terribly difficult to know what the evidence for making that assumption is, which is why I have an innate suspicion of the lexicon of common religious language. It seems to me that there is very little evidence that would say that we can know that we are on about the same sort of thing at all.

207

Dr Morais: You mentioned the very good case of St John Chrysostom doing awful things to the Jews. I am a great admirer of St Teresa and St John of the Cross, and yet they were contemporary with the worst of the Inquisition in Spain. The way perhaps one could look at it is going back to one of the questioners here who asked about the relation between the evolution of society and our own individual evolution. There is no doubt that there has been progress in religious tolerance; I mean the things that even St Teresa could accept, say that the Jews could be burnt at the stake in Madrid or Seville and this was accepted quite naturally by all Catholics in Spain, nowadays we just consider this abominable, entirely unchristian or anti-religious. So there has been progress, but the fruits depend, not only on the progress of the individual, but on the society in which he lives. Even Jesus, of course, was a man of his own time. He was very much a devout Jew who thought that Gentiles were not quite the thing; you have to consider the two poles of the matter in order to look properly at the truth.

Angela Tilby: A further problem that arises from that is that we simply do not know, just as St Teresa or St John of the Cross may have had no idea, of the actual sins and the disharmonies that were present in their own time. We have no guarantee that we are not harbouring the most appalling and outrageous sort of sins or difficulties or problems in our own time. What is the evidence, how do we know that people won't look back in 300 years' time and say do you realize people then believed that they were religious, believed that they were Christians or Buddhists or tolerant people and yet all that time – the neutron bomb. Where else does one need to look?

dom Silvester: One is perfectly certain that in 300 years' time people *will* look back in horror. I think that is what gives us confidence to go on.

Colin Wilson: I have always felt that this religious emphasis on love is a mistake. I have always had a pragmatic approach to the question. I was fascinated by that story of the psychologist, Victor Frankl, who during the war was in a Nazi concentration camp. He noticed that the people who managed to survive the hardship were those who possessed any kind of purpose whatsoever. There was even a man called Trachtenburg who worked out an interesting system of speed calculation in a concentration camp and it provided him with motivation to survive. Frankl discovered that it was the prisoners who had any kind of drive or purpose – in other words, a tomorrow – who survived. The ones who had no purpose tended to die of quite minor illnesses. One day they were being shifted from Auschwitz to Dachau. They were on the train for two days and when they got there they were forced to stand out in the rain for the whole night and the whole of the following morning because one of the prisoners had fallen asleep in the lavatory and was not there for the roll call. And yet, Frankl says, they were all intensely happy standing outside Dachau because they saw *it didn't have a chimney*. This one fact – that they had a tomorrow, that they had gone to a camp that did not have an incinerator – was enough to make them intensely happy standing there in the freezing rain for twelve hours. He said they were nudging one another and making jokes and laughing. They had found a set of circumstances that raised their inner pressure. Man is precisely like those tyres on cars that say 'Keep inflated hard'. For most of the time our minds are flat and soggy, and if you drive a flat and soggy tyre, it will wear out in no time at all. And if you drive a completely flat tyre you will ruin it within five minutes. The problem is how do we inflate the tyre? And it seems to me that love wouldn't have done them a great deal of good in Auschwitz or Dachau. Trachtenburg's mathematics did *him* a great deal of good. So I have a certain prejudice against religious notions as such. My feeling is 'Let's get down to this practical problem of how to raise our inner pressure.' Have a universe, a world full of people with high inner pressure and you will have a universe of good loving people at the same time.

dom Silvester: But surely our divine and neptic fathers would have said that Trachtenburg's mathematics was the expression of *agape,* of love. This is the fruit coming out; he's got something inside him, he's got a root which is able to produce something decent, something worthwhile which is going to have effect.

Q. What evidence have you that man can be more highly developed? Do you know such persons and how did you decide that they were more developed?

Dr Morais: Well the persons we know about are mostly through reading about them, through their fame, the facts they have produced, the great spiritual figures of mankind, the people who really produced changes in history. People like Jesus Christ, the Buddha, the saints, the great yogis did change history, they did change people, they made profound changes in the world around them and to me this is the proof. Also the great creators, the people who created great works of art, when you are listening to a Beethoven symphony or to Bach's St Matthew Passion, that is again a soul who created something; what it created is still alive and its love is coming through, in that music which is again, as we were saying about contemplation, beyond words. It is an international language. You can see it also in people who may not have reached very high levels of development and yet are faithful to their task, somebody who is a loving mother, who is really very faithful to her children, and looks after them with loving care, even when the children are handicapped, or a man who is handicapped himself and yet manages to live through that handicap; all these examples are inspiring – you don't only have to look at the Everests of human achievement, you can look at very humble examples around you and be inspired by them. People can be changed and people can live by their fidelity to certain principles, and to see someone who is faithful and persevering even when they have tremendous problems to confront is in fact very encouraging; sometimes it is by these most humble examples that one sees that one is most inspired.

dom Silvester: Do you remember the mediaeval story from the 15th century or maybe a bit earlier, in those collections of moralities and moral tales about the person who got to heaven because of one act of charity, which was throwing a stale loaf at a beggar who was bothering him. Some of these stories are very similar to the Zen ones; they put an extreme case in order to teach something which is quite true. But there can never be surely any one person about whom we can say 'Now that is the absolute ideal.' Everybody is aiming at some sort of perfection. Angela Tilby spoke about the two people, the believer and the unbeliever on the same road; they can only tell when they get to the end, but only one will then say I was right, the one who said there was an end to the road; but the one who believes there is no end to the road, that the path is the goal, when do you know that he is right? This is the problem, this is the way we have to live.

Angela Tilby: My problem is with this notion of the desirability of being highly developed. I have known extraordinary people who were capable of extraordinary physical endurance and also of mental power which could affect things. There was no doubt to me that the person I have in mind was living on a higher level of consciousness than I was or than most people I've met. That didn't stop them from being one of the most outrageously selfish human beings that I've ever met, so where is the desirability in it? If one says what evidence have you that man can be holy, I would refer you probably back to my alcoholic sinner, because that seems to be God's contradiction of our own religiousness and notions of the desirability of being able to manipulate spiritual powers. I think the religious quest and the quest for self development are actually very, very different things.

Colin Wilson: A comment about Gurdjieff once again. When Fritz Peters went to see Gurdjieff immediately after the war, he was in a state of shell-shock and nervous exhaustion. He had had a bad time at the front. Gurdjieff told him to sit down in the kitchen while he went and did something. Fritz Peters sat down and felt so enclosed and suffocated that he had to get up and go and look for Gurdjieff. Gurdjieff took one glance at him, saw what a bad condition he was in and made him go and sit down. Gurdjieff himself, Fritz Peters said, was looking absolutely awful – exhausted and grey – but as Peters sat in the chair in the kitchen he suddenly felt a curious sensation of a warm glow rising inside him. He looked up and found that Gurdjieff was staring at him from the other side of the kitchen with a peculiar intensity. Quite suddenly Peters was fine. All the exhaustion and misery had gone, and he was once again on top of the world. But Gurdjieff looked absolutely drained and pale. At this moment there was a ring at the front door and a great crowd of people turned up. Gurdjieff went out of the room to let them in and then to Peters' surprise came in about five minutes later looking absolutely splendid, glowing with health once again. He then said a very interesting thing to Peters. He said 'Thank you for reminding me.' Now I think the significance of this story is this: it was again a question of inner pressure. Peters had allowed the inner pressure to drop until it was at a dangerously low level; there was no possible feedback inside him, so to speak, no way of building it up once again. Whatever Gurdjieff did to him, I don't think he transmitted energy, I don't think he shot a beam of energy into him; in some peculiar way he touched the natural self-inflator that we all have inside us for raising our own inner pressure. Then having got Peters properly inflated and exhausted himself in the effort of doing it, Gurdjieff suddenly thought 'You fool, why are you letting yourself feel exhausted. You've got one too', and immediately touched it himself as he went to let the people in at the door. It seems to me that *this* is really what religious experience is about, the divine afflatus, the intensity, the something that flows into you and that ultimately with a little luck can perhaps raise you to God, or at least to a contemplation of something much broader than our normal narrow and hysterical perspective. Because there is no doubt whatever that, in Janet's terms, we are all hysterics.

Q. Rumi in his poem, the *Masnavi*, has spoken of the elephant taken into captivity, never losing its memory of the forest, longing to return. Idries Shah, in *The Sufis,* speaks of man's deepest yearning in the search for an inner meaning to life and Dr Morais talks about the child who forsakes play and demands its mother. Are those responses from the same side of the brain or do they represent a common Sufi ecumenical language?

Dr Morais: There are many ways of expressing this: Paradise Lost, the myth of the island, the happy island where we can all be happy without any effort, All these are myths, if you like, of a lost past that is sometimes projected into the future. You can see in all folkore, in all mythology, reflections of this ideal of something that has been lost and one never knows whether it was in the past, will be in the future or is in fact, or could be recoverable in the present. All religious traditions have got an idea of this; in the Jewish-Christian tradition it is very obvious, in the Garden of Eden where primaeval man was in fact in direct contact with God; he lost the contact through his disobedience. If you look at the beliefs of a lot of so-called primitive tribes, I think the man who has gone most into this is Mircea Eliade; in his books on comparative religion, you will see that there are very similar myths in primitive tribes, how in the old days the gods were much more accessible than they are now, or in the old days you could even talk to the animals, the animals could talk to people and so on. This sort of primaeval, paradisiac state has been destroyed somehow or other. This is really part of something like a pseudo-memory of mankind. It may be that only at a later period of our own development shall we be able to know what exactly this myth of the lost paradise means. Essentially they are all symbols of the return or elevation to this higher state of consciousness, which gives you bliss and ecstasy. There is a beautiful science fiction story, perhaps one of the best works of science fiction, by Arthur Clarke, *Childhood's End*. In *Childhood's End* a superior race comes to earth in order to save us, reform us. They never appear because they are afraid of frightening mankind with their appearance; it is only after two generations of contact with them that they dare to make themselves known in the flesh and when this being from the stars actually descends from the aeroplane he has got two horns and a tail: he looks like the devil. So the author makes the speculation that the myth of the devil is in fact a prefiguration of something that was going to happen to mankind, it was projected into the future, and not something that had happened in the past. The same may happen to the dream of the Garden of Eden, we don't know.

dom Silvester: There are surely two problems here. The return to the forest, is it the return to childhood that we are thinking about? The return to 'les vieux temps', the return to the forest of Broceliande, in Brittany, near where my ancestors came from. Or is it the return to the centre? One is a return in time to the beginning, the other is a return psychologically to where we exist in order to produce fruit, in order to produce activity – the Wu way of Taoism; by reaching the centre of the mandala, the wheel which is turning, you are at the still centre and the wheel cannot turn unless there is that point of nothingness which doesn't turn. The vase can't hold any water unless it's got a hollow space inside. This is the return to the centre which is going to be fruitful, so the return is in fact part of the activity; if

213

you are off centre, you can't be quite so efficient; you can't do your work in the office. One of the reasons why in Japan they have these two minute breaks every few hours is to be more effective. So that is perhaps the return of the elephant to the forest.

Angela Tilby: The problem is, in the Christian tradition, the way back to Eden is barred by an angel with a fiery sword, and the Fall story is also interpreted as 'Oh happy fault' without which there would not be any redemption, so I suggest the way to Eden is barred for the future and perhaps what is required is not a return but an acceptance of the weary struggle out of Eden into whatever lies ahead.

Colin Wilson: The recognition that keeps coming back to me is that, oddly enough, I tend to be a natural optimist. So I feel very cheerful about these problems. They no longer seem to me as depressing as in the days when I wrote *The Outsider*. In 1959, I was greatly cheered when I received a letter from a professor named Abraham Maslow, who told me that, as a psychologist, he had got sick of studying sick people, because he said sick people talked about nothing but their sickness. And so he looked around for the healthiest people he could find and studied them instead. He immediately discovered a very interesting thing that nobody had ever discovered before, because nobody was interested in healthy people. He found that all the healthy people he talked to had, with a fair degree of frequency, what he called 'peak experiences' – a sudden bubbling over of overwhelming happiness. They were *not* mystical experiences. A young mother watching her husband and kids eating breakfast when suddenly a beam of sunlight came into the window, and she bubbled over into the sheer delight of the peak experience. A hostess looking round a room when she'd just given a very successful party, with all the cigarette butts trampled in the carpets and empty glasses, nevertheless suddenly went into a peak experience. They appear to be a function of normal healthy people. Now the interesting thing is that when Maslow began talking to his students about peak experiences they not only remembered peak experiences that they had had, but had not noticed at the time – things which they had just allowed, as it were, to pass through them and forgotten about instantly – they also started *having more peak experiences*. In fact talking about them made them begin to have them. It was this curious matter of self-reflection, of self-consciousness. In the way, when you are lying in bed on a freezing winter morning and have to get up in one minute's time, the bed is never so deliciously warm. You just cannot experience that same warmth on a Sunday morning when you can stay in bed as long as you like. It is the peculiar act of self-reflection that in some way starts off this process of intensifying consciousness. And finally one cheering thought: during the Korean war the Americans discovered that there were no escapes of American soldiers because the Chinese had made a rather interesting discovery. Instead of keeping all the soldiers under a heavy guard, they realized that all they had to do was to watch them carefully for a few days, remove from them the soldiers who seemed to have any kind of discipline or originality, and put them in a separate compound under heavy guard. They found that as soon as they had taken these men away, the rest of the soldiers became a kind of inert mass who made no attempt to escape; they could leave them without any guard at all. So they were able to economize on guards and there were no escapes of American soldiers. They had rediscovered an interesting fact of zoology: that the members of any group who possess originality and drive are always precisely five per cent of the total number. Zoologists have discovered that the dominant minority among animals and birds is precisely five per cent: one in twenty. The people who are deeply interested in questions of consciousness and awareness are once again precisely five per cent. The interesting thing is that you all clearly belong to this dominant five per cent or you would not be here, so you are already so to speak on the basic step of the way to salvation.

Further Reading

ABD AL-RAHMAN AZZAM *The Eternal Message of Muhammad* London, 1965.

CARMEN BLACKER *The Catalpa Bow* London, 1975. *A Study of Shamanistic Practices in Japan* London, 1975.

LIONEL BLUE *To Heaven with Scribes and Pharisees* London, 1975.

R. MCAFEE BROWN *The Spirit of Protestantism* Sudbury, 1966.

HARIDAS CHAUDHURI *Integral Yoga* London, 1965.

ALAIN DANIÉLOU *Yoga: The Method of Re-Integration* New York, 1955.

J. M. DÉCHANET *Christian Yoga* London, 1960.

A. O. DYSON *We Believe* Oxford, 1977.

RIADH EL-DROUBIE *Islam* London, 1970.

MIRCEA ELIADE *Yoga: Immortality and Freedom* New York, 1958.

ISIDORE EPSTEIN *Judaism* Harmondsworth, 1970.

ALTAF GAUHAR *Translations from the Koran*, London, 1977.

MICHAEL GREEN (Ed.) *The Truth of God Incarnate* London, 1977.

BEDE GRIFFITHS *Return to the Centre* London, 1976.

JOHN F. X. HARRIOTT *Fields of Praise* Southend, 1976. *A Pride of Periscopes* Southend, 1976.

JOHN HICK (Ed.) *The Myth of God Incarnate* London, 1977. *Truth and Dialogue: Relationship between World Religions* London, 1974.

CHRISTOPHER ISHERWOOD *Vedanta for the Western World* London, 1951.

LOUIS JACOBS *Jewish Theology* London, 1973.

R. E. O. JAMES *Comparative Religion* London, 1961.

PHILIP KAPLEAU *The Three Pillars of Zen* New York, 1967.

C. W. KEGLEY *Protestantism in Transition* New York, 1965.

TREVOR LEGGETT *Zen and the Ways* London, 1978.

DOW MARMUR (Ed.) *A Genuine Search* London, 1979, *Reform Judaism* London, 1973.

E. A. MASCALL *Theology and the Gospel of Christ* London, 1977.

ABUL A'LA MAUDUDI *Towards Understanding Islam* Karachi, 1960.

SWAMI NIKHILANANDA (Transl.) *Ramakrishna: Prophet of New India* London, 1951.

M. PICKTHALL *The Meaning of the Glorious Koran* London, 1957.

IRMGARD SCHLOEGL *The Wisdom of the Zen Masters* London, 1975. *The Zen Way* London, 1977.

IKBAL ALI SHAH *The Spirit of the East* London, 1973.

HARI PRASAD SHASTRI *Yoga* London, 1974.

R. H. TAWNEY *Religion and the Rise of Capitalism* Harmondsworth, 1969.

SHIVESH THAKUR *Christian and Hindu Ethics* London, 1969.

P. TILLICH *The Protestant Era* Welwyn, 1966.

E. TROELTSCH *Protestantism and Progress* London, 1912.

SWAMI VIVEKANANDA *Raja Yoga* Calcutta, 1970.

CHARIS WADDY (Ed.) *The Muslim Mind* Harlow, 1976.

C. E. WELCH (Ed.) *Protestant Thought in the 19th Century* London, 1972

J. S. WHALE *The Protestant Tradition* Cambridge, 1955.

COLIN WILSON *New Pathways in Psychology* London, 1972.

THE INSTITUTE FOR CULTURAL RESEARCH

The Institute is an educational charity which was founded in 1965 to promote study, education and publication in the field of human thought. It concerns itself with the rise and development of ideas and their action and interaction within and between communities. The principal objective of the Institute's programme is the fostering of interdisciplinary studies and the promotion of cross-cultural research and discussion in a diversity of fields. To this end it organizes lectures, seminars and symposia designed to make available to the general public the results of research on many aspects of human thought and behaviour. Much of the material disseminated in this way is published in the Institute's Monograph Series of which the current list of titles is given below.

While the principal sphere of the Institute's activity is the United Kingdom, it has since its foundation made and maintained contact with scholars all over the world and has promoted interchange between them and between the world of learning and the general public. Specialists in a wide range of subjects, including anthropology, sociology, psychology, medicine, science, history, oriental studies and religion have made valuable contributions to the work of the Institute.

The Institute for Cultural Research P.O. Box 13, Tunbridge Wells, Kent, England.

I.C.R. MONOGRAPH SERIES
ISSN 0306-1906

No. 1 *Vico's Theory of the Causes of Historical Change* Professor Leon Pompa
2 *Some Unusual Aspects of Communication* Edward Campbell
3 *The Indian Guru and his Disciple* Peter Brent
4 *Exploring Human Behaviour in Groups* Professor John Allaway
5 *Education and Elitism in Nazi Germany* Robert Cecil, C.M.G.
6 *Cultural Imperialism* Robert Cecil, C.M.G.

218